MODERNISM AND BEYOND

Women Artists of the Pacific Northwest

MIDMARCH ARTS BOOKS
Documenting Women in the Arts

Modernism & Beyond: Women Artists of the Pacific Northwest

The Lady Architects:
Lois Lilley Howe, Eleanor Manning, and Mary Almy, 1893-1937

Camera Fiends and Kodak Girls:
50 Selections by and about Women in Photography 1840-1930

Yesterday and Tomorrow: California Women Artists

No Bluebonnets, No Yellow Roses: Texas Women in the Arts

Pilgrims and Pioneers: New England Women in the Arts

Women Artists of the World

American Women Artists: Works on Paper

other MIDMARCH ARTS BOOKS

Beyond Walls and Wars: Art, Politics, and Multiculturalism

Mutiny and the Mainstream: Talk That Changed Art, 1975-1990

Voices of Women: 3 critics on 3 poets on 3 heroines

Illuminations (for *Asphodel, That Greeny Flower*)

Images From Dante

Artists and Their Cats

Whole Arts Directory

Guide to Women's Art Organizations and Directory for the Arts

MODERNISM AND BEYOND

Women Artists of the Pacific Northwest

Edited by
Laura Brunsman
&
Ruth Askey

MIDMARCH ARTS PRESS
New York

Cover photo: May Day scene at Mt. Rainier, early 20th century, artist unknown. From the Pemco Webster & Stevens Collection, courtesy of Museum of History & Industry, Seattle, Washington.

Library of Congress Catalog Card Number 92-062399
ISBN 1-877675-13-X

Published in 1993 by
Midmarch Arts Press
300 Riverside Drive
New York, New York 10025

Printed and bound in the United States

Contents

Introduction

by Laura Brunsman

Modernism & Beyond: Women Artists of the Pacific Northwest begins with the stirrings of modernism in the teens and continues through to contemporary developments and postmodernism of the early '90s.

As part of a series published by Midmarch Arts Press celebrating women artists in regions hosting the College Art Association and the Women's Caucus for the Arts meetings, the book focuses on developments in Seattle and Portland, with some coverage of Vancouver, B.C. and outlying areas.

The evolution of modernism in the Pacific Northwest is explored in five parts: Women Defining Themselves — Modernism 1900 to the 1940s; Regional Modernism and the Mainstream — 1930 through 1960; Grandes Dames of Craft-Related Traditions; Contemporary Northwest Art — Pluralism and Postmodernism; Feminist Spin-offs — 1970 through the Present.

The thematic essays convey a chorus of voices that reflect the pluralism which is part of, and inseparable from, this regional perspective, as issues of regionalism intersect with complex developments from modernism until the present in what we now call postmodernism.

The cities of the Pacific Northwest were not settled before the mid-1850s. Until the late 1920s and early '30s they remained remote from — but not untouched by — mainstream modernist movements circulating in Paris, New York City, Chicago and Los Angeles. Since then, interaction between regional art and modernism has expanded. Northwest women artists have a long history of achievement inside and outside the region, with connections nationally through birth, education, travel, and association.

One truth emerging in these pages is that the Northwest is not as isolated as suggested by persistent patriarchal modernist myths surrounding the "Northwest School" since the '40s. Economic development and regional growth in the post-World War II era led to increasing support of the arts and a burgeoning art scene. The rise of the women's movement in the early '70s activated new networks and communities. Today women artists travel and exhibit outside the region and continue to be included in numerous group exhibitions around the country.[1] The question of how distinctive or innovative they have been within the regional context is one level of analysis presented here. Another question is whether these women have reflected a distinctive regional sensibility. As Patricia Failing suggests, artists manage to balance provincialism with adaptations of mainstream developments.[2] What emerge as distinctive to the Northwest are contemporary developments in narrative and figurative painting and sculpture, particularly in ceramics and glass, as well as alternative forms like installation or performance art. The basic premises of this work, however, are still tied to the mainstream.

Although presenting a cogent look at women artists of the region, we can only begin to investigate the still mostly unwritten history of Pacific Northwest artists. Nor is there any pretense of covering every woman artist who has contributed to the Northwest art scene.

The fact that women other than visual artists have been active in modernist developments is seen throughout, particularly in the conversation with arts activist Anne Focke. Women have been catalysts within museums, galleries, and the educational system.[3] Art schools founded by women continue to have a presence, including Cornish College of the Arts (formerly Cornish Institute), founded by Nellie Cornish in 1914. In an afterword, Julie Anderson, corporate curator for SAFECO Insurance, explores the role of women arts administrators.

While several authors mention significant exhibitions by women artists, many competitive regional exhibitions have been and continue to be venues for women as well.[4] There are also alternative exhibition spaces and public art programs notable for support of women artists: and/or presented unique opportunities for women artists, writers, and administrators from its inception in 1974 until its demise in 1984 (as it branched out into 911 and COCA). The Portland Center for the Visual Arts (PCVA) has also provided an important exhibition space for women artists in the 1970s. Here Lucy Lippard curated the pivotal exhibition, "In Touch: Nature, Ritual and Sensuous Art from the Northwest," in 1976. Seattle's excellent public art patronage system continues to present an alternative patronage system that has benefited many women — especially in Washington's One-Percent for Art funding.

An area yet to be adequately addressed, yet beyond the scope of this book, is women in arts education. Women artists have long worked as instructors within traditionally feminine areas, like design. Since the women's movement, colleges and universities have hired more women, although there is still an imbalance, as for instance at the University of Washington: After Viola Patterson's retirement from the Painting and Printmaking Department in 1966, there were no women in tenure track-positions until the late 1980s, when two women artists from outside the region, Karen Ganz and Shirley Scheier, were brought in.

Perhaps the fact that this book cannot hope to cover all the accomplishments of any one artist will spur authors and publishers to produce monographs on women of the region. Monographs on Northwest artists are few — historically only Emily Carr, along with Morris Graves and Mark Tobey, have been written about consistently. There is also a dearth of major retrospective exhibitions, as well as catalogues on women artists, although small catalogues have been published on Oregon's LaVerne Krause and Washington's Helmi Juvonen and Patti Warashina.[5] There is also a recent monograph on intermedia artist Doris Chase by art historian Patricia Failing.[6]

Moreover, the few publications on regional art history are mainly exhibition catalogues, such as Martha Kingsbury's essay in *Northwest Traditions,* which explains the relationship of male "Northwest School" artists to international developments, and places Margaret Tomkins and Hilda Morris within this context.[7]

In the past, writers on art of the Pacific Northwest have attempted to identify just what Northwest regional art is — or is not.[8] But few major publications have focused on contemporary Northwest art. Peter Plagens's book, *Sunshine Muse: Contemporary Art on the West Coast,* practically ignored living artists working in the Northwest, women artists in particular.[9] A recent book on public art by James M. Rupp, with photographs by well-known Northwest photographer Mary Randlett, *Art In Seattle's Public Places: An Illustrated Guide,* catalogs over 300 public art projects in a state recognized for its public art patronage; of these only 40 are by women.[10] This figure however, doesn't reflect developments within design teams, a major component in Seattle's public art programs of the late 1980s and early '90s, and thus, the rise of a new breed of public artist, like Vicki Scurri. There is also the well-illustrated *50 Northwest Artists* by former Seattle Art Museum curator Bruce Guenther and photographer Marsha Burns, which covers 14 women artists and features incisive portraits by Burns.[11]

Modernism & Beyond: Women Artists of the Pacific Northwest begins to examine how women artists working within the context of the Puget Sound,

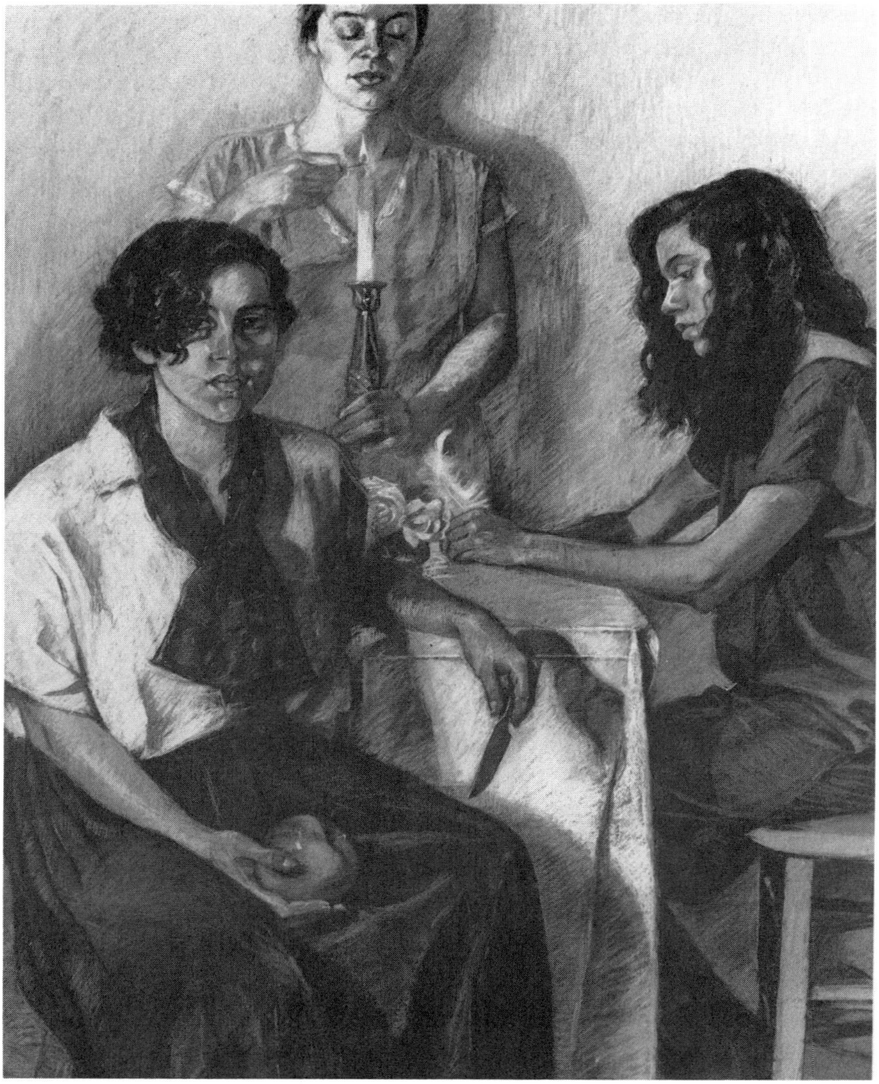

Terry Furchgott, *Psyche and Her Sisters*, 1989, 47 x 36. Courtesy of Lisa Harris Gallery, Seattle.

Eastern Washington, Oregon, and British Columbia have made significant contributions to the Northwest art scene. This dialogue may initiate a re-examination of regional art history as well as inform the broader community of the many achievements of these women.

NOTES:

[1] Perhaps one of the most important recent exhibitions provided national exposure for women artists of Washington state when the National Museum of Women in the Arts (NMWA) presented its Washington centennial-related exhibition, "Washington to Washington: Women in Art Today," 1989. The show focused on the work of 15 women artists working in ceramics, painting, mixed media, photography and fiber art, and opened at Washington State University's Museum of Art in Pullman before traveling to the NMWA's Washington, D.C. gallery, then returning to Washington for an extensive tour through the state.

[2] Patricia Failing, "Temporary Indulgences: Exotic Cuisine and Regional Art," *Reflex*, May-June 1989.

[3] Many women museum curators have been active in the Northwest, including Rachel Griffen (formerly at Portland Art Museum), LaMar Harrington (formerly at Henry Art Gallery and Bellevue Art Museum), Beth Sellars (Cheney Cowles Museum), Barbara Johns (Tacoma Art Museum), Sarah Clark-Langager (Western Washington University), Susan Sagawa (Bellevue Art Museum), Vicki Halper (Seattle Art Museum). Independent curators — men and women — have organized exhibitions in more populist venues, like Seattle's arts festival Bumbershoot: critic and curator Matthew Kangas has exhibited numerous women artists in his large-scale "Bumberbiennale" exhibitions, such as "Seattle Painting: 1925-1985"; other Bumbershoot curators like Ruth Askey have included more than 50% women artists in exhibitions.

[4] Founded in 1914 and active until 1975 (reactivated by the Center on Contemporary Art in 1990 as a biannual), the Annual of Northwest artists was held in Seattle, at the Seattle Art Museum in Volunteer Park (after its construction in 1932). This open competition pre-dated the gallery scene and was evenly balanced in jury and participants between men and women; in 1937 all prizewinners were women.

[5] Karie Nicholson, Ken Paul, Darcia Krause. *LaVerne Krause: Painter and Printmaker (1924-1987)* (Eugene, Oregon: University of Oregon, 1991). Martha Kingsbury, *Helmi Juvonen: Observations and Transformations*. Edited by Wesley Wehr (Olympia: Washington State Capitol Historical Association, 1983). Vicki Halper, *Patti Warashina: Ceramic Sculpture 1962-1991* (Washington: Bellevue Art Museum, 1990).

[6] Patricia Failing. *Doris Chase: Artist in Motion* (Seattle, University of Washington Press,1991).

[7] Martha Kingsbury. *Northwest Traditions*. Exhibition catalogue essay (Seattle Art Museum, 1978).

[8] Past publications, notably Peter Plagens, *Sunshine Muse: Contemporary Art on the West Coast* (New York: Praeger, 1974), have considered Washington, Oregon and British Columbia to be the Pacific Northwest. Art historian Martha Kingsbury's *Northwest Traditions* centered on artists of the Puget Sound area. *Kingsbury's Art of the Thirties: The Pacific Northwest* (Seattle: University of Washington Press, 1972) focused on artists from the Puget Sound, with examples from Oregon and Central Washington. Discussing developments in Washington and Oregon, an essay by Portland Art Museum curator Rachel Griffin, "Portland and Its Environs," accompanied Kingsbury's essay, "Seattle and the Puget Sound," for The National Collection

of Fine Arts exhibition, *Art of the Pacific Northwest from the 1930s to the Present* (Washington, DC: Smithsonian Institution, 1974). In the history of ceramics, the area of Washington, Oregon, Idaho, and Montana has been considered the Pacific Northwest, as in LaMar Harrington's *Ceramics in the Pacific Northwest: A History* (Seattle and London: University of Washington Press, 1979). Former Seattle Art Museum curator Bruce Guenther's *50 Northwest Artists* (San Francisco: Chronicle Books, 1983) included selected artists from Washington, Oregon, Montana and Idaho. In Susan Biskeborn's *Artists at Work: Twenty Five Glassmakers, Ceramists and Jewelers* (Seattle: Alaska Northwest Books, 1990) 15 of 25 artists are women. Artists, museums, and galleries in the cities of Vancouver, Seattle and Portland were the recent focus of Patricia Failing's "Sex, Landscape, and Videotapes" (*ARTnews*, December 1991, 88-93).

[9] Plagens, 1974.

[10] James M. Rupp, with photographs by Mary Randlett. *Art in Seattle's Public Places: An Illustrated Guide* (Japan: University of Washington Press, 1992).

[11] Bruce Guenther and Marsha Burns, 1983. The women artists included are: Joan Ross Bloedel, Deborah Butterfield, Judy Cooke, Fay Jones, Diane Katsiaficas, Nancy Reddin Kienholz (with Edward Kienholz), Sheila Klein, Sherry Markovitz, Hilda Morris, Lucinda Parker, Mary Ann Peters, Norie Sato, Margaret Tomkins, Patti Warashina.

Acknowledgements

The editors would like to thank all those who played a role in the development of *Modernism & Beyond: Women Artists of the Pacific Northwest.* In particular, we are grateful for those who helped to sponsor this publication, including: SAFECO Insurance Co., Microsoft Corporation, Sally Brunsman, Dale Chihuly, Patricia Failing, Lois Graham, Karen Guzak, Carolyn and William Staley, Joan Wahlman, Wesley Wehr, and all the others too numerous to name.

We are appreciative of the Seattle Art Museum, Henry Art Gallery, Cheney Cowles Museum, Vancouver Art Gallery, Oregon Historical Society, King County Historical Society and other institutions who have assisted the authors and provided illustrations from their collections. We would also like to extend our appreciation to the many art galleries in Seattle and Portland who were instrumental in providing information.

Special thanks goes to those who assisted the editors in the Seattle end of production, notably Wallis Bolz, Diane Testa, and Heidi Myer.

Part I:
Women Defining Themselves: Modernism 1900 to 1940

The seeds of modernism in the Pacific Northwest were sown by numerous women artists from 1900 to 1940. The history of notable achievements by these regional women began around the turn of the century and expanded during the depression era, when it was nourished by support from the government-sponsored Federal Art Project. Art historian Lynn McAllister describes the background and lives of these artists and their relation to unfolding modernism within the embryonic Northwest communities.

Stirrings of Modernism in the Northwest

by Lynn McAllister

Art is not created in an historical vacuum, but grows out of individual works within the context of artists' intentions and experiences. The artist's experience inevitably brings her into contact with her environment and existing art traditions. My essay addresses individual histories of women artists in this context in two major sections: the Early Period from 1880-1920 and the Inter-war Period from 1920-1940.

THE EARLY PERIOD (1880-1920)

The fact that the Northwest region was enriched by women residents interested in the arts was not unique in the West. Men of the frontier regions were developing the land and commerce. This left to women the responsibility of developing art and culture.

Unfortunately, information about these early Northwest women artists is meagre.[1] Among women artists recognized nationally, *The American Art Annual* listed 20 Seattle women active in the first quarter of the 20th century. The art community in the Northwest had begun to flourish during the last quarter of the 19th century, as Seattle developed from a town to a city. The Northern Pacific railroad in Tacoma in 1885 and the Great Northern Railway built in Seattle in 1893 brought settlers in increasing numbers. The discovery of gold in Alaska in 1897 further enhanced Seattle's position as a thriving city.

The earliest art instruction was attempted by Sarah Cheney Willoughby who arrived in Seattle in 1862 and was hired by the newly formed Territorial University of Washington to teach art classes. However, because there were no students, she taught music instead. The first art classes at the University were taught by Miss Minnie Sparling in 1877 with eight students in attendance. Mrs. Harriet Foster Beecher was added to the 1882-1883 University of Washington catalogue as a new painting and drawing instructor. Seattle's first art studio was opened by Beecher in 1881. In 1912 the University of Washington established a College of Fine Arts.

Private art education also began at this time with the official opening of the Conservatory of Arts in 1890; classes were taught by Jessie Fisken and Ella Shepard Bush. Bush opened the Seattle Arts School in 1894. Private studios were also important. In 1904 Lillian Ann Pettingill opened a studio to prepare students for acceptance by Eastern art schools.

Women artists were instrumental as well in establishing art societies and clubs that eventually became the major art institutions of the Northwest.[2] The Society of Seattle Artists, founded in 1904 with an artist-only membership,[3] was an attempt to provide a forum for artists in the region. The Society held its first exhibition in 1905, achieving national status with inclusion in the American Art Annual.

Women were the mainstay of the Seattle Fine Arts Association, founded to include members of the community interested in the arts, but not necessarily artists.[4] In 1914 women established the Annual of Northwest Artists, which became the annual juried exhibition for local artists. Finally, the Fine Arts Society became the Seattle Art Museum (SAM), founded in 1932 by the donations of Dr. Richard E. Fuller, president of the Society and later director of the museum, and his mother, Mrs. Eugene Fuller.

Other artist societies founded in large part by Northwest women artists made major contributions to artists' education and support and increased exhibition opportunities for Northwest residents.[5] Twelve charter members of The Northwest Printmakers (NP) formed in 1928 were women. The society continued until 1971, with internationally recognized artists regularly exhibiting in annual shows. Still active today, the Women Painters of Washington (WPW) was founded in 1930 by six women artists.[6] Finally, the Northwest Watercolor Society (NWS) was founded in 1940; several of the women discussed in this article have been associated with the NWS.

Many area women painters studied at the Art Students League [New York City] with American artists Robert Henri and William Merrit Chase, whose teaching incorporated modern concepts. Many founders of the early art societies were themselves teachers, as well as practicing professional artists,who studied with artists like Henri and Chase.

Painter, art critic, and teacher, Ella Shepard Bush was an important figure in the Seattle art scene from 1887 to 1916.[7] Her training was extensive, beginning at the Corcoran Gallery of Art in Washington D.C, continuing at the Art Students League in New York with Henri, Kenyon Cox, Thomas W. Dewing, and J. Alden Weir. She was the first president of the Society of Seattle Artists, and in 1907 wrote an art column for *The Week-End*, a Seattle publication. She took her students on sketching trips and her women's life classes were among the first in the area. Bush's portraits were mainly of notable male figures in the area, including five King County Superior Court judges; in their vivid brushwork and painterly tonal style they reflected her study with Henri.

Emily Inez Denny (1853-1918), daughter of a founding Seattle family, cited Bush as one of Seattle's leading artist-teachers.[8] Denny was a self-taught artist whose Northwest scenes might be called modern primitive paintings. The garish palette of her later large canvases, like *Panoramic View of the Olympics* (1894), shows intense color and simplified, bold composition.

Harriett Foster Beecher (1854-1915) and Abby Rhoda Williams Hill (1861-1943) were early Seattle painters whose landscape scenes in impressionistic brushwork captured the evanescent light of Northwestern skies and water.[9] Beecher was a noted portraitist, who painted intimate natural scenes, including the Calallam and Makah Indians at their daily chores. In 1883 she moved to Tacoma, where she was commissioned by the State, Northern Pacific and Great Northern Railroads to paint the American wilderness. Hill studied at the Chicago Art Institute with William Merrit Chase and exhibited at the Chicago World's fair in 1893, among other major expositions. Her work leaned toward the grand view.

Kathleen Houlahan (1884-1964) was one of the early Seattle artists who achieved recognition in New York and Europe as well as locally.[10] Her range of subjects included florals, seascapes, and rugged atmospheric Northwest landscapes. After graduating from the University of Washington, she studied at the Art Students League with Robert Henri, who singled her out as a gifted portraitist. She painted many children, and her broadly applied color in *Jimmy* (1917) captures emotion and vitality, revealing her debt to Henri's modernism.[11]

Louise Crow (1891-1968) was sought after as a portraitist in Seattle, and a noted teacher at the Seattle Fine Arts Academy and the Cornish School, (founded by Nellie Cornish in 1914).[12] Crow's 1925 portrait of her mother presents virtuoso brushwork in mauve, pink and blue tones. She received her first critical acclaim during travel to Santa Fe from 1918 to 1922 painting the region's Native Americans. Her oil *Eagle Dance* (1919), shown in the Paris Salon d'Automne in 1921, was one of the first modernist works by a Seattle-born artist to be exhibited internationally.[13]

While Seattle's art community was developing, the city of Portland had an equally energetic art scene. In the 1880s Portland proclaimed itself the third richest city per capita in the world. Certainly its residents could travel and collect art from Europe and New York. The Portland Art Association (PAA) was founded in 1892, and the new museum was built in 1905.[14] Out of the PAA grew the Oregon Art Association, which began to hold annual exhibitions in 1896. In 1911 the Portland Art Museum (PAM) held its first invitational show of works by Oregon artists, and in 1912 the PAA held the First Annual Exhibition of Artists of Portland and Vicinity. In 1913 it began the annual series, Artists of the Pacific Coast. Another enduring early art club active from the 1920s to the '70s was The Attic Club, which met once weekly to sketch from live models.[15]

Two major figures in this early Portland art scene were Anna Belle Crocker (1866-1961) and Clara Jane Stephens (d.1952). Crocker's formal art training was at the Art Students League, which she attended in 1904 and 1908.[16] She also studied at Columbia University with Arthur W. Dow. The broad, immediate brushwork of her self-portrait (1910) reflects training with Robert Henri.

After a study trip to Europe in 1909, Crocker was appointed curator of the newly formed PAM, where she remained in various positions for the next 46 years. The PAM and its school were the center of art activity in Portland. Her enthusiasm for modern art was evident when the museum brought Marcel Duchamp's sensational *Nude Descending a Staircase #2* (1912) for exhibition shortly after its controversial appearance in the Armory Show in New York, February, 1913. Crocker also authored a book on ideas in Oregon art entitled, *It Goes Deeper Than You Think,* (1946).

Clara Jane Stephens was another major art influence at the turn of the century. She trained at the Art Students League in New York and studied in France and Italy with Kenyon Cox and William Merrit Chase. Chase painted her portrait and gave it to her as a prize for doing the best work in his class. On her return to Portland, she became active in a variety of art clubs and began an active exhibition schedule which included New York. A French art critic for *Les Artistes D'Aujourd'hui* wrote, "These are modern works, without exaggeration, which immediately separate themselves from the ordinary by their sense of color and the spiritual realism of the persons depicted. . . ."[17]

During this period, Oregon and Washington were home to two outstanding women photographers who achieved international reputations, Myra Albert Wiggins (1869-1956) and Imogen Cunningham (1883-1976).

Wiggins was a member of the Photo-Secessionists, a group formed in 1902 by Alfred Stieglitz[18] to advocate photography as a fine art. Three of her photographs were shown in the 1910 Photo-Secessionist exhibition at the Albright Art Gallery, including *Hollyhocks,* a portrait of her daughter Mildred, a painterly work that emphasizes photography as a medium of personal expression. Wiggins was influenced by the pictorial style of Gertrude Käsebier, a member of the Photo-Secessionists and leader of the Pictorial Photographers of America.

Wiggins was also an accomplished painter who had studied at the Art Students League in 1891 with Chase. She moved to Washington in 1907, pursuing painting as well as photography, and in 1930 helped found the WPW.

Imogen Cunningham was born in Portland, Oregon, but grew up in Seattle.[19] She began her photography career by buying a 4 x 5 inch view camera and taking a correspondence course in photography. After graduating in chemistry from the University of Washington, she spent two years working in Edward S. Curtis's photography studio. In 1910 she opened a portrait studio of her own, working in a pictorial, Photo-Secessionist style influenced by Käsebier. An important early Northwest modernist, Cunningham photographed her then-husband Roi Partridge nude on Mount Rainier, creating a local sensation. Later she began her well-known series of plants and flowers, discovering abstract qualities in natural forms, and creating images that entered the pantheon of modern photography.

Three significant Northwest printmakers from the first quarter of the 20th century are Helen Neilson Rhodes (1875-1938), who taught at the University of Washington, Bellingham-based Helen Loggie (1895-1976), and Elizabeth Aline Colborne (c. 1885-1940s).

Rhodes portrayed regional subjects in block prints, like *The Last Road* (1910) and *Herefords*.[20] The realistic rendering of the former contrasts with broken and flattened forms in the latter. A later linocut, *Windows* (1937), shows a cubist-precisionist style with shallow space and angular, faceted forms.

Loggie became a nationally-known printmaker of distinctively stark, powerful compositions of trees and landscape in intaglio. After studying at Smith College and the Art Students League, she took extended study trips to Europe.[21] Her engravings from the '20s, such as *Mountain Hemlock* (1929) and *Virgin Cedar* (1924), are minimal compositions with strong vertical and horizontal lines accenting dramatic darks and lights.

Colborne, another Bellingham printmaker, studied with Rockwell Kent at Pratt Institute in New York. She worked there as a children's book illustrator before moving back to the Northwest, where she produced landscapes of the area — intimate scenes contrasting the dramatic strength and delicacy of nature.

THE INTER-WAR PERIOD OF 1920-1940

In the period between the wars, American art was dominated by Regionalism.[22] In the Northwest, government-supported art programs were an important response to the Depression of the 1930s.[23] A regionalist presentation of local themes in modern realistic styles was the dominant approach of the government-supported Federal Art Project. Several Northwest women artists participated in the Project, which gave artists professional status and time and money to pursue their art.

Ostensibly rejecting modern European art and theory in favor of American subjects, regionalist painters nevertheless revealed their awareness of European modernist trends. Modernism was not dead; its formal elements were simply couched in realistic terms. Northwest women distilled a regionalism that incorporated Cubism and such American modernist styles as Precisionism, while several Northwest artists moved toward toward non-representation.

Women artists of the area mainly portrayed the environs: landscape, seascape, urban scenes, genre themes, like county fairs or markets, and daily events.[24] Among those who deserve attention are Margaret Camfferman (1881-1964), Elizabeth Warhaik (1880-1968), Dorothy Dolph Jensen (1895-1977), Dorothy Milne Rising (b. 1895), Yvonne Twining Humber (b. 1907), Florence Harrison Nesbit (b. 1910), Anne Kutka McCosh (active c. 1930s-1940s), and Ebba Rapp McLauchlan (1909-1985).

Camfferman painted abstracted landscapes and still lifes. Although few of her works appear to be extant, her compositions, such as *Landscape* (1933) and *View from Old Homestead Ranch* (1936), were usually arranged in systems of interacting cubist planes and organic forms loosely articulated in bold fauvist colors. Her early training was at the University of Minnesota and the Minneapolis School of Art, as well as the New York School of Applied Design and, perhaps most importantly, in Paris at the atelier of Andre L'Hote.[25] When she married painter Peter Camfferman, the couple established an art school on Whidbey Island.

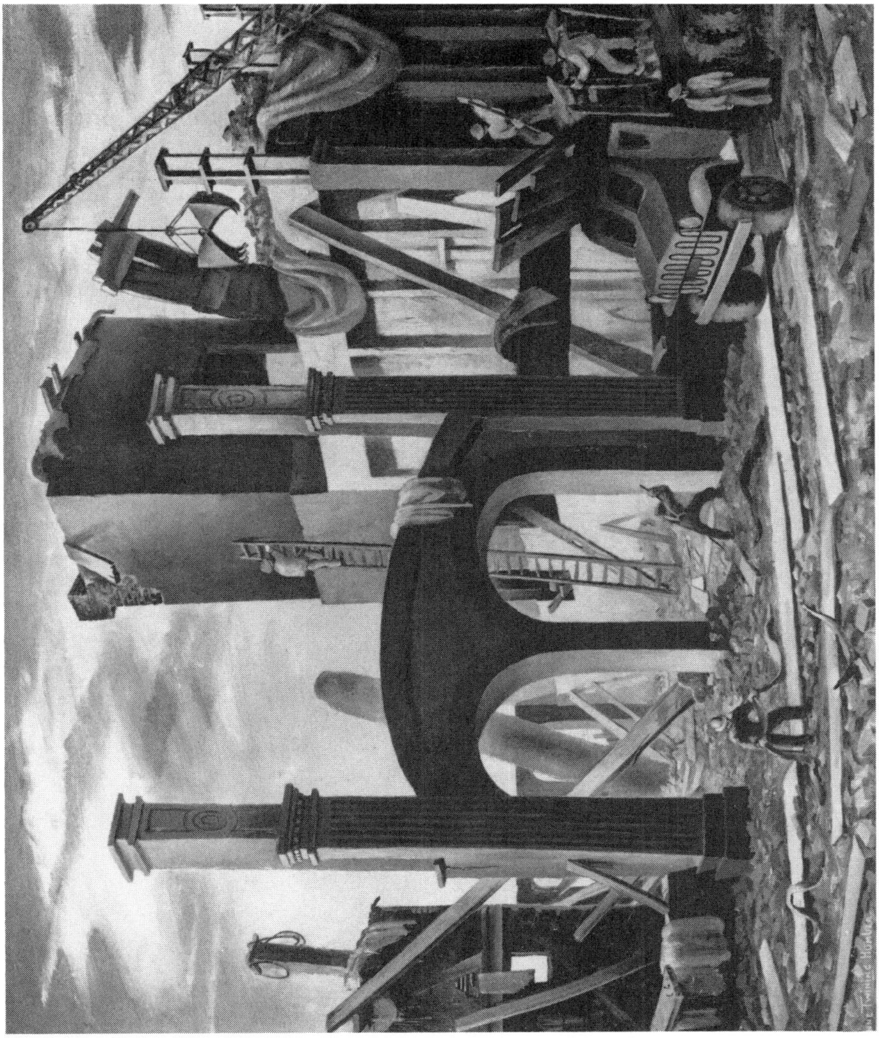

Yvonne Twining Humber, *Demolition*, ca. early 1940s, o/c, 25 x 82.

Elizabeth Warhaik, painter and printmaker, made Impressionistic paintings in the 1920s, like *A View of Lake Union* and *Mt. Shuksan,* vibrant with color and broken brush strokes. She studied at Wellesley College and the University of Washington and was a founding member and first president of the WPW. Warhaik had two solo shows at the SAM as well as one at PAM.[26]

Another painter and printmaker, Dorothy Jensen, painted landscapes, seascapes, and urbanscapes with austere form reduced to essential components.[27] She trained in Antwerp with M. Hanneau and was a student at the Académie Julian in Paris, working with Jean Paul Laurens. Upon her return to Oregon, she studied portraiture with Sidney Bell and landscape

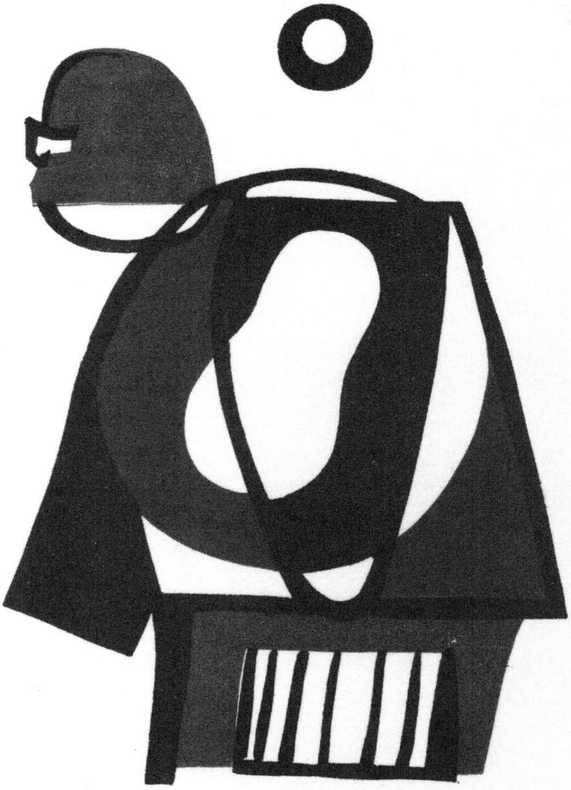

Ruth Penington, ***Still Life***, 1939, color woodblock print, 9 1/2 x 6 9/16. Collection of the Seattle Art Museum (Gift of the Northwest Printmakers).

painting with Harry Wentz. Comparable to Georgia O'Keeffe's landscapes, Jensen's paintings, like *Eastern Washington* (c. 1930), are painted in contrasting colors: tinted golden hills are striped with blue-purple hard-edged shadows.

Dorothy Rising is a painter and printmaker who studied at the Pratt Institute in New York, the Cleveland School of Art, and the University of Washington, where she received an M.F.A.[28] *Mountain Mood*, a landscape, creates rhythm through small staccato accents and sweeping arabesques.

Yvonne Humber became a recognized modernist painter of the American scene. She studied with the American Impressionist, Francis Coate Jones, and Charles Webster Hawthorne in Provincetown, in addition to classes at the National Academy of Design and the Art Students League. After being awarded two consecutive Tiffany Foundation Grants, Humber entered the Public Works of Art Project. In 1943 she moved to Seattle.[29] Her American

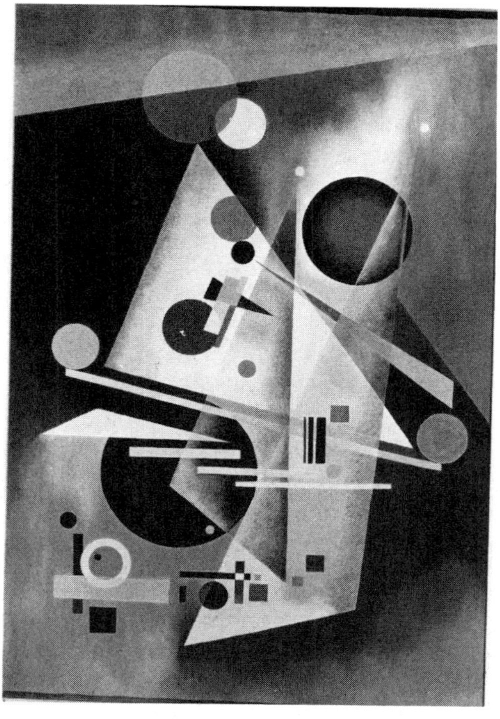

Maude I. Kerns, *Composition No. 27*, 1944, o/c, 36 x 24. Eugene Fuller Memorial Collection, Seattle Art Museum

scenes depict simplified figures engaged in isolated activities in paintings like *Woodland Park Zoo* (c. 1948), *Carnival* (1945), and the *Pike Place Market* (1945). Humber's abstracted genre scenes are compelling modern regionalist paintings.

Ebba Rapp McLauchlan made sculptures that were stylized abstractions, while her paintings were genre scenes with a psychological, Surrealist-inflected edge. She studied at the Cornish School of Fine Art, where she later taught. She also assisted Alexander Archipenko at the University of Washington in 1937-38.[30] Her terra cotta sculpture, *Girl Holding a Mirror,* resembles Picasso's heavy nudes and her two-headed sculpture, *The Gossips,* may have been based on Archipenko's essential forms, but with humorous overtones.

In her genre scenes, Oregon painter Anne McCosh turns the human figure into abstracted shapes that merge with the regional setting of the Eugene area. Studies with Simon Nicolaides (author of *The Natural Way to Draw)* enhanced her unique approach to the human figure.[31] McCosh's paintings, *After the Swim Meet* (1936), *Leg Lock* (1936), and *The Challenger* (1938), depict athletic events, with the contours of the human body composed into concave and convex rhythms.

Constance Fowler is another Oregon artist working during this period who lived in Eugene. She studied at the University of Washington and was influenced by the teachings of the Bauhaus. Fowler later established the art department at Willamette University[32] and in the '30s contributed to a dialogue about modern art on a radio talk show.

Z. Vanessa Helder and Jane Dunning Baldwin were two modern realists of Eastern Washington who worked for the WPA during the 1930s. Baldwin's block prints of the era reflect American values and the rural landscapes of the Northwest's Inland Empire. Helder, a painter and printmaker who was also part of the WPA, worked in a regionalist style with subject matter taken from her Eastern Washington surroundings.[33] Her paintings of the 1940s, such as *Construction Crew* and *Coule Dam Looking West,* incorporate precisionist influences in static forms with crisply defined edges and stable, modulated color.

Ruth Fluno (1923-1974) and Lorna Lowry moved away from regionism, boldly utilizing elements of Cubism in abstracted subject matter. Primarily a self-taught artist,[34] Fluno showed a keen sense of caricature in works like *Gertrude Stein and Alice B. Toklas Arriving at the Chicago Airport* (1934). Lowry, a painter, studied at the University of Washington.[35] In *Birds* (1937), her reduced palette of grey tones in small, fractured brushstrokes evokes the space of Analytic Cubism, while her organic forms recall the abstractions of Arthur Dove.

Three major women artists of the inter-war period developed distinctive non-representational styles.

Ruth Penington (b. 1905) was a printmaker and designer (in metal and jewelry) who taught at the University of Washington. She had studied at the University of Washington, the University of Oregon, Columbia University, and with the modernist artists, including Amadée Ozenfant. In a style related to the bold abstractions of Stuart Davis, as well as European purism, she made brightly colored geometric abstract linoleum block prints, such as *Abstract Forms* (1937), arranged in flattened, often hard-edged shapes printed in contrasting colors against a white ground.[36]

Maude Kerns was an Oregon-based artist who worked in a non-objective style. Her non-objective painting style matured in the 1940s. Her compositions of circles, triangles and rectangles over a field of color are seen in *Composition #12: Forces* (1943). Kerns studied at Columbia University from 1904 through 1906 with Arthur Wesley Dow and E.F. Fenollosa. (Fenollosa taught universal compositional principles of spatial arrangements in line, color and light and dark and espoused a new system of art education in America.) In 1929 she studied with Hans Hofmann, spurring an interest in spatial illusion. Her non-objective style was influenced by Kandinsky, whose work she saw in a 1927 PAM show. Kerns exhibited at the Museum of Non-Objective Painting in New York (now the Solomon Guggenheim Museum of Art), in group exhibitions in the early '40s with artists like Lazlo Moholy-Nagy and Lyonel Feininger, as well as regionally at the SAM and PAM.

Patricia K. Nicholson (b. 1900) developed an Abstract-Expressionist style filtered through Northwest School influences. Her oil and tempera paintings synthesize Abstract Expressionism based on study with painters Peter Camfferman, Mark Tobey and Franz Baum. The large tempera on masonite, *Bright Moon, Clear Wind* (c. 1950s), is a composition of large expressionistic sweeps of color with a halo of gray shadows. The brushwork parallels the calligraphic strokes of Northwest School painters like Tobey and Guy Anderson [37]

The women artists noted here were active in the unfolding scene in the Northwest from 1880 through the 1940s. Undoubtedly there are many more yet to be discovered. Although only a few of the artists mentioned here are well known outside the region, modernist trends they developed are still present in the Northwest.

NOTES:

[1] Anita Galvan Dodds, *Women and Their Role in the Early Art of Seattle* (Master's Thesis, University of Washington, 1981). Much of the information for Part I is based on Dodds's research. Also, see Phil Kovinick, *The Woman Artist in the American West, 1860-1960,* which states that there were approximately 1100 women artists and art educators working in the West by 1890. Also, valuable information on this early period was found in the "Vertical File," Historical Society of Seattle and King County, Seattle.

[2] Dodds, p. 14-19. For information on early Seattle art societies see also Anne H. Calhoun, *A Seattle Heritage,* 1942.

[3] The original 11 founding members were all women: Harriet Foster Beecher, Mrs. E.W. Andrews, Jessie and Mabel Fisken, Emma Small, Mathilda Piper, Ruth Schram, Ella Shepard Bush, Carlotta Blaurock, Florence Curtiss, and Lillian Ann Pettingill. To become a member, the candidate had to be recognized by the community as an accomplished artist.

[4] The Seattle Fine Arts Association was formed in 1908 and shared many members with the Society of Seattle Artists. Important founders were Mrs. Heman Field, an honor graduate of the Art Institute of Chicago, Jessie Fisken, and Imogen Cunningham.

[5] David Martin of Martin-Zambito Fine Art, Seattle, provided essential information on the formation of various societies and the women who were founding members. His biographical files were a major source throughout this essay. See also Bill Lancaster and Clifford Burkey, "Where it All Started," *Northwest Watercolor Society Newsletter.*

[6] The organization is still in operation with more than 100 artist members and both national and international exhibitions during its 62 years. The founding was a response, in part, to the 1928 founding of the Puget Sound Group of Northwest Men Painters, which excluded women.

[7] Dodds, p. 74, and Erika Michael, *Regional Painters of the Puget Sound 1870-1920* (Seattle, Museum of History and Industry exhibition brochure, 1988).

[8] In 1863 she was inspired by Sarah Cheney Willoughby's art exhibition at the University and began to paint using whatever materials were at hand. Dodds, 89, 30. Also see Emily Inez Denny, "Concerning the Development of Art in Seattle, Reminiscences," 1915 (Vertical File, Historical Society of Seattle and King County).

[9] Dodds, p. 68. For information on Abbey Hill, see Jan Budden and Helena Hoyte, *Early Northwest Paintings* (La Conner, Washington, exhibition brochure, Janet Huston Gallery, 1992).

[10] Dodds, p. 100. Also David Martin biographical files. Dodds's 1915 portrait of Puyallup Mayor Ezra Meeker was exhibited at the Panama-Pacific International Exposition in San Francisco. A member of the Society of Independent Artists in New York, she exhibited there from 1917 to 1931.

[11] In 1914 Houlahan returned to Seattle where she exhibited at the first Northwest Annual.

[12] David Martin autobiographical files. Dodds also notes that Crow painted a portrait of Ezra Meeker, as had Houlahan and Beecher.

[13] She exhibited extensively, including shows at the Oakland Art Museum Inaugural, Society of Independent Artists, Corcoran Gallery, and the Seattle Fine Arts Society.

[14] William H. Gerdts, *Art Across America.Two Centuries of Regional Paintings* (NY: Abbeville Press, Vol. III, 1975, 1990). The Portland Art Association was a citizen-directed group whose mission was the cultural enrichment of the region through a permanent collection of art and a suitable exhibition space.

[15] Telephone conversation with Jack Cleaver, Director, Oregon Historical Society.

[16] Gerdts, and Jack L. Joki, Director, The Sovereign Collection, Portland, Oregon, provided biographical information on Crocker. On her return to Portland, Crocker became an active member of the art clubs; she exhibited with the Portland Art Association in 1886, and the Oregon Art Association in 1895-96, and was one of the first four women invited to join the Portland Sketch club, along with Clara Jane Stephens, Carol Dilly and Lillian F. Bain.

[17] Information from The Sovereign Collection. Stephens was honored with a one-woman show in an early exhibition of the newly formed PAM in 1914. She taught at the PAM school from 1917-1938. The other French journal to review her painting of 1925 was *La Revue du Varai et du Beau*. Both journals are mentioned in the *Spectator*, "Paris Notes Miss Stephens' Art," (Oct. 10, 1925).

[18] Information from David Martin's biographical files, with the special assistance of his assistant, Sharon Bearny. See also, Gerdts, Volume III.

[19] Dodds, p. 82. See also Imogen Cunningham, *Imogen Cunningham: Photography* (1970). A collection of Cunningham's work is in the Museum of Modern Art, New York.

[20] Biographical information from the Henry Art Gallery, University of Washington, which also has a collection of her prints. See also Marion Appleton, ed., *Who's Who in Northwest Art* (Seattle, Frank McCaffrey, 1941).

[21] Receiving numerous awards, she had several one-person shows, among others at the Smithsonian Institution, the National Academy of Design, and the SAM. Loggie exhibited widely at American museums like the Whitney Museum of American Art and the Carnegie Institute, and was a member of the Northwest Printmakers (NP).

[22] Mathew Baigell. History of American Painting (New York: Praeger Publishers, 1971): pp. 227, 232.

[23] The two major programs were the Public Works of Art Project, started in 1933 and funded by the Federal Treasure Department, which stresses art based on the American scene; and the Works Progress Administration established in 1935 with the intention to support local and regional artists in need.

[24] David Martin, Martin-Ambito Fine Art, and Jan Budden, private dealer, were very helpful in identifying modern Northwest women painters, supplementing information from regional museums and literature.

[25] A member of the loosely organized Group of Twelve and the WPW, Camfferman had a one-person exhibition at SAM in 1935.

[26] Warhaik exhibited on both the East and West Coasts, winning several awards.

[27] Jensen was a founding member of the WPW and charter member of the NWS as well as belonging to the Northwest Printmakers (NP). She had solo exhibitions at the SAM, the Charles and Emma Frye Art Museum.

[28] Rising was a charter member of the NWS, and an early member of the WPW, as well as exhibiting nationally in various group shows. Information from Martin's biographical files. Also, see Appleton.

[29] Humber served as president of the WPW from 1947-48. She had a solo show at SAM, and exhibited at the National Academy of Design and the New York World's Fair of 1939.

[30] Rapp exhibited at the SAM, the Frye, PAM and the Henry Art Gallery.

[31] McCosh began exhibiting in 1931 at the New School for Social Research after she met Diego Rivera while in Mexico on a scholarship.

[32] Fowler exhibited in the 1939 World's Fair and had a solo show at SAM in 1942. Biographical information was provided by David Neckak.

[33] The Cheney Cowles was a resource for the artist's paintings. (Biographical information from Appleton.)

[34] Fluno did take part-time and night-school classes at Minneapolis Institute of Art, Walker Art Center, Heatherly's College of Art, London, and Washington State University's Summer Program, studying with Kenneth Callahan. She exhibited throughout the Northwest, including Expo '74 in Spokane, the Governor's invitational, at the University of Oregon, and the University of Washington. (Biographical and visual information from the Henry Art Gallery, University of Washington.)

[35] The Seattle Art Museum provided visual information. See also Erika Michael, *Northwest Cubism: The Heritage of Cubism in the Pacific Northwest from the 1920s through the 1960s* (Tacoma Art Museum, 1991). Lowry's painting *Birds* is in Michaels' brochure. She had a solo show at SAM in 1937. She was an elementary school teacher at Bailey Gatzert School, Seattle, Washington.

[36] Penington belonged to the NP and exhibited prints in various regional group shows.

[37] Nicholson was a member of the WPW and had a solo exhibition at SAM in 1933. See Northwest Art Today, Adventures in Art, Seattle World's Fair, 1962.

Part II:
Regional Modernism and the Mainstream: 1930 to 1960

Women artists who were pivotal figures from the 1930s through the early '60s, a time when few women artists received attention either in or out of the region, are examined here in three essays. Historian Kazuko Nakone discusses three artists working from the period of the 1940s through the '60s: Viola Patterson, Margaret Tomkins, and Hilda Morris. Art historian Martha Kingsbury describes what loner Helmi Juvonen had in common with other modernists of her generation. Critic Ron Glowen looks at the career of influential Canadian painter Emily Carr.

Washington and Oregon Independents: Individual Paths Along a Northwest Landscape

by Kazuko Nakone

Three Northwest women,Viola Patterson (1898-1984), Hilda Morris (1911-1991), and Margaret Tomkins (b. 1916) began careers in art from the 1920s to the late 1930s. Forging different paths in the landscape of Northwest art, they sought visions uniquely their own, yet registering outside influences.

Most area literature has focused on artists like Mark Tobey and Morris Graves. Saturation coverage of these few individuals has ignored the accomplishments and diversity of many artists of the period. A multiplicity of art styles flourished in the region simultaneously with the predominant "Northwest School."

Today, in a time of internationalism, young Northwest artists look beyond the region for inspiration. But Patterson, Morris and Tomkins's stories, and the course of their artistic development, reveal the ongoing flow of American art movements into the present.

VIOLA PATTERSON

Viola Patterson was a graduate of Lincoln High School in Seattle. When the Seattle Fine Arts Society established the Annual Northwest Artists competition 1914, she was not yet part of the local art scene. She didn't take her first drawing class until beginning a master program in librarianship at the University of Washington. In 1922, she married Ambrose Patterson (1877-1966), who taught the drawing class. He had joined the faculty at the University of Washington in 1919, already an accomplished painter who had trained in his native Australia as well as in Paris and shown in Paris, London, and Brussels.

Raymond Hill, Annette Eden, and Eugenie Worman were on the faculty when Viola studied art at the University of Washington and her social circle centered around the University. She often painted alongside Ambrose, whose influence during her formative years is not entirely clear. His painting, especially his "light-hearted color range," clearly intrigued her, and she retained this love of color throughout her life. Among her earliest works known to the public, *Victoria B.C.* (1928), published in a chapbook series with Ambrose, featured 12 monochromatic woodcuts of literally rendered scenery.

During the 1920s it was still rare for American artists to have years of training, and those who wished to be modern looked toward Paris. In the fall of 1929, Patterson traveled to Paris to study art, accompanied by her husband. Andre L'Hote, a prominent teacher who worked with many international students, had a class of about 40 which Patterson joined at his atelier in Montparnasse. L'Hote would set poses for nude and costumed life models on Monday morning and leave them until Saturday.

In Paris of the '20s, Matisse and Picasso were influential figures. Yet, as late as 1930, color in L'Hote's painting was conservatively structured and relatively naturalistic. Patterson's landscape, *Portofino* (1929-1930), also retains an illusionistic depth. *Seated Nude* (1934), however, has a subtle geometric structure which divides a surface of harmonious color.

A review of a show the Pattersons had together in Seattle (*Town Crier*, January 16, 1932) noted that "Both the Pattersons reflect Europe and particularly France, not only in subject matter, but in feeling." Viola wrote an article on "Craftsmanship" (*Town Crier*, May 14, 1932), stressing the importance of learning over a long period and proper handling of media.

In 1934, the Pattersons travelled together to Mexico. Viola was impressed by the Mexican muralists' fresco technique, and her paintings captured the ambience of Mexico. By the late 1940s, however, her orientation was to formal issues, especially overall compositional balance, as in *Pike Place Market* (collection SAFECO Insurance Co., Seattle).

Although she associated closely with European artists teaching in the United States such as Alexander Archipenko and Amadée Ozenfant who visited the University of Washington in the late '30s, Patterson still did not follow Ozenfant's purist painting and spontaneous line drawing directly to abstraction.

Her work had more in common with other modernists of her generation in the region, such as Walter Isaacs or Margaret and Peter Camfferman. Many diverse painting styles coexisted among the 124 artists recorded in *Roll of Artists of the State of Washington* (1924-5).

American artists of the era were striving to achieve their own distinctive modern art while learning from the advanced Europeans. Patterson had exhibited paintings, prints, and sculpture early in her career, and in 1937 became, with her husband, a part of The Group of Twelve, a loosely organized local artists group. It was not until 1947 that she became a professor of art at the University of Washington, where she taught until her retirement in 1966.

In the early 1950s, when Abstract Expressionism began to have an effect in the Northwest, Mark Tobey, a friend of the Pattersons since 1923, offered

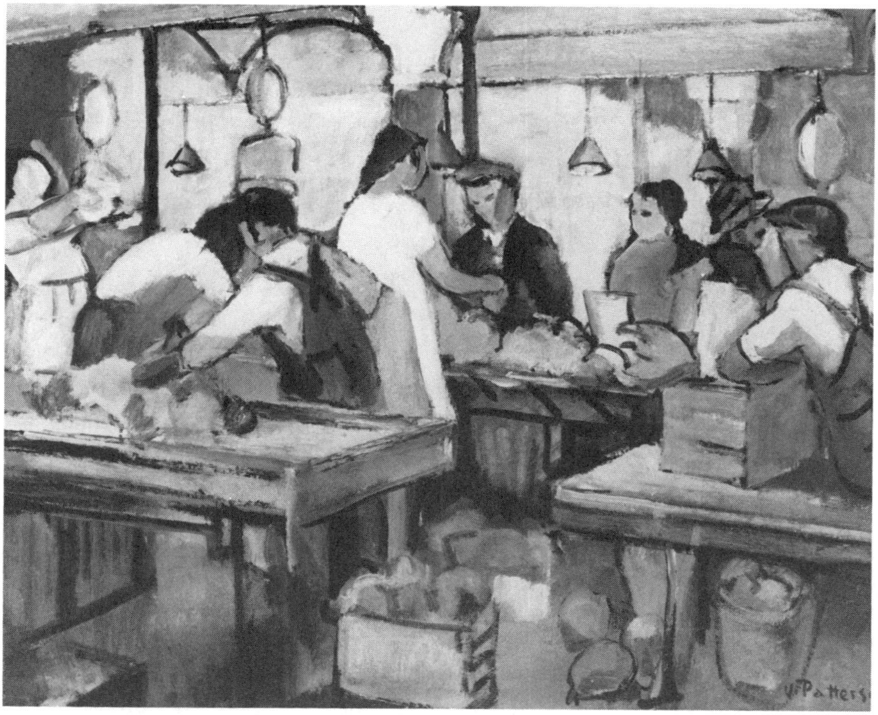

Viola Patterson, *Pike Place Market*, ca. late 1940s, o/c. Collection of SAFECO Insurance Co., Seattle.

to teach her the style. Instead of following the linear abstraction known as "white writing," which Tobey developed in the 1930s and '40s, she began her own approach to abstraction, working with the images of boats, water, and sky. The boats began to change form, as the basic geometric lines of their structure filtered through her imagination. These later calligraphic "signature" paintings of the late 1950s and early '60s might be compared with New York School painter, Franz Kline, who suddenly came into abstraction, propelled by a strong foundation in drawing. However, unlike Kline, Patterson did not create autonomous black brush strokes, rather invoking harmony with colors as part of an overall composition.

HILDA MORRIS

Hilda Morris, born in New York City, began her career in the 1930s when American modern sculpture was still in its formative years. She absorbed art history by visits to the Metropolitan Museum of Art, the Museum of Modern Art, and the Museum of Natural History (all in New York). In *50 Northwest Artists* (1983), Morris discussed the importance of her high school mathematics teacher who introduced ideas of symbolic imagery to her through mathematics. Her father fostered her continuing interest in music.

In 1932, Morris entered the Cooper Union School of Art and Architecture in New York City. Her painting teacher was American Scene painter, John Stewart Curry, yet her favorite painter was Milton Avery, a poetic interpreter of Matisse. A steadily growing interest in Eastern calligraphy and the ideography of non-Western cultures, as well as differences with her instructors, led Morris to leave the school just before graduation.

The New York art scene of the mid-1930's was intensely diverse. The Federal Art Project, begun in 1933, promoted the idea that art was for the masses. In 1935 and '36, Morris studied at the Art Students League, where Robert Henri's presence continued to be felt. She also looked to art from other traditions. In 1936, the Museum of Modern Art organized a show from Europe, "Cubism and Abstract Art," which introduced visions of radical abstraction. Morris was impressed by the art of Georges Braque, Constantin Brancusi, Henry Moore, and Julio Gonzales. In 1937, she visited Mexico.

In 1938, she was invited to teach at the Spokane Art Center, organized under the W.P.A. Project in Eastern Washington. Two years later, she married painter Carl Morris, Director of the Center. They shared many fundamental ideas, influencing each other while maintaining the boundaries between their approaches.

Excited by the natural environs of the Northwest, Morris initially painted realistic landscapes. In the 1930s, her sculpture began to move toward abstraction and a search for more organic forms. She explored a multitude of sculpture media, including wood, terra cotta, plaster and cement as models for bronze casting. The cement and plaster *Singing Woman* (1939-40) portrays music emanating through the figure's tilted shoulders and outstretched neck.

Giving birth to a baby boy in 1945 started Morris on a series of thematic "Mother and Child" sculptures in addition to her ongoing musical interests. These small-scale works retained a bold presence. Negative space, volume defined by light, deep cuts and the hollowed-out passages were integrated in richly textured, often flowing surfaces with a frontal focus.

The concave skeletal body of *Ancient Fish* (1952-3) flows throughout its sweeping curvature. In the cement and metal poles of *Early Voyagers* (1954-5), uplifted figures seem to dance in orbit. Morris's sculpture and mixed-media brush paintings were exhibited in 1955 at the Otto Seligman Gallery [Seattle].

Although working and exhibiting in the Northwest, Morris felt her native New York was never very far away. She kept abreast of current developments and often visited the city. She knew sculptor David Smith, and was attracted to the work of Reuben Nakian. Her husband became well acquainted with Mark Rothko, who had relatives in Portland. Her work was shown at the Metropolitan Museum of Art; she showed a watercolor at the Brooklyn Museum of Art and at the Kraushaar Gallery, prior to a 1958 one-person show at New York's Barona Penthouse Gallery (*The New York Times*, September 14, 1958). She received a Ford Foundation Grant in 1960.

Though the Morrises were close to Mark Tobey and had lived on a houseboat in Seattle in the 1940s, she never thought her work was part of the "mystic" Northwest School or that she was part of the politically powerful circle surrounding the Seattle Art Museum. At the end of the 1940s, the Morrises moved to Portland and built their own home, isolated on a quiet hillside. Although she was well established in Portland for over 30 years,.Morris longed to return to New York. Instead, she periodically left for Italy, to work in a foundry near Pisa.

By 1965, Morris moved toward bronze casting in Italy, and had already produced one of her seminal works, *Muted Harp* (Opera House, Seattle,

1962), using cement, brass powder for surface reflections, bronze, and copper. Here a balanced, arched sweep opens to a forest of cemented metal poles. An Alaskan trip to see totems in 1963 accentuated Morris's use of symbolic forms to reflect visual experience as a cognitive process.

By the early 1960s, the New York art scene had changed dramatically. To Hilda Morris, art was something sacred and personal beyond commodity. She did not feel part of the generation of artists who emerged with Minimalism or Pop after the heyday of Abstract Expressionism.

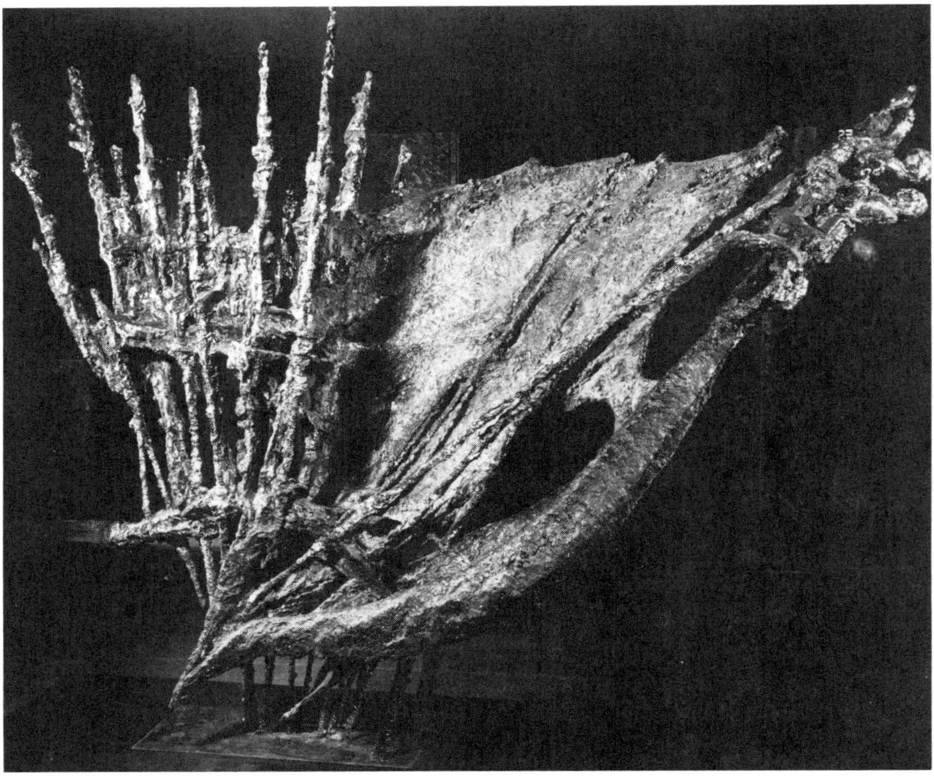

Hilda Morris, *Muted Harp*, 1962-63, cement, metal, color. Seattle Opera House (commissioned by Mr. and Mrs. Kenneth B. Colman).

MARGARET TOMKINS

Born in Los Angeles, Margaret Tomkins spent the first two decades of her life there, earning B.A. and M.A. degrees in fine art from the University of Southern California. She also attended summer sessions at Chouinard Art School. The University did not impose strict academic training, she recalled, aiming instead to enhance the students' individuality.

While an assistant instructor at graduate school, Tomkins experimented with tempera. Then, painstakingly, over the next 20 years, she developed her own style of tempera painting. In the late 1930s her work was included in museum group shows in San Diego, Oakland, San Francisco, Seattle, and New York, where it was exhibited at the World's Fair of 1939.

That same year, she was excited by Pablo Picasso's *Guernica* (1937), when it and related drawings were exhibited at Los Angeles's Stendahl Art Galleries to raise funds for the Spanish Civil War. Throughout the '30s a social consciousness was prevalent among artists and Tomkins was no exception.

With a continuing interest in European artists like Joan Miró, Paul Klee, and Marcel Duchamp, Tomkins was also drawn to paintings of artists recently arrived in the United States as refugees, notably Matta, Max Ernst and S.W. Hayter. Their work communicated subconscious psychic images and Tomkins began to look into the meaning behind formal attributes. The fractured, cubistic structure of early Duchamp interested her, and she was perhaps influenced by Hayter's automatic lines and Matta's bright, transparent color.

Tomkins taught briefly at the University of Washington in 1939. In 1940 she married painter and sculptor James FitzGerald (1910-73) with whom she raised two daughters and a son. A student and friend of Thomas Hart Benton, FitzGerald took over the directorship of the Spokane Art Center after Carl Morris.

From the late 1930s through the '40s, Tomkins's visual expression was influenced by the war experience. In *Metamorphosis* (Seattle Art Museum, 1943), light escapes as though from another world, illuminating unidentified organic form. Her psychological state also illuminated *Night Bondage* (1947), which toured with "Abstract and Surrealist American Art" in 1948. Through these works she became associated with Surrealism.

Tomkins, however, was concerned less with communication of an inner vision than one related to the world around her. In *The Prophesy* (1944), figures were structured by scraping solids with angled outlines and incising cuts with a blade. She described the painting as "a sort of a symbol of the laceration and tortured distortion in the world today" (*Seattle Times*, October 18, 1946). *Tragic Balance of Destiny* (1945), in tempera on paper, is an abstracted landscape with free black lines. Tomkins continued in the tradition of automatic drawing and abstracted structural form well into the 1950s.

After World War II, she felt the urge to create powerful statements rather than withdraw into delicate washes. From then on, she said, color became an essential part of her painting. In *Sign of the Sun* (1957) human figures are

Margaret Tomkins, *Assassination*, 1963, o/linen, 77 1/2 x 86 3/4. Collection of Tacoma Art Museum

assembled from volumes fused with dense, free lines. Cross-hatched, independent lines and color ranging from umber to earth and white to black create structural tension.

During the 1950s, the number of galleries in the region was still very limited and regional artists still relied on the Annual of Northwest Artists at the Seattle Art Museum for exposure. Tomkins and her husband boycotted this competition for ten years to protest the museum circle's control of the local art scene and its connection with the outside art world. In 1958 Tomkins and FitzGerald took matters into their own hands and organized a cooperative gallery on Seattle's East Olive Way. Louis Bunce, William Ivey, Manuel Izuquierdo, and Alden Mason were members for the year of the gallery's survival. During the '50s, Tomkins continued to send work outside the region and was exhibited at the Metropolitan Museum of Art, the Whitney Museum of American Art, and other major American museums.

In 1959 a tragic fire in their home, destroyed 250 paintings and scores of art objects Tomkins and FitzGerald had spent 30 years creating. Soon her painting became a monochromatic landscape of dark fields. In 1961, she and FitzGerald visited Europe and New York. She was overwhelmed by their praise for American art next to age-old European art.

A transition toward dramatically rich color fields in her large oils followed, as Tomkins abandoned the small easel, tempera, and preliminary drawings. One of her major works, *Assassination* (1963), was painted over 20 times after President John F. Kennedy was killed. Both she and her husband continued to be strongly affected by social concerns. FitzGerald made a series of sculptures protesting the Vietnam War. She assisted him with public commissions in the 1960s and '70s, eventually making sheet metal sculpture of her own.

After FitzGerald's death in 1973, Tomkins continued to live and paint in their Lopez Island studio. Her increasing fascination with light is evident in the painting *Passage* (1975, collection SAFECO Insurance Co., Seattle), as translucent color lifts the weight of opacity and layers of subtle pinks and pastel blues and greys bring infinite depth to a frameless sky.

The World's Fair of 1962, held at the Seattle Center, provided an international showcase that accelerated growth of the regional art scene. The reputation of the "Northwest School" was firmly established, and many artists of the generation came to maturity. At the same time, new art movements began to widen the concept of art.

Many older Northwest artists were buried under the media barrage of these new movements. In her Laurelhurst studio residence, Patterson painted flowers in her French garden in the late 1970s. Morris struggled with cancer the last ten years of her life, concentrating on abstract Sumi painting. Tomkins lived alone on Lopez Island, without electricity, until she had a stroke in 1988. Even then she continued to paint.

Though there were professional women artists before the turn of the century in the Northwest, well into the 20th century they were categorized in genres like "flower painting" and "portraiture." Many never received the respect they deserved. These three women lived through a transitional period in American art, fighting for recognition as independent individuals. Morris and Tomkins particularly resisted the category "woman artist," preferring to let the art speak for itself.

REFERENCES:

Laura Brunsman, *Viola Patterson* (Seattle: SAFECO Insurance Co., 1991).

Bruce Guenther, *50 Northwest Artists*, San Francisco: Chronicle Books, 1983.

Sue Ann Kendall, *Hilda Morris* (Master's thesis, University of Washington, 1986).

Martha Kingsbury, "Art of the Thirties: The Pacific Northwest," *No. 4, Index of Art in the Pacific Northwest*, Seattle and London: Henry Art Gallery with the University of Washington Press, 1972.

Viola Patterson, Interview by Martha Kingsbury, Northwest Oral History Project, Archives of American Art, Smithsonian Institution, 1982.

Viola Patterson, Interview by William Hoppe, Archives of Northwest Art, 1972.

Seattle Art Museum, "Northwest Traditions," essay by Martha Kingsbury Washington: Seattle Art Museum, 1978.

Margaret Tomkins, Interview by Bruce Guenther, Northwest Oral History Project, Archives of American Art, Smithsonian Institution, 1984.

Patricia Grieve Watkinson, "Margaret Tomkins," Pullman, Washington: Washington State University, 1977.

Helmi Juvonen (1903-1985)

by Martha Kingsbury

Helmi Juvonen was preoccupied with human culture. Her art dealt with the objects made by cultures, with the symbols and the sign systems of cultures, and occasionally with the creators themselves. In her most vigorous and complex period of work, around the 1950s, she wove the "categories" of creator, symbol, and object into a continuum. Likewise, she interwove allusions to various world cultures with the practice of different genres of art. Her own relation to human culture was highly integrated into the artistic modernism and humanist internationalism characteristic of the avant garde of her time; but, conversely, her relation to culture was extremely marginal in personal and practical ways.

Helmi — as she signed her work and was consequently known by her admirers — was born in 1903 in Butte, Montana, and moved with her family in 1918 to Seattle, where she went to Queen Anne High School. Her parents of Russian/Finnish origin valued the arts, and her sister was later a commercial artist. Helmi's art training continued at the Cornish School, a private institution founded on the integration of the arts — theater, music, design. Her long interest in puppetry probably originated there. From the school's Amilio Amero, Helmi learned lithography and probably the foundation for her rich block prints. She was with the Federal Arts Project in 1938-40 and put her sound technical skills to use as a draftsman at Boeing Aircraft Company during World War II.

Helmi's memories of art school training included a slightly dismissive note that the students did hundreds of portraits and were much too busy to think about the sorts of things interviewers ask about. Certainly her art was directed toward the human, but not as direct portraiture. A series of delineations of shacks and huts in Seattle's Hooverville is perhaps the closest she ever came to landscape. More like surrogate-portraits of human lives, the constructions are described with spare elegance, isolated and centrally placed on the white of the paper. Likewise, her many drawings and paintings of Native-American carved objects might be considered a form of still-life, but they are much more "portraits" of inspirited objects. For many years, she scrutinized masks and other artifacts in the

Washington State Museum (now Burke Museum) at the University of Washington and such other sites as the Provincial Museum in Victoria. In drawings, water-base paintings, and block prints, Helmi usually placed the object-images centrally on a neutral ground (like the shacks) and powerfully modeled them in modes ranging from literal to interpretative.

Although she continued to value and practice conventional techniques of precision, focus, and three-dimensional illusionism through the '50s, Helmi also developed a range of strategies much closer to graffiti and cartoons, with room for spontaneity. Her largest works from the later '40s through the '60s (about 20" by 30", as a rule in tempera, gouache, and ink) tend to some version of this mode. Their lateral organization, shallow indeterminate depth, and "all-overness" are characteristically modernist. A frequent light or white delineation on a darker ground suggests chalk on blackboard and other vernacular references, as well, inevitably, as the "white writing" identified with Mark Tobey and Morris Graves. These two closely linked Seattle painters were at the height of their creativity and national renown during this period and Helmi knew them and their work well. She lived not far from Tobey through much of the '50s, was a warm friend of his close associate Pehr (also a painter), and had an amiable relation with the witty and eccentric Graves.

In her works in this second mode, Helmi introduced words and phrases, along with a wide variety of human figures or faces and bits of architecture as well as other human constructs. In many works, the surface is filled with frontally arranged and laterally dispersed crowds at some ceremony or celebration. In contrast to her meticulous scrutiny of objects in museums, these works are partly grounded in Helmi's drawings of Bon Odori, the Japanese summer festival in Seattle's International District and her trips (sometimes with other local artists) to witness tribal ceremonies in the Long Houses of coastal tribes north of Seattle. Allusions range from Christmas and crucifixions to a widely eclectic selection of circuses, parades, dances, and pancultural gatherings. Angels mingle with totems and exotic gods. The essential content is a fantasy of community and human energy. There is considerable joking in the words and the sometimes cartoonish or clumsy figures, but also poetry in the broken phrasings, and reverence in the accumulated religious references.

These works participate strongly in avant-garde modernism. For example, their pan-culturalism is voracious, eclectic, and partly historical, but more ethnographic. Helmi's extensive notes about a variety of world religions and cosmologies, and her attendance at Baha'i meetings with Tobey and other friends, were both source and expression of this drive, as was her deep love of the museums' ethnographic art. In addition to these non-western sources so frequent among modernisms, from Cubism and Expressionism through Abstract Expressionism, Helmi also undercut the respected genres of western high art with a dismissive indifference worthy of the Dadaists. She sold her block prints from a clothesline with a can for the money, like produce; she made some of her largest works on battered packing-crate material (in one incorporating its tattered labels); she erased distinctions between her greeting cards and her larger paintings. Her few collages — more "conventionally" modern than these practices — reveal a sprightly wit in their use of vernacular images and materials.

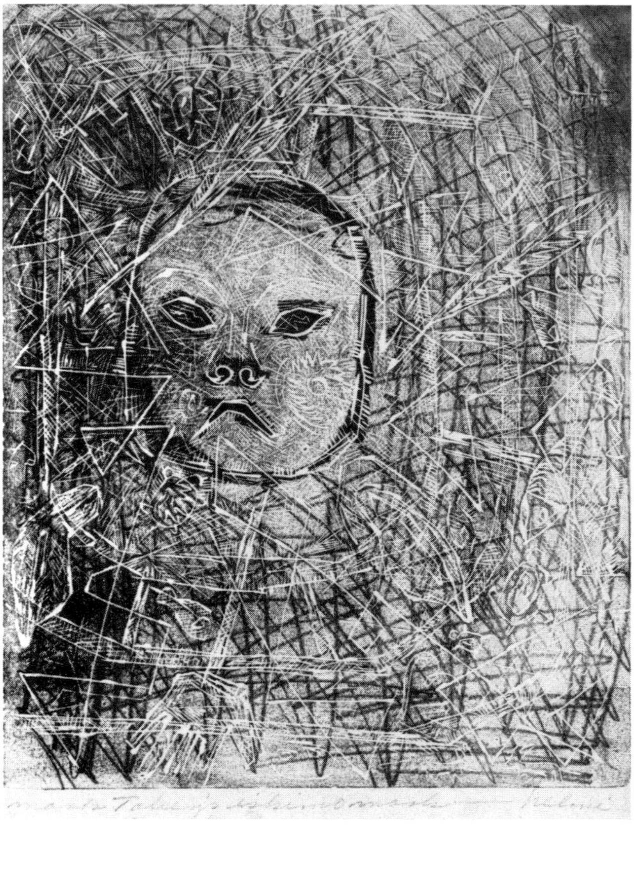

Helmi Juvonen, ***Mark Tobey's Eskimo Mask***, ca. 1953-54, monoprint on newsprint. 13 11/16 x 10 5/8. Collection of Henry Art Gallery, University of Washington (Gift of Neil Meitzler).

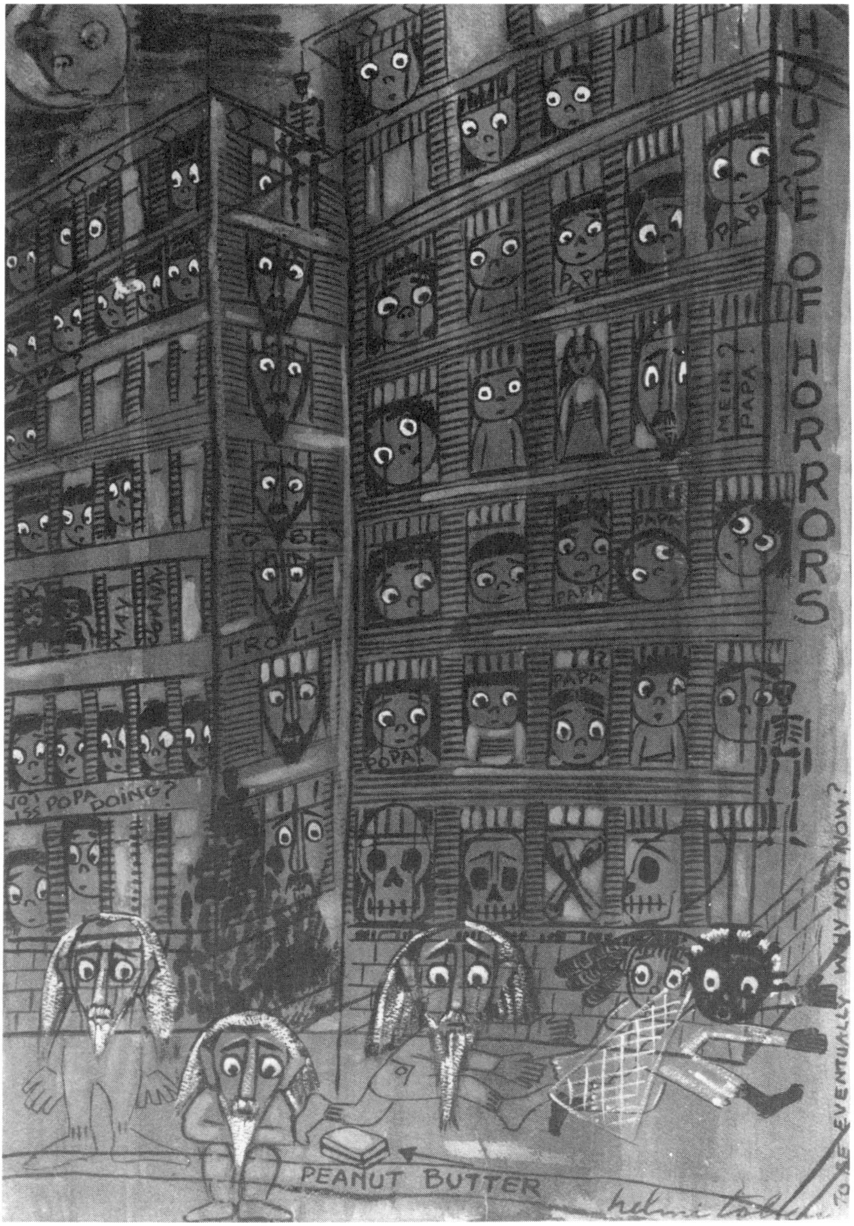

Helmi Juvonen, *House of Horrors*, 1955, gouache on paper, 22 x 14 3/4. Collection of Henry Art Gallery, University of Washington (Gift of Dr. and Mrs. Ulriche Fritasche)

In her active rejection of art protocol, Helmi parted company with artists like Tobey and Graves who were unusually fine craftsmen. Her model for cultural eclecticism, visual diversity, and flouting of convention was probably Picasso, whose name appears in Helmi's works in a variety of humorous ways. And also, while the overall gestural web and the calligraphic details of her work may owe a great deal to her Northwest colleagues, her droll figuration, inventively full of mutation, transformation, and almost hallucinatory fantasy, are much closer to Picasso. (The essentially transformative imagery of the Northwest Native-American art enters here, again, as well.)

Thus Helmi participated in the idealizing internationalism of modernism and in its devaluation of local illusionism in preference to form itself. But another aspect of modernism is often described as its deep alienation from ordinary life in the modern bourgeois West, and ultimately Helmi exemplifies this, too. While she spent all her adult life in the Seattle/Puget Sound area, her connections became more and more marginal. Almost all women artists here of her generation or earlier had the operating framework of a husband (often an artist-husband) or of some institutional affiliation (for example, at the University of Washington, in the high schools, or at Cornish School). Helmi lacked such helpful entries to artist's groups, and her relations with her family of origin are not clear (perhaps ceased altogether).

The artists most linked to Helmi are Mark Tobey, Morris Graves, and others of their associates often designated "Northwest School." Besides being personal acquaintances, they shared pan-cultural sympathies and at heart a gentle but visionary sense of the world's unity. Yet even these links were tenuous. Like women Surrealist artists of her generation or earlier, Helmi was drawn toward a group with an anti-academic stance who valued internal personal realities; but, like women Surrealists, Helmi situated her art more toward fantasy, whether symbolic or narrative, than her male associates did. In addition, women Surrealists had to deal with the exclusionary eroticism of male Surrealists' idealizations and objectifications of women; while in any event Helmi would have been excluded beyond a certain point by the homoerotic currents among some of the Northwest group. Ultimately, the Surrealist women defined themselves as outside that group, and ultimately Helmi remained a loner, apart from the inner circles of any Northwest School.

In 1950, Helmi was apparently a vigorous, down-to-earth, energetic individualist — a woman of wit, imagination, and resourcefulness who had held a number of small jobs and made a modest living through a variety of pick-up work. Over the next decade (her late 40s and 50s), her course appeared to travel from individualist to eccentric to crank — a person of whimsical but obsessive ideas and far too many cats; a person believed unable to manage and/or unmanageable. In the early '50s she was temporarily declared legally incompetent; in 1958 she was in an institution for the mentally ill; and from 1960 to her death she lived in a group home outside the city as a ward of the State. Helmi remained a voracious reader — she "ransacked" the world, according to one friend. She corresponded with friends, and continued to work. Patterns and symbols of her Nordic heritage sweeten and lighten some of these images. In her last decade, serious attention to her art somewhat reconciled Helmi to her life and encouraged her further work.

BIBLIOGRAPHY:

Helmi Juvonen: Observations and Transformations, edited by Wesley Wehr, Olympia: Washington State Capitol Historical Association, 1983.

Martha Kingsbury, *Northwest Traditions*, Seattle: Seattle Art Museum, 1978.

Martha Kingsbury, "Seattle and Puget Sound" in *Art of the Pacific Northwest*, Washington D.C.: National Collection of the Fine Arts, Smithsonian Institution, 1974.

William C. Seitz, *Mark Tobey*, NY: Museum of Modern Art, 1962.

Ray Kass, *Morris Graves: Vision of the Inner Eye*, NY: George Braziller, 1983.

Emily Carr (1871-1945)

by Ron Glowen

Emily Carr (1871-1945) ranks among the greatest modern artists of her native Canada. Her Expressionist paintings of the forests and log-hewn native artforms of West Coast British Columbia belong to the 20th-century tradition of landscape painting identified with Canada's "Group of Seven" painters. She also made a sizable contribution to Canadian art literature with the publication during her lifetime of her journals and five books of autobiographical stories and recollections. Fiercely independent and spirited, yet isolated and vulnerable, Emily Carr followed an erratic and unconventional trajectory as a painter that stopped in mid-arc, then propelled upward in an energetic burst of late activity.

True to its namesake, Victoria (Carr's birthplace and home for most of her life) as the capital of British Columbia province was isolated and constrained — socially Victorian and culturally provincial. The strong-willed Carr rebelled against the social and religious hypocrisy of her family life and of Victoria town society. In her late teens she traveled to San Francisco to attend the California School of Design (now the San Francisco Art Institute). She returned to Victoria three years later, then left for five years of studying and painting in England (1899-1904). Apart from gaining some academic proficiency in drawing and watercolor, Carr's work of this early period was conventional and revealed little of her latent powers.

Her resistance to Victorian propriety probably increased her attraction to the Native Canadian peoples of Vancouver Island, especially the distinctive and powerful images of totems, masks and other sculptural forms that eventually provide the thematic core of her work. Carr would later date her commitment to Native art and themes to 1907, though she had seen and sketched Native villages and peoples as early as 1898.

A sojourn in France in 1910-11, financed by teaching art in her Vancouver studio, brought Carr into contact with the "new art" she had heard about. Unaffected by the innovations of Parisian art (Cubism in particular and urbanism in general), Carr would gravitate to the provinces and study with fellow English-speaking artists who had adopted the style and mannerisms of Post-Impressionist and Fauvist art. The experience developed her vivid color sense and bold brushwork in landscapes and interiors of rural France reminiscent of André Derain. Before returning to Canada, Carr had two works accepted into the 1911 *Salon d'Automne* in Paris, a show that highlighted the Fauves (but not the Cubists, who emerged that same fall in the separate *Salon des Independents*).

Though she felt rejected by her audience and peers back in Vancouver, Carr found her "French style" helped free her color and manner of painting from the task of visual depiction as she moved to formal translation of her emotion and mood. She began to visualize, rather than optically record, and her paintings began to assume more painterly feeling and greater compositional assurance. Returning to Victoria in 1913, Carr entered a long period of artistic dormancy and personal frustration as economic and family matters forced the suspension of her painting career. She did in fact continue to paint, but only sporadically, and resorted to making ceramic pots decorated with Native designs as a source of income.

Carr seemed destined to only a brief moment as a regional artist. As it happened, however, despite the isolation of Victoria, she had several enthusiastic supporters who eventually brought her to the attention of the director of Canada' National Gallery in Ottawa and to the modernist landscape painters known as the Group of Seven. In 1927, at age 56, Carr made a crucial and fruitful journey to eastern Canada. She had been unaware of the institution and the group; each of them (especially painter Lawren Harris who immediately accepted her as "one of us") had an indelible impact on her art and vision, which were amazingly revitalized. Unsophisticated in art theory, she struggled to understand Harris's interest in Theosophy, but she found a deeper spiritualism and moral purpose for her art. She renewed her contact with the dark forests of western Canada and the Native art that had nourished her long before.

The later phases of Emily Carr's paintings saw a rapid assimilation of conceptual and formal ideas. Cubist elements of geometric faceting and simplification, Futurist notions of pulsating energy vectors and Expressionist ideas of immediate brushwork and color now underlay her hom-

opposite:
Emily Carr, *Scorned as Timber, Beloved of the Sky*, 1935, o/c, 112 x 68.9 cm.
Collection of Vancouver Art Gallery, Emily Carr Trust.

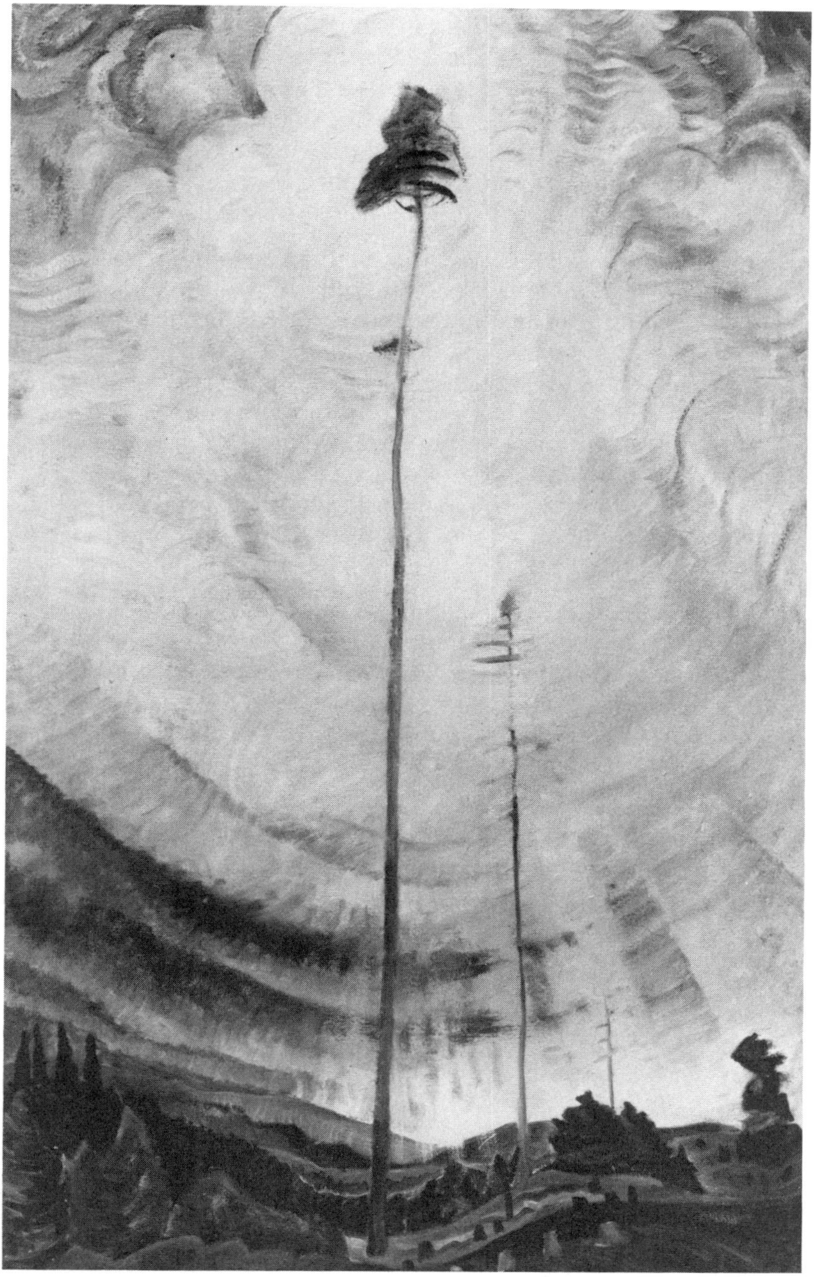

ages to the primordial ancient forests and the vanishing culture of the Native. These distinct phases invoked comparison with the styles of earlier European modernist painters — van Gogh, Gauguin, Munch, Marc, or the Americans Dove, O'Keeffe and Burchfield. But Carr's virtual isolation in Victoria prevented direct links to these modes; instead they suggest a personal discovery of these modernist idioms. (Harris and the Seattle painter Mark Tobey would be Carr's only direct connection to such sources.)

The late paintings feature thick, simplified volumes depicting the forest canopy and the shapes of Native totem forms, or swirling linear patterns that translate natural forms into essences of pulsating life. At the same time, Carr's colors often conveyed the brooding, shadowy stillness and density of the forest in somber earth, green and deep blue, the lush surfaces a contrast to the desolation of forest clearings and abandoned villages. No figures populate this terrain, only the visages of ancient totems standing guard over primordial stands of timber under turbulent skies. Carr's occasional sketch-like paintings of the panoramic seas, inlets and mountains near her hometown instill the feeling of creation, both in the moment and in the act.

In her last years Emily Carr reaped the rewards of her individualistic art, nature and spirit. Major exhibitions in Toronto, Ottawa and elsewhere, and the 1940 radio broadcast and publication of her stories (notably *Klee Wyck*, describing her relationship to the Native people and their art, the title being the name given Carr by her Native friends) made Carr a national celebrity. Her youthful rebelliousness had grown into an irascible countenance, yet her last works depict a tranquil grandeur as the culmination of her artistic journey. She died in Victoria on March 2, 1945 at age 73.

Part III:
Grandes Dames of Craft-Related Traditions

Several women artists stand out as "grandes dames" of traditional craft media who have expanded these media into contemporary art forms important to the region's identity. An overview of ceramics by critic and editor Ruth Askey places this sculptural medium within the contemporary context, focusing on Patti Warashina. Women glass artists prominent within the burgeoning regional and international glass-art scene are described by arts advisor Margery Aronson. Developments in fiber art are discussed by writer Cherry Partee. The proliferation of women book-artists working in the Northwest is surveyed by Sandra Kroupa, artists' books curator at the University of Washington. These essays examine the dynamic role of Northwest women in erasing boundaries between art and craft.

Ceramics in the Northwest

by Ruth Askey

From the close of World War I to 1939, all major colleges in Idaho, Montana, Oregon and Washington taught ceramics. In addition, Ebba Rapp (1909-1985), taught ceramics in the 1930s at the Cornish Institute of Allied Arts. Until the mid-'40s, Western ceramics followed the standard craft techniques of the day — vessels were thrown on the wheel, hand built, in press-molds or slip-cast. Kilns, whether oil, woodburning, or electric, were small, and glazes were the glossy brilliant surfaces achieved by then relatively low temperatures. Then in 1946 the University of Washington Ceramics Department brought in Paul Bonifas, a recognized Swiss artist and ceramicist, to build a top-quality ceramics facility at the School of Art.

As the ceramic scene grew, faculty at most institutions was male: Peter Voulkos and Rudy Autio at the Archie Bray Foundation in Helena, Montana; Paul Soldner at Scripps in California; and Robert Sperry and Howard Kottler at the University of Washington were major influences on Northwest ceramic artists. In the post-World War II era, the liberalizing views of the Bauhaus, along with an Abstract Expressionist freedom gave a higher status to the crafts, linking them closely to the fine arts. By 1960 issues of major and minor arts or functional versus sculptural began to be addressed regionally through the annual Northwest Craftsmen Exhibition at the University of Washington.

Also in the 1960s, Northwest art dealers began to take an interest in ceramics. In Portland, the Fountain Gallery opened. In Seattle, Hall-Coleman, the Phoenix, the Beck Galleries, Polly Friedlander, Penryn & Cone 10 all exhibited ceramics. Gail Chase, a potter, founded The Crockery Shed in Bellevue. The Pacific Northwest Arts and Crafts Association (PANACA), an all-volunteer organization, had established the annual summer Pacific Northwest Arts and Crafts Fair in Bellevue, Washington in 1947, the first market in the Northwest where "production" potters could show. Currently Northwest Craft Center, under the guidance of Ruth Nomura, is an outlet for traditional ceramics. Barbara Rauscher, credited with uplifting the design consciousness of Northwest potters, organized the first traveling exhibition of handcrafts sponsored by PANACA. Since 1975 the Bellevue Art Museum has been an important venue for ceramic artists of the area.

California Abstract Expressionism, (Peter Voulkos), was a major influence, and later the use of common objects in Pop art and the attitudes of Funk artists based at the University of California, Davis. Such "Funk" qualities as gaudiness, irreverence, and erotic references (Robert Arneson and Ken Price) combined with hobby-shop materials — bright colors, glazes, lusters and acrylic paint — changed the emphasis of West Coast college curricula from the precious vessel to open-ended experimentation.

The shift toward Funk sensibility is best exemplified by Patti Warashina, a pivotal American artists who elevated clay from crafts material to the stuff of sculpture. Her work evolved from the functional clay bowl in the early 1960s to life-size ceramic figures in 1991. The bare bones of pottery vessels culminated in the psychic musculature of large narrative figures.

By the time Warashina received her B.A. (1962) and M.A. (1964) from the University of Washington, Abstract Expressionist macho had begun to crumble under the influence of Pop, exemplified in ceramics by Arneson and Price. During her graduate years, Warashina experimented with full-size clay chairs supported by three hand-turned legs and decorated with clay applied in baroque designs. Inspired by Louise Nevelson's work at the 1962 Seattle World's Fair "Art Since 1950," these clay structures were unique in size and scale. Warashina also admired Ken Price, finding his delicate geometric shapes, clear colors and play with worms and eggs particular appealing.

In a catalogue essay for the Bellevue Art Museum, "Patti Warashina: Ceramic Sculpture 1962-1991," guest curator Vicki Halper writes that Warashina and her first husband, Fred Bauer, experimented in 1967 with acrylic paints on clay surfaces before discovering low-fire ceramics and electric kilns two years later. In *Ketchup Kiss* (1969), she incorporated a squat, stacked, jar-like head with oversize lips and surfaces as slick as an album cover.

Warashina's hilarious sculpted kilns (1971) were a response to the unpredictability of gas firings and a pot-shop culture that stressed the plumbing and mechanics of firing rather than the ceramic objects.

She made her first altar images in the 1970s, and continued with them in 1976. These table-top altars combined autobiographical references to found objects, obscure personal symbols and religious images. "I was dealing with this clay object and fighting to get it off the ground and and up in the air. I was playing around with a Japanese cup and put it on a table with four legs and it became an altar." The series refers to Warashina's childhood discovery of her Christian grandmother's hidden Buddhist altar.

Each piece features a woman's carefully painted face on a flat surface with three-dimensional nose and hands and flowers, hearts and carrots as offerings. Shuttling between two- and three-dimensions, these altar/alter images suggest the shifting identity of women.

The monochromatic tableaux of the "little people" began in the late 1970s and continued for over a decade. The elegant, devilish figures appeared when Warashina made a small ceramic car and wanted to mold riders. Critic Lyn Smallwood described them in *Seattle Weekly:* "They seem inevi-

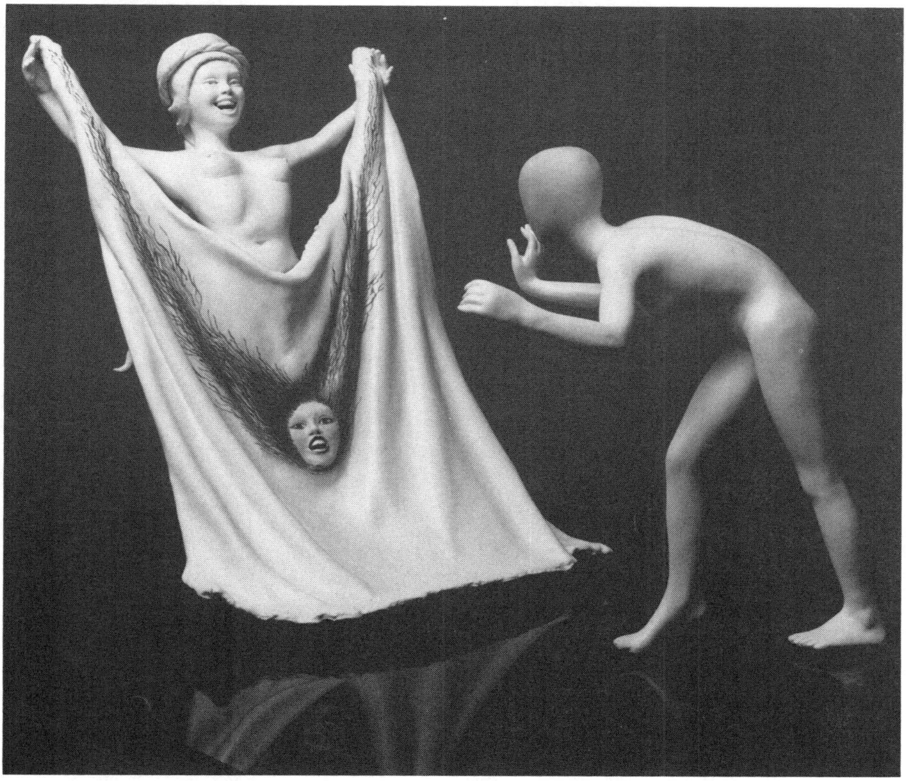

Patti Warashina, *Loss of Identity*, 1978, clay, 19 x 22 1/2 x 15.

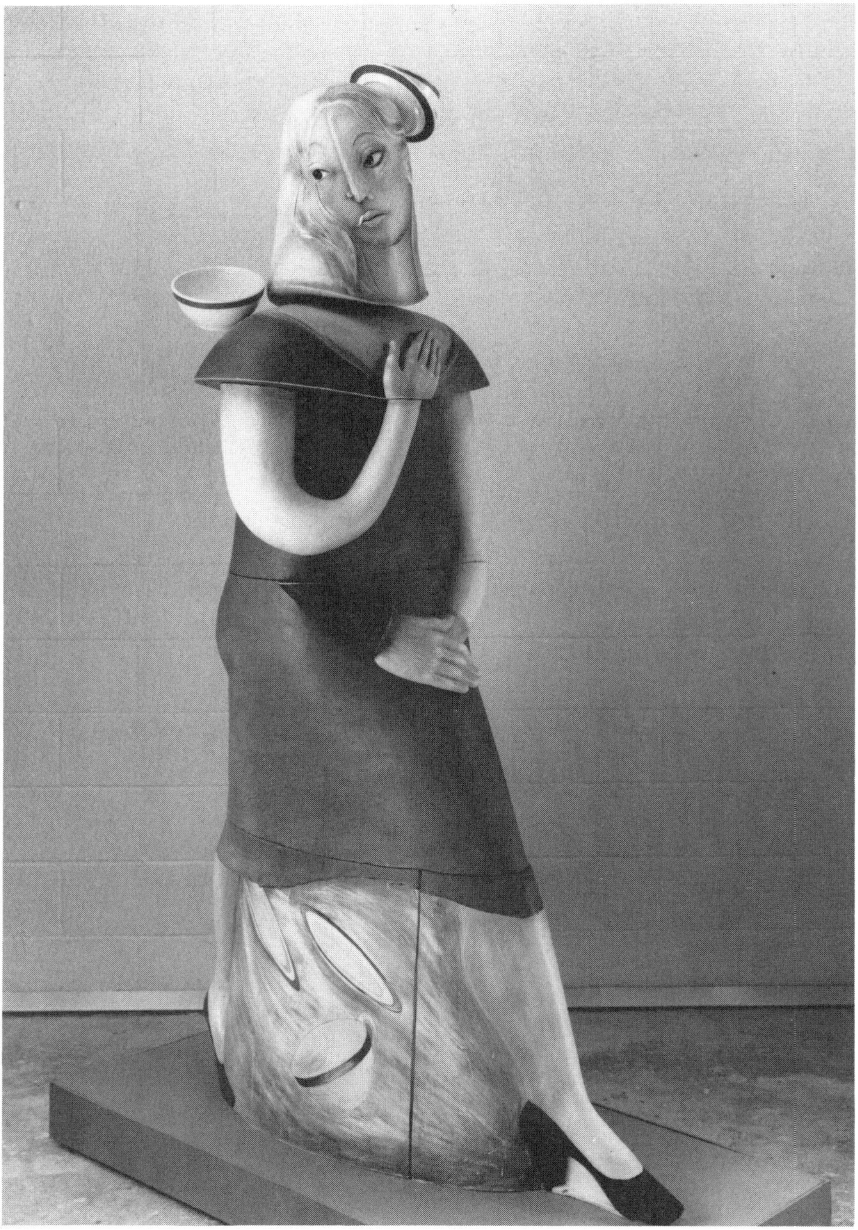

Patti Warashina, *Friendly Persuasions*, 1991, clay, 78 x 42 x 28 (approx.).

table rather than made up, as if wiggling out of some not-so-distant region of the psyche." Full of allegory, the slightly mad, but delicate creatures are shown in frenzied activity — jumping around flames, cavorting outside a burning car, gleefully overturning a cup, and climbing up a pole only to be trapped under a plexi-*Glass Cage* (1982). Warashina says, "I want my work to be dreamlike. I want to deal with reality, but take it back and forth between real and a dreamlike state."

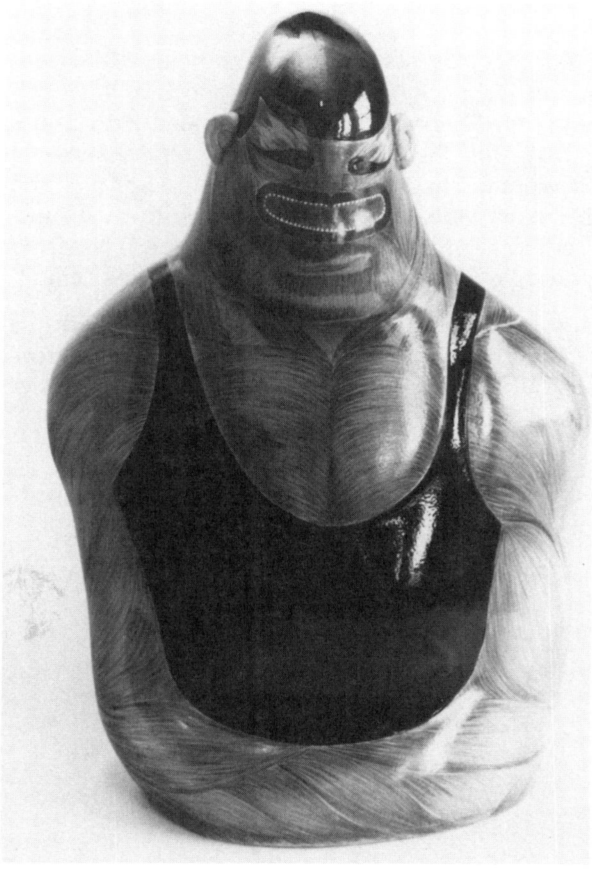

Joyce Moty, *Muscle Lady*, 1977, earthenware, china paint, 22 x 16 x 8.

In the late '80s she turned from small to large pieces and from white to polychrome surfaces. After the death of her friend and colleague, Howard Kottler, she began experimenting with three-foot figures, which developed into covered jars in the form of heads, then evolved into larger-than-life-size figures devoid of the surreal.

Warashina's career has been a series of surprising leaps: The round stoneware pots of the early '60s, to the ceramic altars of the mid-'70s (intervening years included marriage, children, divorce and a second marriage to Robert Sperry), then the miniature white figures in tableaux, to, currently the jar heads and life-size personages, lively icons for the chaotic 1990s. At first, as an instructor at the Cornish Institute and, since 1971, as professor at the University of Washington, Warashina has transferred physical and psychic energy to her students, setting a remarkable example with her own prolific production.

The younger generation of women artists thus inspired include Margaret Ford, Lauren Grossman, and Debra Sherwood; in the work of such colleagues as Ann Perrigo and Joyce Moty we see a like-minded irreverence and wit. Perrigo's *Wash That Man Right Out of My Hair* (1988) shows a three-foot clay torso of a woman shampooing toy men on springs and baby-doll heads out of her hair. Moty's impudent attitude toward functional objects is seen in a series of human-form, hand-built cookie jars (mid 1970s) depicting stereotypes like *TV Mom, Muscle Lady*, and *Snake Lady*.

The special skills and edgy vision of these women have contributed to a distinctive Northwest sensibility which may have been spawned from West Coast Funk attitudes but has been enlarged to include questions of reality and representation.

BIBLIOGRAPHY:

Halper, Vicki, *Patti Warashina: Ceramic Sculpture 1962-1991*, Bellevue Art Museum, 1991.

Harrington, LaMar, *Ceramics in the Pacific Northwest: A History*, Seattle: University of Washington Press, 1979.

Kangas, Matthew, *Patti Warashina, Recent Work*, Tucson Museum of Art, 1982.

Smallwood, Lyn, "From Jars to Jarheads," *Seattle Weekly*, October 2, 1991.

Translucent and Opaque: Women and Glass

by Margery Aronson

Recently a group of West Coast writers observed the team of glassblowers working on *Macchia* vessels at Dale Chihuly's hotshop in The Boathouse, his studio on Lake Union in Seattle. A woman writer from the group asked why all but one member of the seven-person team was male. She was told that it was considered a significant honor to be a part of the Chihuly team, and that although there was an important and growing community of women artists in the field, most were making their own works rather than concentrating on making art for others. In fact, women artists have been involved with the creation of studio glass in the Northwest since 1971, the first summer of activity at the now internationally renowned Pilchuck Glass School.

Although people have been making glass for at least 35 centuries (it is generally acknowledged to have originated in the Middle East), glass as a medium for American contemporary artists working outside a factory context is traced to the efforts of glass scientist and artist Dominick Labino who in 1962 was able to develop a formula for glass which would melt at a relatively low temperature. This meant that a small glass furnace could be built in an artist's studio, permitting individual experimentation and creation. Simultaneously, artist Harvey Littleton began a series of workshops at Ohio's Toledo Museum of Art, which engendered a renaissance in glass and engaged the energies of many artists like Chihuly. Chihuly's impact in the field is significant not only because of his glass sculpture and installations, but also because of his vision in establishing the Pilchuck Glass School on 40 beautiful acres in the middle of a tree farm 55 miles north of Seattle. Many now acknowledge that the Pacific Northwest has become the spiritual and geographic center of America's contemporary glass movement, due in large part to Pilchuck and the remarkable group of artists who come to teach and learn there summer after summer, many of whom decided to stay because of the hundreds of glass artists working in the region.

Now in its third decade, the Pilchuck Glass School was started in 1971 by

Tacoma-born artist Chihuly with the generous support of patrons John Hauberg and Anne Gould Hauberg. Not only did the Haubergs provide a site for Chihuly's educational innovations, but they also augmented his $2,000. seed grant from the Union of Independent Colleges of Art and continued to support Pilchuck for many years. The first summer was a rainy one, and the initial task for the small group of artists enlisted by Chihuly was to build a hot shop, a cooking area, and shelter from the weather. The core group consisted of a number of Chihuly's colleagues from the Rhode Island School of Design (RISD), including James Carpenter, John Landon, and Art Wood, with Buster Simpson (then from Michigan) and a ceramic artist from Hawaii, Ruth Tamura. Toots Zynsky, originally from Massachusetts, today an important glass artist living in Paris, was at Pilchuck the first summer; Dutch artist Barbara Vaessen and Kate Elliott, Seattle private dealer and owner of RegaloVetro, were involved in the early years as well.

The new world of glass art began to attract artists from the ceramics field to its programs as well as from other disciplines, but Pilchuck's records from the first decade indicate that until 1979, Swedish artist Ann Warff (now Wolff) was the only woman on the faculty after Ruth Tamura. 1979 was also the year that Flora Mace and Joey Kirkpatrick met at Pilchuck and they have been collaborating on artwork ever since. In 1980 and in 1981, Swedish artist Ulrica Hydman-Vallien taught at Pilchuck; in 1981 Mace and Kirkpatrick were faculty members as well, and Susan Stinsmeuhlen, an artist from Texas, was an artist-in-residence. The gender barrier was down at last, but women artists were still in the minority.

Due in large part to Chihuly's idea of teaching the medium by having artists and students observe and work alongside the best international artists in the field, The Pilchuck Glass School has been a magnet attracting an extraordinary group for whom glass is central to artistic production.[1] Pilchuck, like the Haystack Mountain School of Crafts in Maine, is primarily a summer school, but for the last several years its facilities have been used in the off season by artists for their own work, and there is now an Emerging Artist-in-Residence Program on campus in the autumn. The Pacific Northwest has become the center of American contemporary glassmaking because of its strongly developed community of artists working in the medium. Their numbers now include a significant proportion of women.

Among the leaders and innovators in this community are Sonja Blomdahl, Flora Mace and Joey Kirkpatrick, Ginny Ruffner, and Catherine Thomp-

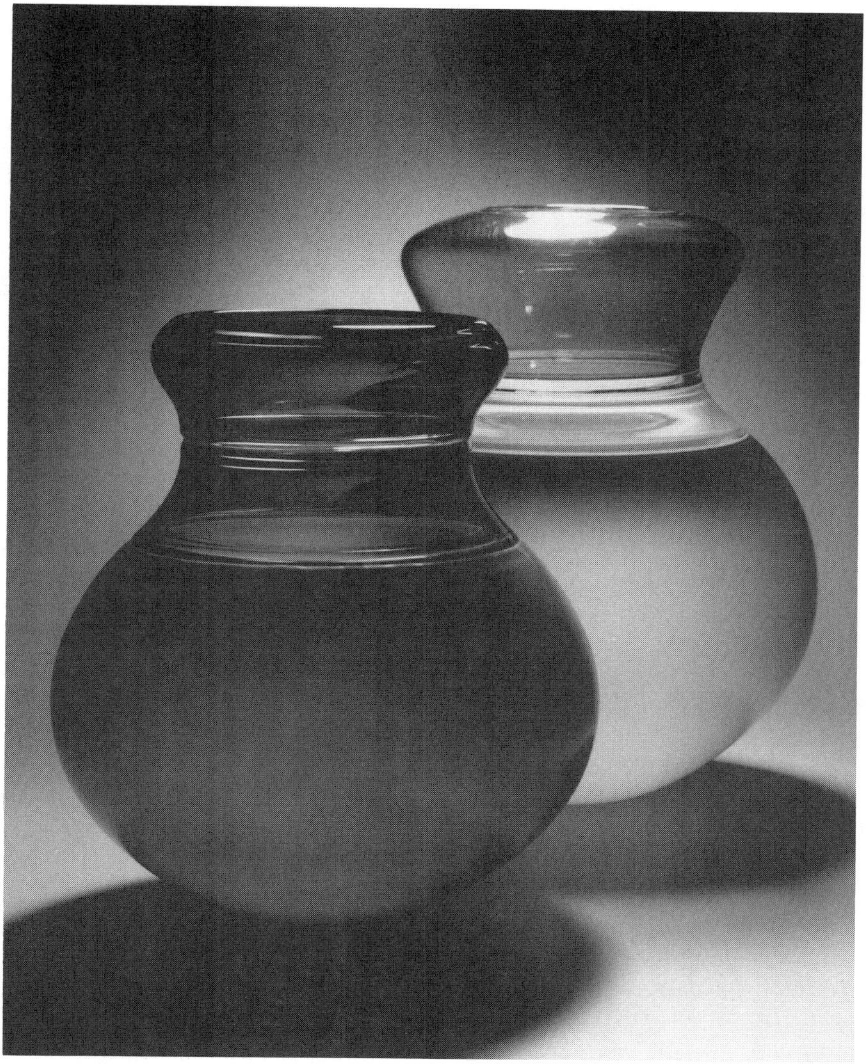

Sonja Blomdahl, *Violet/Yellow/Green*, and *Scarlet/Ruby/Amethyst* 1991, hand blown glass, 16" high, in collection of Tacoma Community College (Washington State Arts Commission Art-in-Public-Places Program).

son. A growing number of other artists have made glass the core of their sculptural work, like Nancy Mee, Ann Gardner, Norie Sato, Susan Plum, Jill Reynolds, Mary Van Cline, Amy Roberts, KeKe Cribbs, Ruth Brockman, Patricia Davidson, Ann Troutner, and Judith La Scola. Also working in the region are Karen Willenbrink, Sabrina Knowles, and Kelly McClain.

Sonja Blomdahl changed the focus of her curriculum at the Massachusetts College of Art to glass when Dan Dailey came there to teach in her senior year. After graduation, she and a friend set up a small blowing studio in the Berkshires and made production glass to sell at craft fairs. Tiring of making the same thing over and over, she applied to Sweden's Orrefors Glass School, where she studied for six months before embarking on a tour of Europe. When she returned to the United States, she worked at a series of odd jobs until 1978 when she was invited by her former teacher Dan Dailey, to be his teaching assistant at Pilchuck. Blomdahl accepted the offer and became a member of the Pilchuck kitchen staff for the rest of the summer, enabling her to continue blowing glass.

She has commented that even in the late '70s women in the glass field were relegated to peripheral roles — opening and closing furnace doors, preparing color rods and generally assisting gaffers, who were responsible for all activity on the hot-shop floor. Blomdahl moved to Seattle after her Pilchuck summer and began to work days at Rob Adamson's Glass Eye Studio and to teach glassblowing at night at the Pratt Fine Arts Center. She was introduced to William Traver by glass artist Dick Weiss and had her first gallery exhibition in 1981. By 1983, she was ready to make the next major career step, that of building her own studio near Seattle's Lake Union, where she still works. Blomdahl's work has always been concerned with symmetry and the pure seamless union of form and color. She has often talked about how she lets color dictate her form and her sense of dialogue with the material. From her first bowls and spheres made in the early '80s to her more recent pear and hour-glass shaped vessels, she has utilized the *encalmo* or double or triple bubble technique to make resonant, luminous objects. Her work is remarkable for its ability to simultaneously unify and separate color and to appear both simple and complex.

Flora Mace and Joey Kirkpatrick had worked with the medium of glass independently of one another before they met at Pilchuck in 1979. Mace developed her technique of essentially drawing with threads of glass heated by a propane torch and applied to a blown vessel while at the University of Illinois at Champaign-Urbana in 1974. Kirkpatrick had received her BFA degree in painting and drawing from the University of

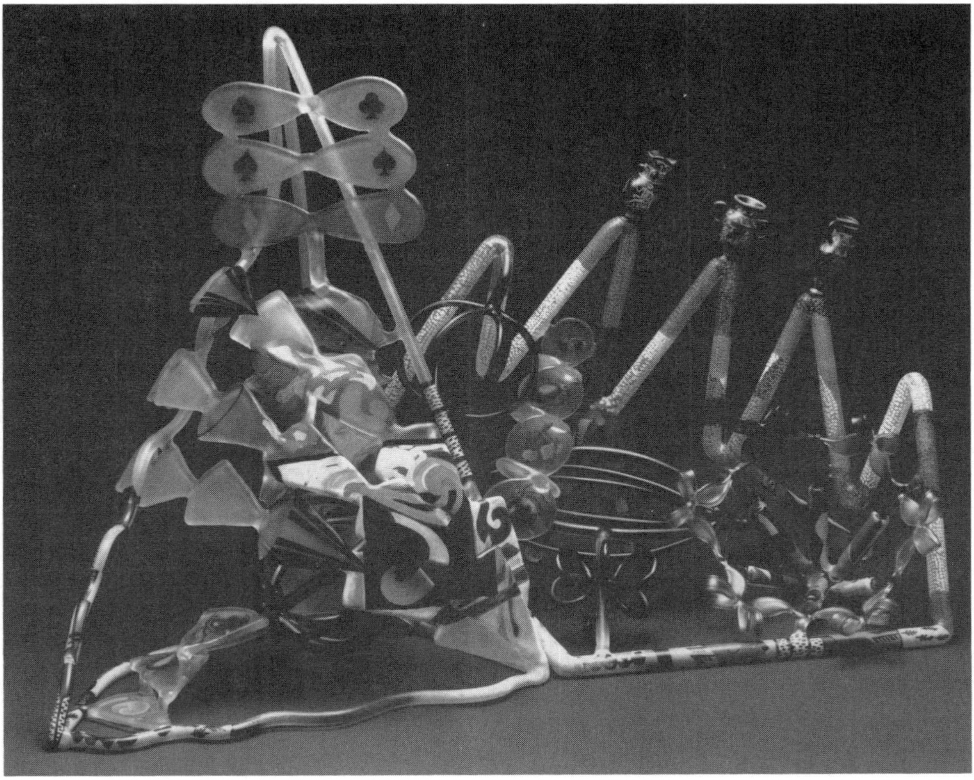

Ginny Ruffner, *The Invention of Games*, 1991, glass, 25 x 37 x 20. Collection of Mary and Jon Shirley.

Iowa in 1975 and done graduate work in glass at Iowa State in 1978-79. She came to Pilchuck hoping to learn to translate her drawings into glass; Mace had been invited to Pilchuck by Dale Chihuly, who was well aware of her abilities and had already used her "pick-up drawings" on his series of glass vessels related to Navajo blanket designs. Mace and Kirkpatrick soon discovered that, although their skills and the directions of their art up to that point were quite different, both were interested in collaborating and in exploring ideas about relationships between humans and nature. In 1980, they became the first women to teach hot glass at Pilchuck, and also began to build a home there so they could work at the school in the off-season.

The first glass pieces from Mace and Kirkpatrick's collaboration were vessels which infused Kirkpatrick's drawings made from fine wire into the hot glass matrix. After the wire drawings series, the artists developed an innovative technique by which thin threads of glass color were fused to the drawings, with a propane torch, then heated on a steel plate placed over a hotplate to prepare them for pickup during the blowing process. Sometimes the preparation for a piece could take an entire week, and, because this was a new process, the failure rate due to incompatibility of color and other unknowns was high. Eventually the process became too burdensome and Mace and Kirkpatrick began to make sculpture combining figurative elements of glass blown into molds with alderwood culled from trees on the Pilchuck campus with bases made of stone. They continued to develop sculptural imagery and began to include leaves made of glass, glass shards with painted birds and extraordinarily realistic fruit, which ultimately led to their amazing still lifes — assemblages of glass fruit and vegetables on alderwood platters fabricated and lacquered by the artists.

Here Mace and Kirkpatrick again demonstrated the power of their collective sensibilities, devising an almost painterly process for layering color, using sifted glass powders to create depth. Next they explored increased scale, which they resolved through collaboration with their long time colleague William Morris. At first, Morris and his associates Paul DeSomma and Karen Willenbrink worked with Kirkpatrick and Mace to make a series of enormous glass fruits, including pears and apples. Now, Mace and Kirkpatrick make all but the largest on their own. Moreover, their sculpture combining wood and glass elements has also become grander in scale.

In Mace and Kirkpatrick's works, it is impossible to tell where one sensi-

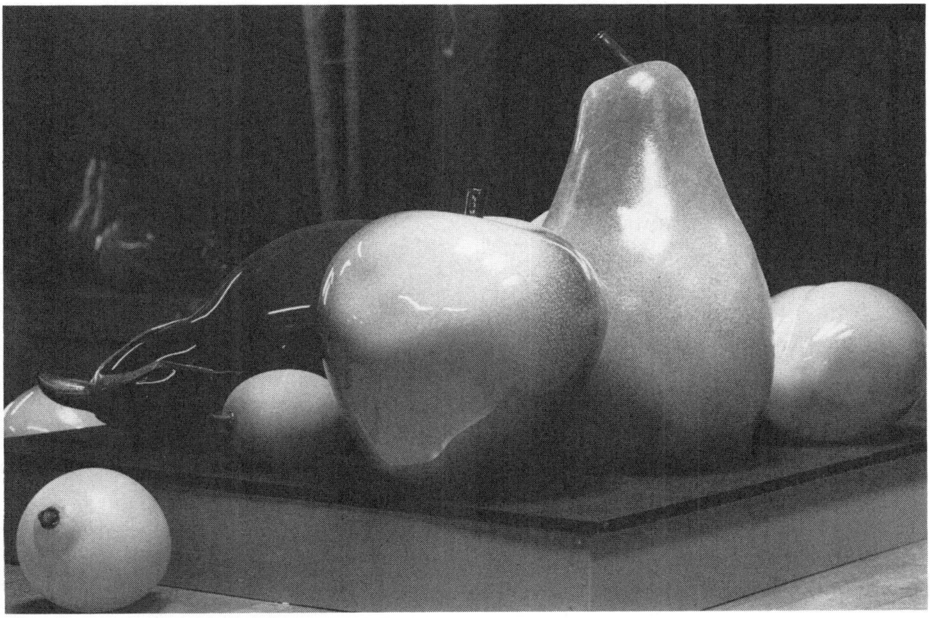

Joey Kirkpatrick and Flora C. Mace, *Studio Installation: Fruit*, 1991, blown glass fruit forms, 9 to 31" tall.

bility stops and the other begins. Both artists say they would not have believed it possible for the collaboration to work as long as it has. They cite their differences as the binding element that makes what they do together completely unlike what they would do as individuals.

Ginny Ruffner was born in 1952 in Atlanta, Georgia. She earned her BFA and MFA in drawing and painting from the University of Georgia and worked there in commercial stained glass and engraved glass companies before moving to Seattle in 1985. Her earliest flame-worked glass pieces dating from 1977 used borosilicate tubes; her first exhibition in Seattle was in a 1984 Pilchuck Faculty group show at the then Traver Sutton Gallery. These pale and ghostly sandblasted works, she said, were "vestiges of the vessel tradition in glass, containers that could hold nothing, shaped as much by what was outside them as by the space within them" ("Ruffner" by Jessica Maxwell, *New Work,* Summer 1988) They seemed to refer to abstracted remnants of another culture. From her triangulated structures of the mid-'80s, Ruffner's vision changed and she began to create recognizable imagery with literary antecedents. The sandblasted tubes, stretched and formed in a most intriguing way, were colored using pastels, acrylics and Prismacolor pencils. These pieces began Ruffner's full-fledged visual assault on language, narrative and the all-too-serious canons of modern art and culture. She remains an innovator in glass sculpture through the complexity, wit, and originality of her ideas, and has taken techniques of flame-working, also known as lampworking, in new directions, infusing the process with energy, and even a great deal of humor.

Ruffner has a well-deserved reputation as a fine teacher, having taught in the Northwest at Pilchuck and Pratt Fine Arts Center, Penland in North Carolina, Cal Arts in Oakland, Summervail in Colorado, New York Experimental Glass Workshop, NYC, and in France and Australia. At home and abroad, she has lectured widely, been on design teams as artist and advisor for public art projects, and served as juror for many competitions. In addition, her article in *American Craft,* "Speaking of Glass/Women Sculptors," surveyed artists, curators, educators, writers and gallery owners on the topic of women making glass sculpture.[2]

1991 was a pivotal year for Ruffner. She curated an important exhibition for the Tacoma Art Museum, "Glass: Material in the Service of Meaning," and exhibited painted wood and aluminum panels and flame-worked glass constructions in Seattle and Chicago. Then, in mid-December 1991, she suffered a disabling automobile accident; after several months in a coma she is now undergoing intensive rehabilitation in New York.

Catherine Thompson (known to all as Cappy) is also an innovator who has found an application in the glass arts for her skills in drawing and painting. At the core of her work is an abiding interest in mythology, in medieval imagery derived from illuminated manuscripts and woodblock prints, and in folk art from many cultures, such as *Aesop's Fables* and the *Fables of Bidpai*, miniatures from India and Persia, and Japanese woodblock prints. In 1975, she began to work in a production stained glass studio in Olympia, WA. Finding that resources and technical information about combining her shaded drawings with areas of pure colored illuminated glass were not available, she had to learn by trial and error. She succeeded in sufficient measure to gain a commission in 1978 for a window using the image of the Virgin of Guadalupe.[3]

In 1984, Cappy was invited to be an artist-in-residence at Pilchuck, where she taught glass painting in 1988 and 1989. The hot-shop gaffers at Pilchuck offered her "blanks" — vessels blown in opalescent white glass.— which she used to make imagery in the round rather than on a flat surface. She was able also to make singular objects for sale, rather than solely on commission. Cappy appreciates both the challenges of the vessel form and the relative immediacy of the process. For the most part, she paints inside the forms, firing many layers of applied pigments as the images develop. Working in Czechoslovakian glass factories in 1989 she experimented with opaque enamels on the surface of colored blown vessels, as well as images incised into blown forms through acid etching and sandblasting.

Cappy's painterly skills permit a kind of storytelling about her faith in the strength of the earth. In 1983, she said, "We are in great need of images that give us a sense of the integrity and beauty of the earth and that make us think about important issues. I want images that have all the humor and conflict . . . that make you laugh and cry at the same time."[4]

Nancy Mee, Norie Sato, and Ann Gardner are contemporary artists who use glass as a prime sculptural material but do not consider themselves glass artists. In the late '70s, Nancy Mee began to incorporate scraps and shards left over from her work as a framemaker into her mixed media pieces, and glass became one of her key materials. At first, she used silicon to bind the glass elements together. Following a stint as artist-in-residence at Pilchuck in 1984, she began to use the technique of fused glass in her sculptures and, ultimately, built a very large kiln to fuse and slump glass. The early work also had brass, copper, and steel elements, some of which were fabricated by others to her specifications. Since then, Mee has learned to do her own welding and forging of steel components. Her proficiency in fusing, sand-blasting, and photo etching glass bring sophistication and elegance to her sculptures, which eloquently explore relationships between beauty and deformity.

Norie Sato came naturally to glass in her investigation of effects of light transmission and relations between abstractions derived from the language of television, in which light literally travels through the air, and images from the video screen. Over the last decade, she has progressed from occasional use of glass shards as reflective and accentuating elements to more frequent inclusion of extremely large-scale sandblasted and acid-etched panels of glass sometimes combined with video monitors or neon. The play of light moving through glass panels into the artwork's environment has become increasingly important, as these days she is more concerned with large-scale installations around the country than making objects per se. Her use of glass in both sculpture and two-dimensional work can be compared to a veil or curtain expertly manipulated to trap, project, and alter light. Sato continues to combine glass with other materials to elucidate the mysteries of the mutable video images she has explored for years.

Ann Gardner's interaction with glass emerged from a background in ceramics and a wish to push the boundaries of mosaic and tile work. Until recently, she made large works cast from molten glass — first, heads of cast glass combined with copper and other materials nearly three feet tall, designed to be hung on a wall, and then translucent cast wings mounted on minimalist metal bases, sometimes combined with found objects, reaching a height of six feet. She has spoken of her affection for molten glass and the necessity for direct intervention and immediate decision. Lately Gardner has returned to large-sized vessel forms in clear glass (usually fabricated for her by gaffers like Seattle's Richard Royal), which she then elaborately embellishes with fragments and shards of Depression glass plates, cups, and bowls. She continues to interweave both hot and cold glass elements as she explores the limits of the medium.

As the Northwest has become a center for glass in all forms, artists from other places have come here to live and work. Susan Plum moved here in 1985 from Mexico City, became a teaching assistant for Ginny Ruffner's flame-working class at Pilchuck and now exhibits throughout the United States and abroad. Jill Reynolds is another artist who had a "Pilchuck experience;" since then her work has incorporated elements of flame-worked and blown glass. Mary Van Cline uses photosensitized glass in sculptural work primarily concerned with time and its emotional and psychological implications. Amy Roberts-Chamberlain began as a glass-blower, then progressed to mixed media sculpture in which glass is only one of several materials. Her recent work combines and contrasts cut and stacked glass with wood, concrete, and stone. Her interests include the conflicts inherent in the glass itself and contrasts and tensions between the beautiful and the mundane. KeKe Cribbs, after a stint out East, returned to the Northwest and began to make figurative work including sandblasted glass components she has compared to windows within painted wooden structures. Her sculptures range from two to six feet tall, and often the glass parts depict figures inscribed with abstract imagery and symbols. Ruth Brockman, currently of Portland, Oregon, has made fused and slumped glass masks as well as cast glass sculptures which address self-discovery and nature. She commonly includes references to other cultures' myths and symbology. Over the last few years, Ann Troutner has moved from making blown glass objects to creating sculptural installations, both as an individual and with her partner, Paul Marioni. Their impact in the arena of public artworks is significant. Patricia Davidson came to the Northwest as a 1991 recipient of a Pilchuck Emerging Artists-in-Residence fellowships, and has stayed on both to continue her own sculpture, which combines mold-blown glass with copper, wood and other materials, and as a member of Dale Chihuly's blowing team and other teams in the region. Judith LaScola also moved to the area after studying at Pilchuck and Pratt Fine Arts Center. Her work consists of ritual objects of blown glass combined with sand-carved, embellished and polished plate glass panels. Karen Willenbrink, Sabrina Knowles and Kelly McClain are Pilchuck staff members who have greatly benefited from the school's creative environment and whose work is becoming recognized beyond the boundaries of Snohomish County.

The symbiotic relationship between the extensive community of women in the Northwest who make artworks with glass — the "old/new material" — and the institutions of the Pilchuck Glass School and the Pratt Fine Arts Center is no accident. Because of the region's vital and supportive creative environment, a disproportionate number of internationally recognized women artists working with this extraordinary material are based here. As Thomas Buechner, an artist and former president of the Corning Museum of Glass, said, "From the beginning of the history of the studio glass movement, some of the most powerful figures in the field have been women. They came on strong early in the game. As a matter of fact, glass is one of the rare fields I don't think of as predominantly male or female."[5]

As we move through the 20th century's last decade, the Northwest is likely to further solidify its position at the center of the American glass art universe, and the remarkable women who are challenging this material will continue to gain international recognition.

NOTES:

[1] When the Glass Art Society held its annual meeting in Seattle in 1990 (the conference was subtitled "Pacific Lip Rap"), a survey indicated that over 300 artists were working with glass in 30 hotshops and more than 50 studios in the region from Bellingham, Washington, to Portland, Oregon.

[2] Her research revealed more contradiction than consensus, while raising the issues of physicality, technical ability and mechanical skills required by the medium, and exposing some of the sexual stereotyping long felt by women in the field. She concluded: "I was struck by the determination — not mere hopefulness — of the women I interviewed. It is a determination which carries connotations of both action and expected results: a direction, a goal and a journey already underway. To risk an oxymoron, I felt part of a community of isolated individuals, and I sighted once again the goal of the quest — the grail. It's out in my studio, it's called perseverance, and I'm working on it right now" (*American Craft*, October/November 1988, p.64).

[3] In this work, she made her first attempts at the grisaille technique, using dry brushes to remove pigment applied in washes, a technique she eventually combined with more traditional applications of fired-enamels painted on glass.

[4] Virginia Painter,"Catherine Thompson's Painted Glass is Much More Than Pretty Pictures," *The Olympian*, July 17, 1983.

[5] Thomas Buechner, quoted in "Speaking of Glass" by Ginny Ruffner, *American Craft*, October/November 1988, p.34.

Fiber Arts

by Cherry Partee

The past 30 years have seen such an upheaval in the field of needlework/fiberart that the word "change" hardly seems to do the event justice. Fiber artists, along with other women artists, are questioning what it means, what it looks like, and what it feels like to be an artist. Continuing to identify the work as fiber art, needlework, or textile art, although organizationally convenient, is as descriptive as calling a Judy Pfaff installation woodworking.

However, there are important historical and developmental differences between this work and traditional "malestream" art. Such differences as class, gender, locus of production, have been known, well-described, and documented by several outstanding critics. But the implications of this different relation to art, one created and codified by women, have been neither fully explored nor understood.

At least two aesthetic trails appear in contemporary art. One is dominated by a Duchampian attempted anti-aesthetic, heavily language-dependent and therefore culturally compatible. The other is consciously aesthetic, sensual, and evocative; its meaning is far less stable (of course, all meaning is unstable) because of its greater distance from language.

The art world's critical sense of rightness seems to be still centered on the idea of a traceable line from Impressionism, Abstraction, Surrealism, Abstract Expressionism, with Duchamp/Cage/Rauschenberg found objects, and Installation with Performance art branching off somewhere along the way. It may be time for advocates of each trail to follow Leo Steinberg's advice and perform that "leap of faith" which enriches our intellectual context.

For example, an undeniable case has been made for 18th- and 19th-century landscape as a reflection of the bourgeois accession to the economic throne and consequent possession and subjection of the earth. The association of women with those landscapes and with nature is a symbol of their supposedly natural and continuing subjugation to male hegemony. Yet landscape continues to be the subject of a tremendously large percentage of contemporary fiber art.

Historically, one of the few areas in which women exercise control was the domestic flower and vegetable garden and at least a portion of the home. There can hardly be, in Western, industrialized countries, a woman alive today who is not aware of and has not been influenced by feminist thinking. Reinterpreted in this other historical and contemporary context, might not work such as Karen Perrine's *Rain* and Nancy Erickson's *Sanctuary* be read as assertions of the right and ability of women to exist in the world on their own terms? Perhaps, even as in Gerry Chase's *Best Beloved*, it is necessary to pass judgement and call the world to account. The frequent appearance of doorways and passages such as Erika Carter's *Transition*, Dina Barzel's *This is the Gale*, and Linda McFarland's *Figure/Doorway*, are surely markers of a changed and changing perception of social and cultural place.

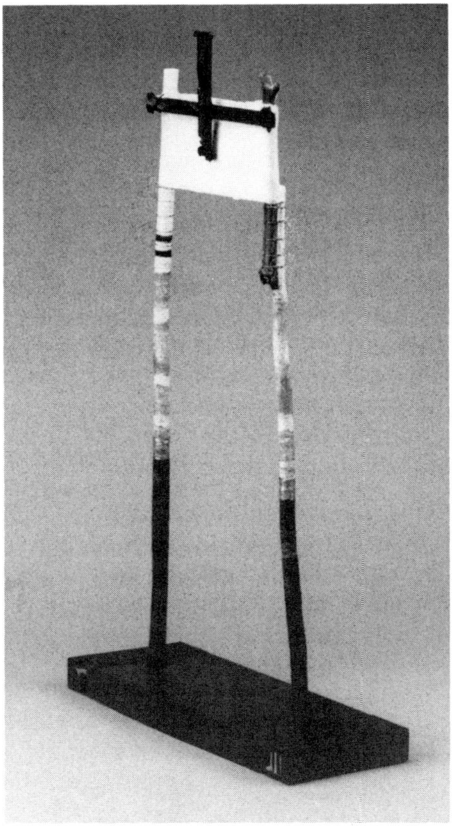

Dina Barzel, *This is the Gate*, 1988, 39 x 22 x 8, wood, flax, found objects, paint, gold.

A major factor in these changes has been the increasing exposure of needle workers/fiber artists to academic discipline. The Costume and Textile Study Center was developed under Virginia Harvey in the Department of Home Economics of the University of Washington, Seattle, during the '60s through the '80s. Textile design was first a B.A. program as a division of Art Education, becoming part of Fiber Arts in the School of Art in 1962

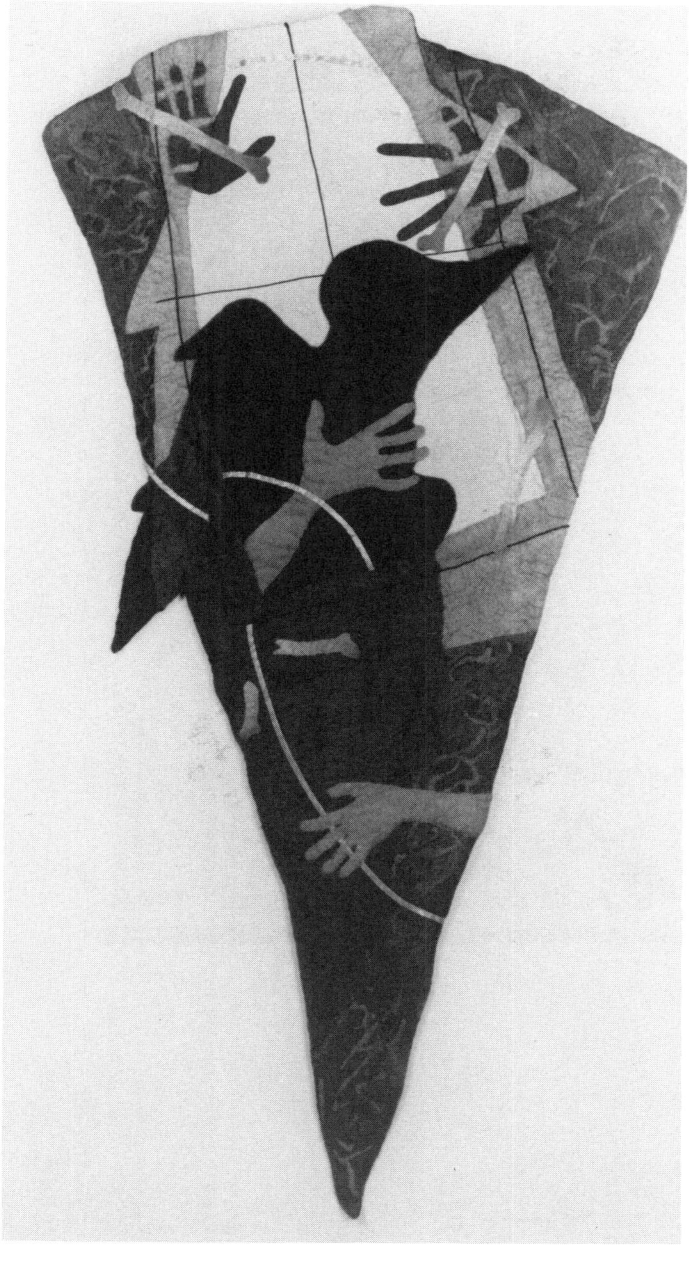

Layne Goldsmith, *The Fury of Restraint*, 1987, wool felt, mixed media, 60 x 30 x 6.

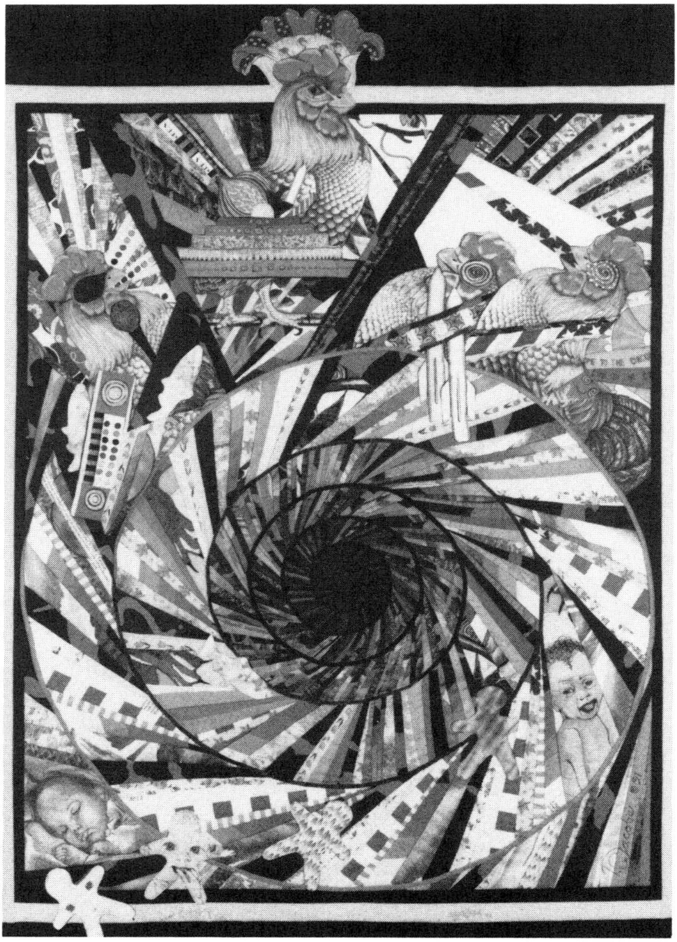

Teresa Cooper Jacobs, *New Reports*, c. 1991, mixed media, 44 x 35.

under Richard Proctor, where the program is today. *Surface Design for Fabric* by Richard Proctor and Jennifer Lew and *Crafts Design* by Spencer Moseley and Hazel Koenig were two influential books in the Pacific Northwest, and Proctor and Lew are still cited. Currently, Layne Goldsmith is an active force teaching textile art at the University of Washington.

The University of Washington's textile collection, originally housed by the Home Economics Department, now under the care of the Henry Art Gallery, is one of the best in the world, available for research and is accessible to students.

Lyn Basa as art curator for Safeco Insurance Company (1981-1986) and currently as Director of the University of Washington Medical Center art program has been a solid presence in the Pacific Northwest. Herself a tapestry weaver, she has brought historical understanding and a sensitivity to contemporary fiber to institutional acquisition.

The Oregon School of Arts and Crafts also has a strong fiber program. Newer museums, such as the Bellevue Art Museum and the Tacoma Art Museum, have given tentative support to the field. Cultural evolution, like biological evolution, makes use of old systems not designed for current function. Fossil traces of "Home Ec" and "fabric design" blind both artists and critics to the current state and possibilities of the art.

In addition to budding academic support, there has grown up a parallel education system, a loosely tied network of guilds and organizations which have taken the place of mother-to-daughter instruction. The Pacific Northwest Needle Arts Guild, The Contemporary Quilt Association, Quilters Anonymous, Northwest Designer Craftsmen, The Embroiderers Guild of America, Surface Design Association, and the National Standards Council of American Embroiderers, to name a few of the larger groups, have kept fiber art alive during long, dry seasons of disregard. Nationally, such groups and academia snipe at each other, arguing over who are the professionals and who are the real artists, who is folk and who is fine, who is high and who is low. Such wrangling mimics wider debates brought about by economic and social changes and subcultural clashes. But for the moment, in the Northwest, there seems to be a delicate, exploratory truce. Self-portraiture such as Carol Bennett's *Mute Series*, Janet Boguch's *Emerging From Underneath*, Layne Goldsmith's *The Fury of Restraint*, and Betty Brown's *Portrait Figure* would have been at least improbable without academic exposure. Similarly, Brown's *To Hell in a Handbasket (Teresa of*

Avila) and all Elly Smith's work on the contemporary sampler would have been impossible without the preservation of historical context and technique made possible by those to whom the work is more than status or paycheck.

The political work of Stephanie Cooper, Mary Hanson-Spofford, and Teresa Cooper Jacobs obviously shares this multiple consciousness. Nowhere is the new pluralism closer to realization than in the world of fiber. Fiber travelers to other cultures return with stories of mutually respectful exchanges of knowledge, country to country, gender to gender, and class to class. Who, after all, is brave enough to hope in a world such as this? For a while at least, this one spot seems to be working.

Book Arts: Rock, Paper, Scissors

by Sandra Kroupa

A large percentage of artists in the book arts in the Pacific Northwest are women. At workshops and lectures all over the country, the prevalence of women in the field is noteworthy. Why are women drawn to these elements of image, text, and structure? Many reasons are suggested: the form's accessibility, its tactile and secretive nature, and its personal and autobiographical aspect.

Because artists come from many different but equally important paths, bookworks appear in a variety of formats, from traditional to experimental. Each aspect of book arts has fine practitioners among women in the Pacific Northwest and this brief essay can only focus on a few. Most of the artists discussed have work in the Book Arts Collection at the University of Washington Libraries, where many of the pieces described herein can be seen.

In defining "book," form, content, materials, and structure are factors usually considered. Handmade paper was once only a means to an end, carrier of the printed image. Today paper can become image. In her long career, Margaret Ahrens Sahlstrand (Ellensburg, WA) has worked in cast and embossed paper, collage, pulp painting, sheet forming in Japanese and Western styles, combinations of elaborate and autobiographical drawings and relief prints with decorated paper to form the central image; *There Is No Ocean In Ellensburg* (1900), also one-of-a-kind, has complicated drawings with a handwritten text in a sculptural binding. Through teaching and workshops, Sahlstrand has shared her expertise with many artists.

Suzanne Ferris (Seattle, WA), another artist long associated with handmade paper in the Northwest, and her husband, Neal Bonham, are known for their expertise in sheet forming and watermarks. In addition, Ferris has been a letterpress printer (Sea Pen Press and Paper Mill) since 1975, focusing on limited editions and broadsides of poetry. In over a dozen books and as many broadsides, Ferris either creates the images (*Portable Kisses*, 1978) or collaborates with another artist, such as wood-engraver Gretchen Daiber (Leavenworth, WA) (*A Tree Sequence*, 1984). A regular collaborator is Judith L. Johnson (Seattle), a bookbinder since 1978, who designed and executed many of the Sea Press edition bindings, such as *Our Lady of the Harbor* (1986).

Margery Hellman (Seattle) is also a papermaker/paper artist, whose collage pieces and innovative sheet forming are notable. Hellman also does one-of-a-kind bookbindings, sometimes incorporating her textiles. Mary Slowinski's (Seattle) pulp paintings have already drawn attention and the Summer 1992 issue of *Hand Papermaking* has a paper sample from her mill with an embossed design by Margaret Ahrens Sahlstrand. Lilian Bell (McMinville, OR) has created paper to use in her sculptural books for over 15 years. Dorothy Field (Cobble Hill, B.C.) is another notable paper artist from the Northwest.

Both letterpress and high quality offset printing are thriving in the Pacific Northwest with many outstanding women in the field. Some letterpress printers publish limited editions of poetry, an historical mainstay of book arts. Besides Suzanne Ferris, there are Sally Green, who prints while her husband Sam binds editions (Brooding Heron Press, Waldron Island, WA); Rayner Holtz and Mary G. L. Shakleford (Laughing Dog Press, Vashon Island, WA), printing for 15 years; and Jan Elsted (Mission, B.C.), printing Barbarian Press editions since 1977 with her husband Crispin doing editorial and design work. Megan Benton (Tacoma, WA) runs the Elliott Press at Pacific Lutheran University and teaches book arts. Marion E. Cluff (Portland, OR) prints, (*A Seasonal Rhythm*, Instar Press, 1989), binds, and does artists' books. Sandy Tilcock (Eugene, OR) is known for her fine editions and custom binding.

Some book artists both print the text and create the images. Sarah Chamberlain (Chamberlain Press, Portland) and Maralyn Crosetto (Seattle) reprint favorite texts to which they add appealing illustrations, such as *Mother Goose* (Chamberlain, 1987) and *White Horse Girl and the Blue Wind Boy* (Crosetto, 1990). Chamberlain works primarily in wood-engravings and lino-cuts; Crostto creates mezzotints and paper-cuts. Patricia Grass (Bank, OR) illustrates her own text, *Culinary Seeds* (1983), a portfolio of broadsides. Susan Lowdermilk (Eugene) also wrote her own text to accompany her woodcuts in *Interior Passage* (1991).

Mare Blocker (Ames Lake, WA) has gained national attention with over 25 letterpress limited editions and 150 one-of-a-kinds in a dozen years. Blocker is easily one of the most prolific book artists in the country, combining technical excellence with diverse texts and images. Her books vary from black and white textless lino-cuts of skeletons (*Dance of Death*, 1991) to unconventional bestiary alphabets in miniature (*Animal Facts*, 1985), from handcolored accordion books with beads (*Dinner at Café Sport*, 1983) to a traditional language-of-flower book bound in a 14th-century limp vellum style (*Reeta's Garden*, 1987.).

Blocker has collaborated with several noted Seattle visual artists as well as with other book artists: Dennis Evans (*Seminary*, 1984), Lauren Grossman (*Did You Bring the Matches, Hon?*, 1986), Carolyn Law (*Home Book*, 1985), Mary Slowinski (*Dalmatian Fixation*, 1992), and Rita Tollefson (*Tale's End*, 1986). In 1991, Blocker produced *The Mystery Girls' Circus* in collaboration with Portland writer Katherine Dunn on a production grant from the National Museum of Women in the Arts.

Several regional artists work comfortably in both letterpress and offset printing. Tree Swenson (Port Townsend, WA), who with Sam Hamill started Copper Canyon Press in 1972, has inspired and trained a number of traditional letterpress printers active in the Northwest. Now the Press focuses on publishing first edition poetry and poetry in translation by offset. The offset books of Lesley Link-Moore and John Ellison (Broken Moon Press, Seattle) have won a number of design awards. Seal Press (Seattle), a leader in feminist publishing, has a large output of well designed books. Ruth Hayes (Seattle) is known for her humorous offset flip books, such as *Flip Book of the Dead* (1990).

Elsi Vassdal Ellis (EVE Press, Bellingham, WA), currently teaching offset and letterpress printing at Western Washington University, has been a mentor to beginning book artists. Known for extensive variety in her work and interested in myth, legend, non-Roman alphabets, and typographic history, Ellis writes or translates texts, creating both editions and one-of-a-kinds in innovative bindings. *Genesis* (1991), a one-of-a-kind, is a sequence of Prismacolor images of the creation myth in a shaped double concertina stick binding. Mary Ann Warner (Bellingham), a former student of Ellis's, produced a fine offset book using her own text and graphic black and white images, *The Gift of the Crow* (1988).

Judy Anderson (Seattle), who teaches design at the University of Washington, also creates letterpress and offset books. Her personal work, such as *The Initiation* (1990), is produced at the X Press. Shirley Scheier (Seattle) has been involved in the book arts since the early 1980s, currently teaching printmaking and book arts at the University of Washington.

Some artists use calligraphic texts, such as Jocelyn Curry (Seattle) in *So, I Want To Thank You* (1991), combined with images in interesting bindings.

Eileen Canning (Olympia, WA), a major paper marbler in the region works with calligraphers to create one-of-a-kind wall pieces (The Pacific Northwest has many excellent calligraphers, too numerous to mention here.) Bonnie Garlan (Portland) creates bindings and enclosures and artists' books with handwritten texts, drawings, and collage. The work of Edith Carlson (Gig Harbor) WA) has a medieval quality, sometimes including a surprise pop-up.

Images in bookworks can be created in many ways. Charlotte Murray (Everett, WA) generates her book pieces by using photographs and computer typesetting (*Invisible Reality*, 1991). Another photographer making books is Sandy Jackson (Seattle). Joan Cawley Crane (Ellensburg) uses sculptural and accordion forms, monoprints, and dramatic folded constructions. *Monoprint House* (1991) is a good example of a shaped binding viewable page by page and as a whole standing structure.

Artists' books are a form with no easy definition. Many of the books already mentioned can certainly be termed artists' books. Two popular styles are one in which a single artist has a concept but collaborates with other artists on some technical aspects, such as printing or binding; the other, books which are sculptural in nature. T. Ellen Sollod (Seattle) does both kinds of artists' books. Her *A Meditation On Human Rights And a Woman's Life* (1990) combines Sollod's forceful text and dramatic images with expert printing by Shelia Coppola and Charles Matson at Ink On Paper (Seattle). Coppola and Matson also printed Nelleke Nix's (Seattle) *1940-1945 Remembered* (1991), the artist's first book, with text and images recollecting her childhood in Holland. Collaborating on the binding, was Carolina Veenstra (Kingston, WA), who also does artist's books (*Shirt Book*, 1984) and fine designer bindings. Lucie Lambert (Vancouver, B.C.) conceived the idea for *Conversations With a Toad* (1987), created the images and then commissioned the poetry, printing, and binding.

opposite, top:
Mare Blocker, *Dalmation Sensation*, 1992, letterpress and block printed artist book, 7 x 5.

opposite, bottom:
Kathryn Leonard, ***Windows Out of Walls***, 1990, letterpress printed text in a tunnel book format.

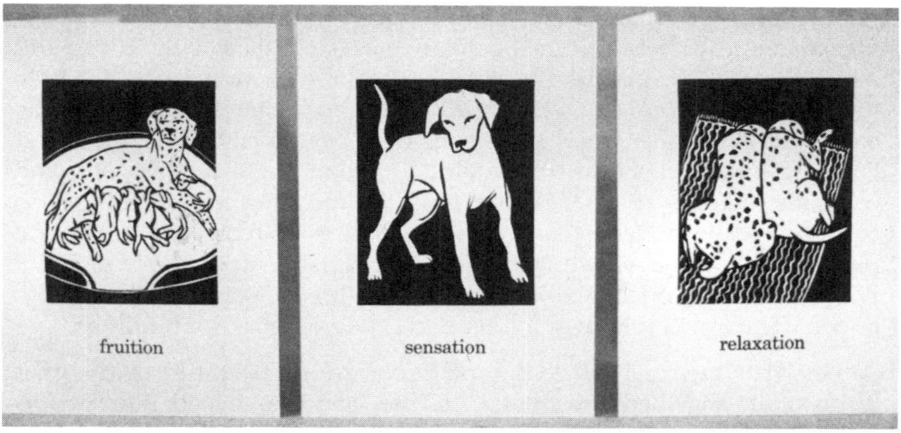
fruition
sensation
relaxation

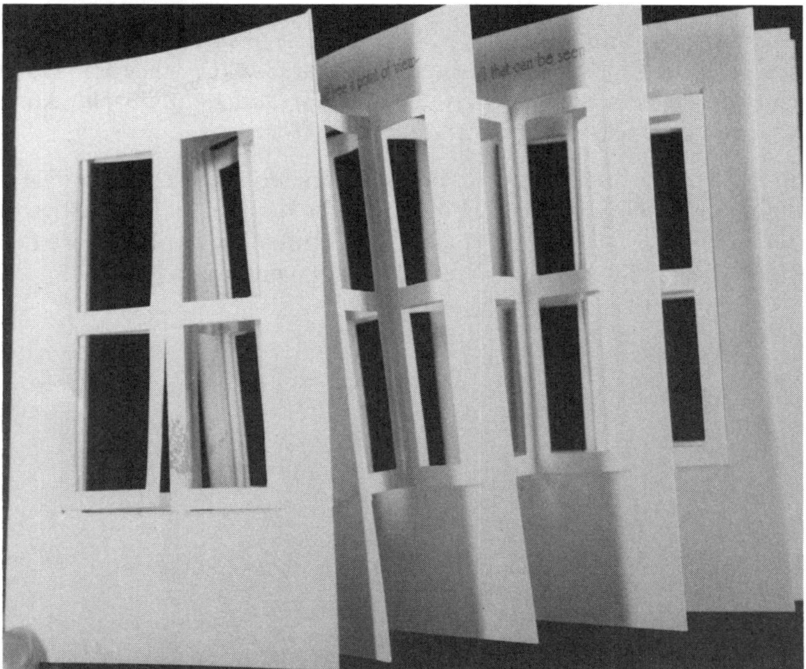

The majority of artist's books are produced by a single artist and can appear in any form. Sculptural books are popular in the Pacific Northwest. Another artist who uses this form is Kate Leonard (Seattle), specializing in tunnel books (*Windows Out of Walls,* 1990) and interesting uses of the concertina, as in her pop-up, *Asparagus Culture* (1986). She writes and letterpress prints her texts, uses folded and cut paper for imagery, and creates structures and boxes to extend the meaning. Leonard has also collaborated with Dennis Evans and Margaret Ahrens Sahlstrand as a bookbinder. Seong-Ae Mun (Seattle) created her sculptural piece, *Pencil Book* (1991), with offset text in an edition of three. Oregon binder Sandra Lopez (Finn Rock) is known for her decorative constructed bindings.

Some artists interested in sculptural books are proficient in many other forms of art and there are crossovers from ceramics, installation, performance, painting, and, of course, sculpture. Artist-of-many-talents Deborah Mersky (Seattle) has worked with one-of-a-kind transformed books (*Blue Key,* 1985) which reflect social and political themes. In *Coffee Table Book* (1986), Barbara Inglis McAusland (Seattle) has relief printed collaged decorations which project from the tooled lead cover to create a forbidding object. Helen Lessick (Portland) makes artists' books and does sculptural installations. Clothing is used by Mary Coss (Seattle) in book pieces. Nancy Cushwa (Portland) has some bookworks which resemble historic wax and clay tablets. Betha Gutsche (Seattle) also uses traditional bookforms in new ways, such as the scroll and Jacob's ladder.

Each artist has a highly personal reason to choose the book form. Here their fears, passions, and possibilities can be explored, then stitched together as books, visual and textual artists' quilts. The book arts are flourishing in the Northwest; the results are unique and memorable

Part IV:
Contemporary Northwest Art: Pluralism and Postmodern

This section offers a variety of critical approaches to trends in contemporary Northwest art in light of pluralist and postmodern tendencies and women artists' involvement in the expanding art scene. International and regional art exhibitions at the 1962 World's Fair in Seattle helped prompt a growing consciousness of the outside art world. New possibilities opened to women artists of the Pacific Northwest with the economic boom of the mid-'60s. In the 1970s, with the rise of commercial galleries in the area, feminism, alternative spaces and public art programs, opportunities grew. In this climate, women artists developed a diversity of approaches to modernism and postmodernism that continues.

Critic Jennifer McLerran's essay on narrative and figurative trends cuts across a range of multicultural approaches that address issues of representation and difference. Examining postmodern theories that have shaped contemporary photography, critic Elizabeth Bryant's essay discusses how artists deal with Self and Other. Critic/curator Matthew Kangas incorporates essentialist gender-based imagery into a formalist analysis of women artists working abstractly. Critic Lois Allan presents an overview of contemporary women who have shaped the Portland art scene. Critic Regina Hackett's essay highlights the importance of sculpture by regional women whose roots are in craft and assemblage. A personal view of postmodernism by artist/critic Pam Keeley looks at collaboration and interaction in the work of women artists in alternative exhibition venues in the Puget Sound area.

Narrative and Figurative Trends: Telling Differences

by Jennifer McLerran

Knowledge and truth in our culture have traditionally been constructed on a male model. A number of prominent Northwest women artists challenge this partial construction of reality. The richness and diversity of their art makes apparent, by contrast, the constraining influence of a culture which speaks of and to a particular race, class and gender.

Nancy Mee, Elizabeth Sandvig, and Fay Jones refuse to position their female subjects as passive objects of male visual pleasure. Lauren Grossman adopts and reworks familiar symbols of Judeo-Christian mythology, thus critiquing one of the most powerful master narratives of Western culture. Sherry Markovitz appropriates materials and techniques of folk art and incorporates design motifs from Native American traditions. Patty Warashina, Marita Dingus, Barbara Thomas, Gwen Knight, Gail Tremblay, and Cecilia Concepcion Alvarez draw on the Asian American, African American, Native American and Hispanic influences which have contributed to their identities. Gene Gentry McMahon and Maxine Martell concern themselves with cultural conflict and the imposition of dominant culture on women and Third-World peoples. In varied ways, all of these artists recognize cultural difference and the diverse cultural traditions which form individual identity. Their work testifies to the importance of "little" narratives, of voices which have been silenced in deference to the "master" narratives of dominant culture.

Nancy Mee indicts a cultural tradition which privileges standards of female beauty based on an unattainable ideal conforming to male desire. Her sculptures contain photographic reproductions of classical Greek goddesses whose images are etched on glass. These are combined with glass constructions representing deformed spines confined within rigid steel braces. Mee's sources include medical photographs of spines deformed by scoliosis, a debilitating condition which predominantly afflicts young women. Metaphors for the physical agony women endure in attempts to conform to a cultural ideal of feminine beauty, her work further comments on the dehumanization of medical technology.

Elizabeth Sandvig presents women in her paintings, not as the typical passive objects of male visual pleasure, but as active protagonists in carnivalesque and dreamlike sequences. Female circus performers, as in *Circus Series: Lift* (1990), may set the terms of the narrative. Though they retain an element of the "to-be-looked-at-ness" characteristic of male-determined images of women, Sandvig's female circus performers are more parody than passive participants in male visual pleasure. Sandvig's paintings often employ a stand-in for the artist in the form of a sleeping figure who dreams the images on the canvas. Accordingly, the stories we see have the disjunctive quality of dreams. Images seem jumbled together,

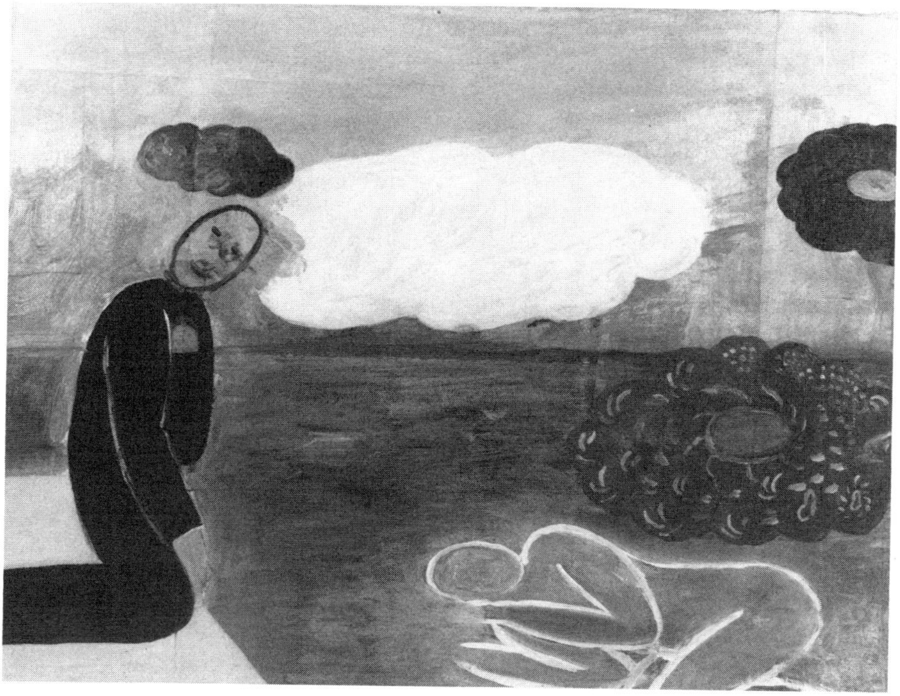

Fay Jones, *Morpheus*, 1991, acrylic/ paper, 11 x 13 3/4. Courtesy of Francine Seders Gallery, Seattle.

nonsensical, nonlinear, not fitting the standards of clarity and linearity established by the Western literary/artistic tradition. They, instead, reflect one woman's inner world of fantasy and reverie.

Fay Jones depicts a white middle-class world inhabited by figures yearning for the exotic. Similar to Sandvig's dreamers, Jones's figures seem to occupy an internal realm. They cast no shadows. Rather than depictions of real people in the everyday world, they signify the exotic of daydreams and fantasy. The object of female desire in Jones's work often takes the form of a sailor, a mysterious stranger and traveler in exotic realms. Although she has never been there, Jones often sets her dramas in, or dresses her figures in traditional attire of, the Far East. *Touch and Go* (1991), a three-panel painting, resembles a Japanese print in perspective and composition. Figures include sailors and a woman in traditional East Asian dress who, while embracing her male partner, drops a handkerchief behind his back in a flirtatious gesture to one of the sailors. This realm of the mysterious, exotic Other offers a space to exercise female fantasy and desire.

Lauren Grossman constructs a world where the illusion of seamless master narratives has fallen away. Her imagery includes figures of Adam, Eve, the Virgin Mary, Salome, and Susannah and the Elders. Her most recent figures, which are bolted together but with a gaping vertical seam, emphasize the cultural construction of mythological types. They literally no longer hold together without gaping holes. In one such figure, *Weeping Eve* (1990), the figure's white body is inscribed with an indecipherable script. Not only are the narratives of Western culture no longer seamless, they have lost accessibility and shared meaning. The objects in Grossman's installation, *Rusted Eden* (1990), are physically chained, bolted and locked together. In the world she presents, which includes the Tree of Knowledge with its fruit securely attached, meaning is locked to referents and free play of difference and marginalized experience are foreclosed.

Sherry Markovitz is best known for her elaborately decorated animal trophy heads, such as *Bow Wow Queen* (1987), a female elk head covered with richly colorful beadwork in a ruffled collar encrusted with glass, plastic and metal beads, shells, bells, miniature toys and jewelry. The intricate beadwork embellishing Markovitz's sculptures draws on traditional women's art, folk art traditions, and Native American techniques and motifs, forms that have been outside the realm of high art. She unites needlework with a trophy head, an object normally associated with masculine prowess. Injecting a little narrative into a male master narrative of domination of the natural world ironically undercuts it.

Patty Warashina similarly draws on traditions at odds with majority culture. She is well-known for her ceramic domestic goddess altar pieces, such as *You Captured My Heart* (1976), in which the arms of a geisha offer us a heart pierced with arrows. Describing a childhood encounter with her Christian grandmother's Buddhist shrine, Warashina says, "When I was in the third grade, I remember going to her house and opening a cupboard, and there was a Buddhist shrine. It was like a little dollhouse with all these little things — hair and beads and pieces of paper. For me to look at that as a Christian kid growing up was like looking at the occult."[1] Products of both dominant culture and Asian-American culture, Warashina's early shrine pieces can be seen as efforts to negotiate and accommodate difference.

As the work of individuals in specific social/historical contexts, visual art is inevitably to some degree a personal narrative. As such, it reflects the constraining influences gender places on women. Narratives of those identified as African-American, Asian-American, Chicana/o, or Native American are, similarly, the stories of individuals who must negotiate a marginalized position in their everyday lives. By listening to their stories, we learn how marginalized individuals have negotiated the dominant culture. Thus the workings of a dominant ideology, normally invisible, are illuminated.

Gwen Knight's work and personal history elucidate such cultural processes. She was an active part of the vital Harlem arts community of the 1930s and member of the circle (including her future husband Jacob Lawrence) surrounding the legendary African-American sculptor Augusta Savage. Knight herself conveys the rich history of efforts by women of color to negotiate difference during a period of great cultural change. In *Ritual* (1987) Knight presents three women in vaguely African dress. The grouping of three suggests a reading of these figures as symbolic of past, present, and future. The woman in the center, corresponding to the present, holds a red flower in full bloom, which, symbol of the richness of the present informed by the past she hands to the future. The image reflects a sentiment similar to that expressed by writer/filmmaker Trinh T. Minh-ha: "To preserve is to pass on, not to keep for oneself. A story told is a story bound to circulate." Like the woman in her painting, Knight also passes to future generations rich and vital cultural traditions and a rich personal history.

One tool of colonialization has been imposition of the dominant culture's literary/artistic tradition. Subordinate groups, however, have retained cultural traditions in folk art and other forms. Individuals pushed to the margins of dominant culture piece together alternate identities from fragments of majority culture and remnants of ancestral cultures. They can be seen as *bricoleurs* — "tinkerers" with cultural images, myths, etc.— as they join fragments and leftovers, those elements of dominant culture to which they are granted access, with surviving elements of subordinate cultural traditions.

Marita Dingus's art constitutes an attempt to reclaim and reconstruct African-American heritage. Dolls are traditionally a means by which cultural values are conveyed to girls. Dingus employs this traditional function to reconstruct African-American identity. Her early dolls made of

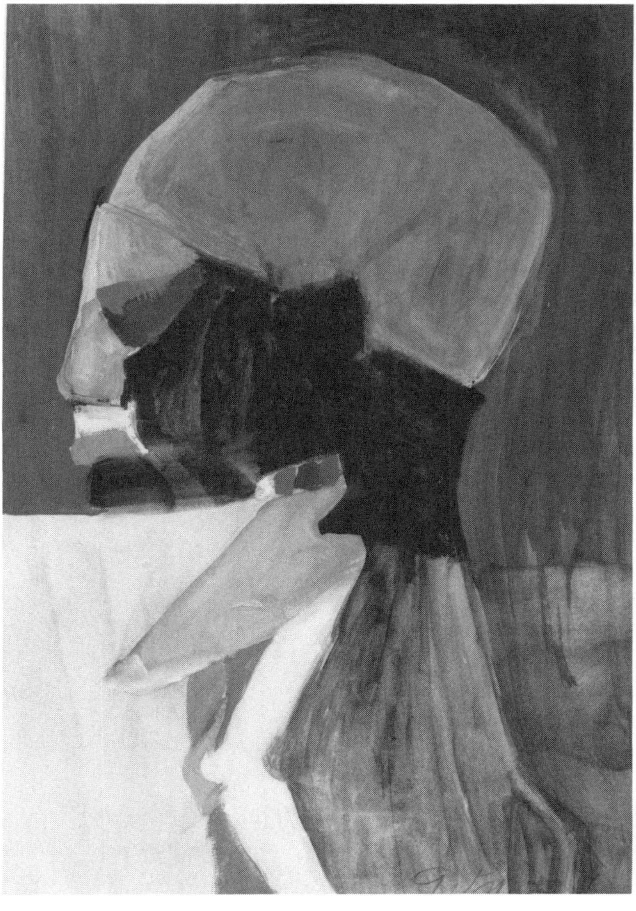

Gwen Knight, *Mask I*, 1940, gouache/paper, 20 x 14. Courtesy of Francine Seders Gallery.

cloth derive from cultural sources including rag dolls of the slave era, fetishes of Caribbean culture, and West African sculpture. In recent constructions composed of materials normally regarded as junk, Dingus again draws on folk art traditions and employs historically significant African-American techniques and forms. She challenges a modernist aesthetic of mastery of materials and boldly violates artificial standards of craftsmanship and excellence. Dingus's dolls and other personages are apt metaphors for the African-Americans construction of identity out of what is marginalized by majority culture. In *Lincoln Logs* (1990) Dingus manages to affirm African-American identity through the "refuse" of majority culture. Lincoln Logs, discarded toys seemingly devoid of cultural value, become significant for their association with Abraham Lincoln, a meaningful figure in African American culture.

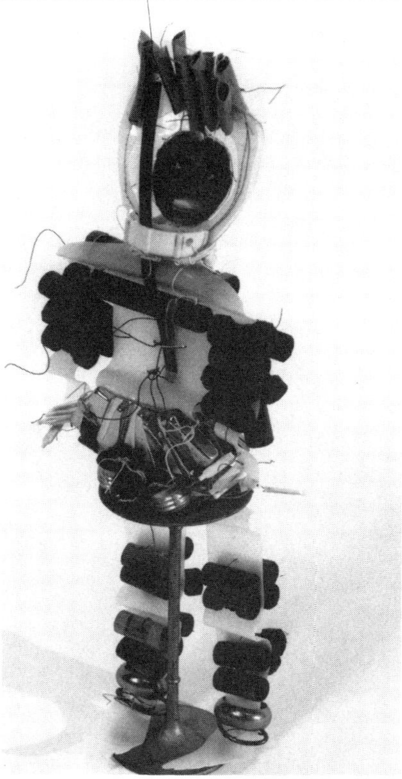

Marita Dingus, *Lincoln Logs*, 1990, mixed media, 21 x 8 1/2 x 4. Courtesy of Francine Seders Gallery.

African-American artist Barbara Thomas draws the viewer into intimate engagement with her small paintings much as one is drawn into engagement by a storyteller. Thomas says of her work: "I like to think of my paintings as short paragraphs. It's always a little story — never a big, grandiose thing."[2] She engages in little narratives. By putting together narrative fragments to make visual stories she practices storytelling as *bricolage*. Through telling stories of individuals previously untold (or at least unheard), Thomas hopes to show that people historically positioned as "other" are not irrevocably different from those who comprise majority culture. She thus hopes to mitigate physical and cultural difference.

Storytelling is also central to the art of Gail Tremblay. In *Sky Woman Falls to Earth Making My Ancestors* (1989), she recounts the creation myth of her Haudenosaunee (Iroquois) ancestors. Sky Woman, the first mother and the agent who makes agriculture possible, appears in Tremblay's sculpture as a doll of constructed felt. Turtle, the creature who carries the newly created North American continent on his back, appears as a beaded image. In another construction, which resembles a Christian altarpiece, *The Things Colonial Angels Witness*, Tremblay depicts the destruction of the Inca and Aztec empires by European intrusion in two panels and, in a third panel, the burning of her Haudenosaunee ancestors' homes. When the altarpiece is closed, the exterior shows the image of three sisters representing Corn, Beans, and Squash. The three, according to legend, grew up from the body of Sky Woman's deceased daughter, making agriculture, hence the sustenance and continuation of the Haudenosaunee people, possible.

Storytelling as carrier and creator of cultural values is equally important to Lillian Pitt, a maskmaker of Warm Springs-Yakima descent. Maskmaking is not a traditional art form of Pitt's ancestors; neither is the process of raku firing which she uses. However, she finds this Native American art form in general, and Inuit masks in particular, well suited to conveying the legends of her people. The stories she makes the basis of her work are those she remembers from childhood as instrumental in disciplining children. The legend of Steahah (Stick Indian) is a favorite. In one of Pitt's hand-built raku masks, *Spirit of the Stick Indian,* we see Steahah with his mouth puckered in a perpetual whistle. Pitt explains: "Indian children are told that if they wander far or misbehave the Stick Indian will get them. He can whistle your name. He can whistle you deep into the forest or he can whistle you to safety if you are good."[3]

Cecilia Concepcion Alvarez sees herself as negotiating three cultural identities and traditions. As a Chicana, her background includes a mixture of Native American, Spanish Colonial and contemporary Euro-American influences. Viewing power struggles as fundamental to human relationships both individually and collectively, she makes issues of power and exploitation her basic concerns. Alvarez draws on Native American legends for imagery, as in *El Danzon del Eternao Sueno de la Unidad* (*The Eternal Dance of Unity*), a painting based on a Mayan legend about a conflict between the sun and the moon in which the sun deity, jealous of the moon deity, plucks out the eye of the moon to make itself more powerful. Alvarez makes another central concern, the dangers of cultural tourism, subject of a codex. In this work in progress, she hopes to interrogate the tendency to translate traditions from other cultures into the dominant culture's terms.

Maxine Martell's recent paintings comment on how the dominant culture requires those who remain irrevocably "other" to configure its power. She further suggests the collusion of the art world in imposition of colonial narratives. The lower half of Martell's paintings depict elegantly set tables.

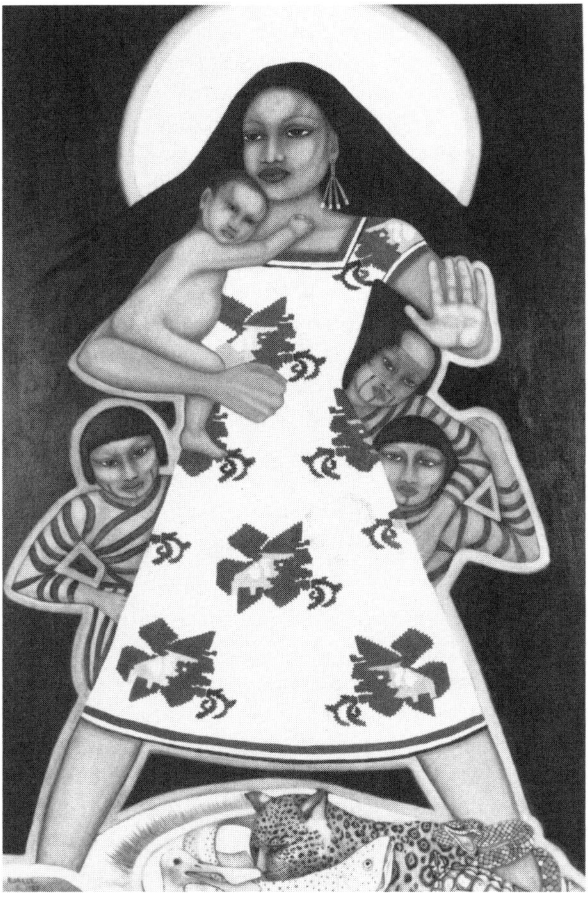

Cecilia Concepcion Alvarez, *La Tierra Santa*, 1990, o/c, 36 x 52.

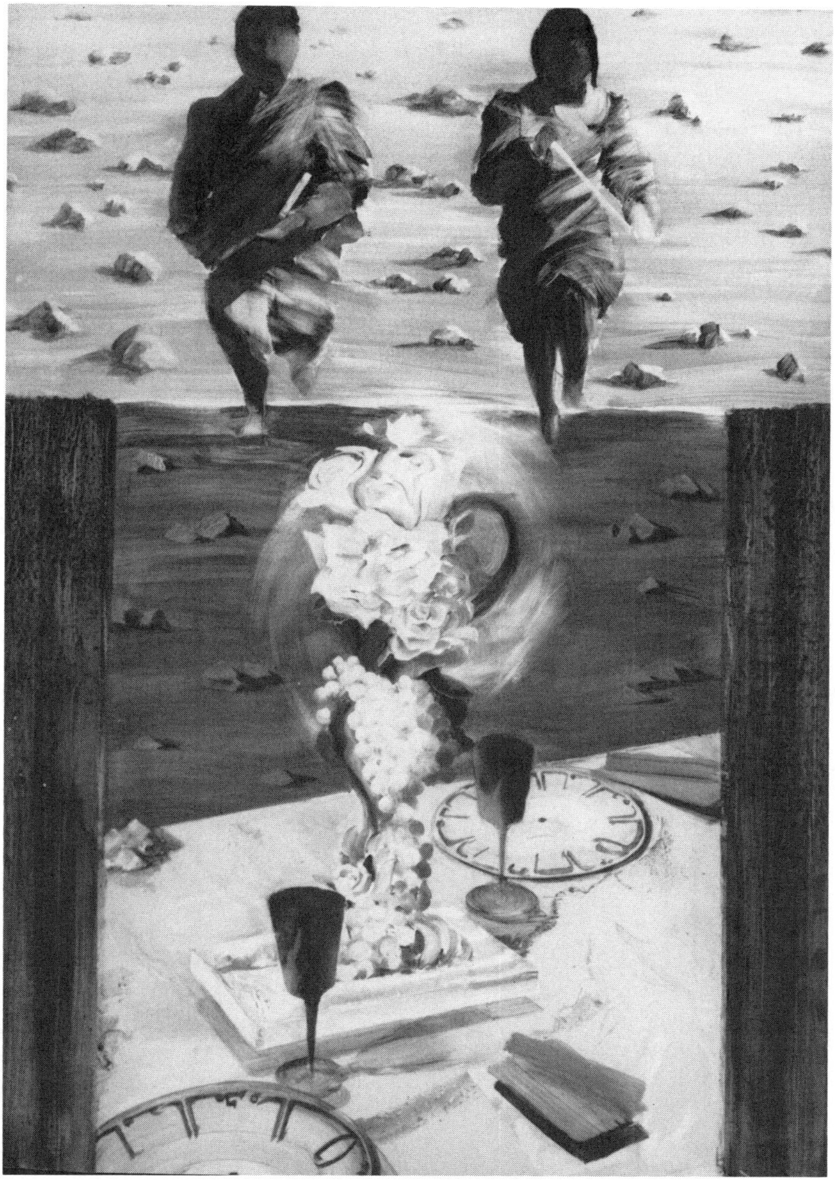

Maxine Martell, ***Red Desert — White Rose***, 1990, a/c, 70 x 48. Courtesy of Grover Thurston Gallery, Seattle.

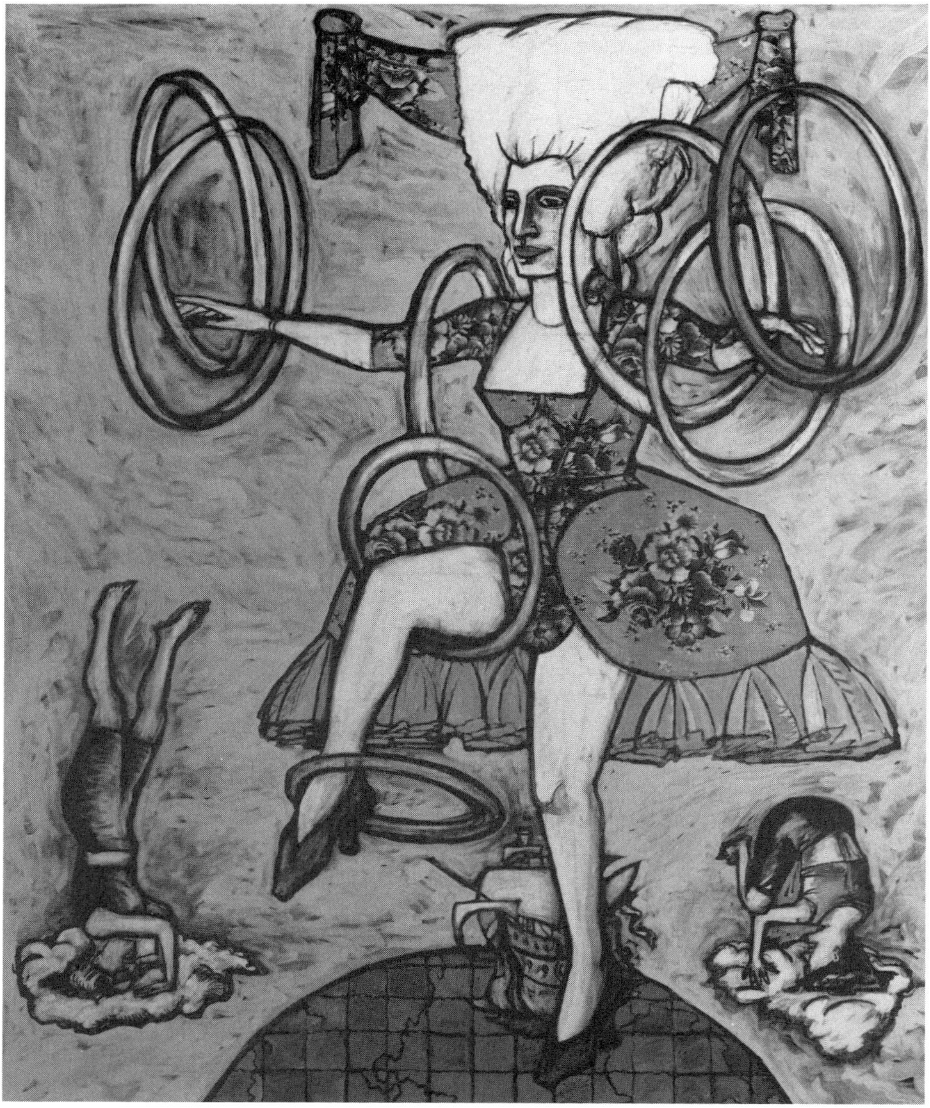

Gene Gentry McMahon, *Rings of Fate*, 1991, o/c with collage, 68 x 56. Courtesy of Greg Kucera Gallery, Seattle.

The top depicts Third-World violence. Her seemingly conflicting imagery reflects the oppositions of a culture that marginalize many and privilege a few. Martell's scenes of violence, like the table settings, are beautifully composed and seductively painted. That the tables are set for those in power suggests an aestheticization of Third-World violence for consumption by the dominant culture. Her painterly handling also obscures her subjects' identities. That which, by First World standards, makes these superior works of art (superior technical facility) serves, at the same time, to position the subjects as irrevocably "other." Martell's paintings point to the dangers of turning Third and Fourth World struggles into objects of First World aesthetic consumption.

Gene Gentry McMahon also explores the issue of colonialization. In her painting *Fate and the Goddess/Rings of Fate* (1991) we see McMahon's version of Fortuna, the European goddess who determines both individual fate and collective destiny by directing the course of the Wheel of Fortune or Wheel of Life. Fortuna stands atop a globe marked out in a Cartesian grid. In an absurd balancing act, reminiscent of a circus performer, she twirls rings resembling hula hoops. Behind her, a Spanish galleon represents Columbus's "discovery" of the New World. McMahon thus presents conflicting views of human enterprise. Fortuna, traditionally portrayed as blindfolded, reflects a view of fate as directed by an indifferent force blind to reason and justice. However, here she stands atop a globe bearing the marks of a civilization founded on rationality and predictability, a known world mapped out in a system of coordinates, conforming to human reason and logic. Once all points on the globe could be mapped, located by a system of coordinates, they could be mastered — and colonized.

The artists discussed here respond to such attempts at mastery. Their individual stories convey the impact of historical contingencies and cultural constraints on individual lives, lighting the intersections of master narratives with little narratives, offering points of local resistance. Although little narratives are shaped by grand narratives as people attempt to make their lives conform to the norm, grand narratives are reshaped by little narratives, as well. Respecting difference can generate tolerance rather than exclusion.

NOTES:

[1] Susan Wechsler, *Low Fire Ceramic: A New Direction in American Clay*, New York: Watson-Guptill, 1981, p. 125.

[2] Lynn Basa, "Three Artists Mix Poetry with their Painted Artwork," *Journal-American*, June 22, 1986.

[3] *Ceramics Monthly*, vol. 32 (June/July/August 1984), pp. 97, 99.

Photography, Media Arts, Self, and Other

by Elizabeth Bryant

The question of representation of women in photography has become increasingly problematic in recent years, so that a deliberate strategy, or a conscious decision to ignore such strategy, is required. The problem is doubled when the photographer is a woman. This is as true for photographers in the Northwest as elsewhere.

In the 1970s, widely influential writings by Susan Sontag and Roland Barthes challenged the traditional view of photography. Rather than an objective document of reality, the photograph began to be seen as a carefully constructed viewpoint. The rise of a "deconstructivist" approach in academic and critical circles during the 1970s and '80s also brought photography's role in mass media as a persuasive, and pervasive, tool for constructing social and political "realities" under intense scrutiny.

The theories of French psychoanalyst Jacques Lacan were of particular importance in this deconstruction and became central to the discourse surrounding photography and film. Lacan regarded both gender and "Self" as socially constructed phenomena. He saw the "Self," not as an essential entity, but as pieced together from what was mirrored back to the individual through the outside world. Lacanian models of the mechanisms of objectification, of the separation of the world into Self and Other, and of the gaze and its relation to maintaining a phallocentric order, closely paralleled the workings of a camera — relied, in fact, on the metaphor of the camera obscura.

Such a parallel raised the stakes for photography: if the creation of a photograph mimicked the construction of self and social "reality," if a photograph was itself a document disguising the construction of a social "truth," then such social "truth," and the selves it created might also be consciously manipulated and exposed through the strategic use of photography. Interrogating photography became a way of interrogating the presumptions of culture. By the same token, Lacan appealed to a certain faction of feminism: if femininity is socially constructed, it might, be reconstructed. For those feminists who found the road of essentialism a dead end, Lacanian theory offered an avenue of attack.

Feminists have long been concerned with the social positioning of women in artistic representation. If the image of women was seen as so conditioned, co-opted, and "colonized" by men as to be untenable in painting, the image of women in photography was even more problematic. While a painter might simply ignore feminist arguments, avoid images of women, or produce essentialist or bio-morphic abstract imagery (as has been done, more often than not, by women's painting in the Northwest), a photographer must deal with the relationship of subject to object, the photographer's controlling (traditionally male) Gaze, the usurping of the photographed subject's identity by the photographer's subjective reality, and all the rest of the medium's ethical baggage. In the Northwest, as elsewhere, moral dilemmas posed by photography force a confrontation with deconstructivist feminist thinking for all but the most naive photographer — even when the origins of such thinking are not apparent to the individual artist.

This is not to say that images of essentialism, or substitution or avoidance of images of women (especially in combination with other media) aren't also employed by women photographers in the Northwest. Heather Ramsey, for instance, uses handcolored 35 mm photography in conjunction with her Cornell-like "dollhouses." Her small, Surrealistic tableaux of displaced chairs and barred windows, apples, ropes, and broken ladders read as portraits of battered wives, or women trapped by societal roles, while sidestepping direct female images altogether.

Peggy Hitchcock uses "fem-tech" to heal the nature/culture split: She silkscreens found photographs — from advertising, art history, pre-history, science, technology, pop culture — onto a variety of supports ranging from paper to wood constructions to copper. Each individual screen is stretched on an embroidery hoop; then overlaid and juxtaposed with other images to create a pieced-together, "quilted" effect. The works, from microscopic images of bloodcells to telescopic images of galaxies, electron microscopy to atomic cloud-chambers, share archetypal significance as essential, female symbols—spirals, circles, wheels—and yet place women squarely within culture and history. The female fundamentals of culture are revealed in the spirals of an Assyrian beard. The "zero" of a mannequin's moonface is worked through to the symbol for infinity.

Susan Seniuk, while a painter, employs photography to comment on the mechanisms of culture. She projects newspapers and magazine photos onto canvas in order to recreate them in thin, flat acrylic paint. She alters the screen-dot pattern of media reproductions with optical pattern systems taken from military camouflage and color-vision tests, mixing in an overlay of text, to challenge our ability to perceive media messages and cultural assumptions. A recent painting featured text from the cover-jacket of a woman's self-help book on "loving too much" juxtaposed with text from a SWM's personal ad overlaying the camouflaged "photographs" of a man and a woman.

If Seniuk uses painting like photography, Barbara Noah's work uses photography like painting, recombining both original and found photographs to express a universal, if increasingly female, life experience. Noah, who has taught at Cornish College of the Arts in Seattle since 1979, is perhaps the most significant Northwest woman photographer in the use of substitute representation. Her early work combined a preoccupation with images of natural power (volcanos, lightning, fire) with a playful approach to materials and sophisticated political awareness. An ironic sense of the smallness of human experience in the vastness of the universe—and the potential for disaster in our disregard of nature—has long been an aspect of her work. She has avoided the human image in favor of the primal ability to perceive faces in a three dot pattern: bowling balls became startled "oh no" visages; a ballooning volcanic mushroom-cloud beneath the dual windows of a flaming house reads as a comically stoic portrait.

Noah's immaculately crafted, hand-tinted photographs splice together images of the vegetable with the animal and mineral to form the human: Two holes in a close-up of weathered driftwood form eyes over a galaxy "mouth"; the hair a shot of Mt. St. Helen's eruption. Or the hair is a microscopic view of an ovum bristling with yellow sperm, the red mouth a circular nebula and the eyes two pebbles flung into a lake: one pebble just touches the water, the still frame splash surrounding it like lashes, while the other hangs suspended just above the surface. Personal references run throughout: the imprint in the sand of a dearly loved, recently deceased dog becomes one of the primordial three spots, for instance. Images read at times as infants, at times as self-portraits: A cactus holds out its arms like a prickly child; an accompanying set of mixed media "vanity" mirrors and compacts offers photographs of nebulae where reflections of self should be. Noah's recent work speaks of an awareness of life in mid-generation: caught between the possibility of procreation and the certainty of death.

Lyn Hamrick is another Northwest photographer whose awareness of the problems inherent in photographic representation more often focus on the correct ethical stance towards the world than on the specific representation of women. Yet, one could argue, the very careful nature of Hamrick's

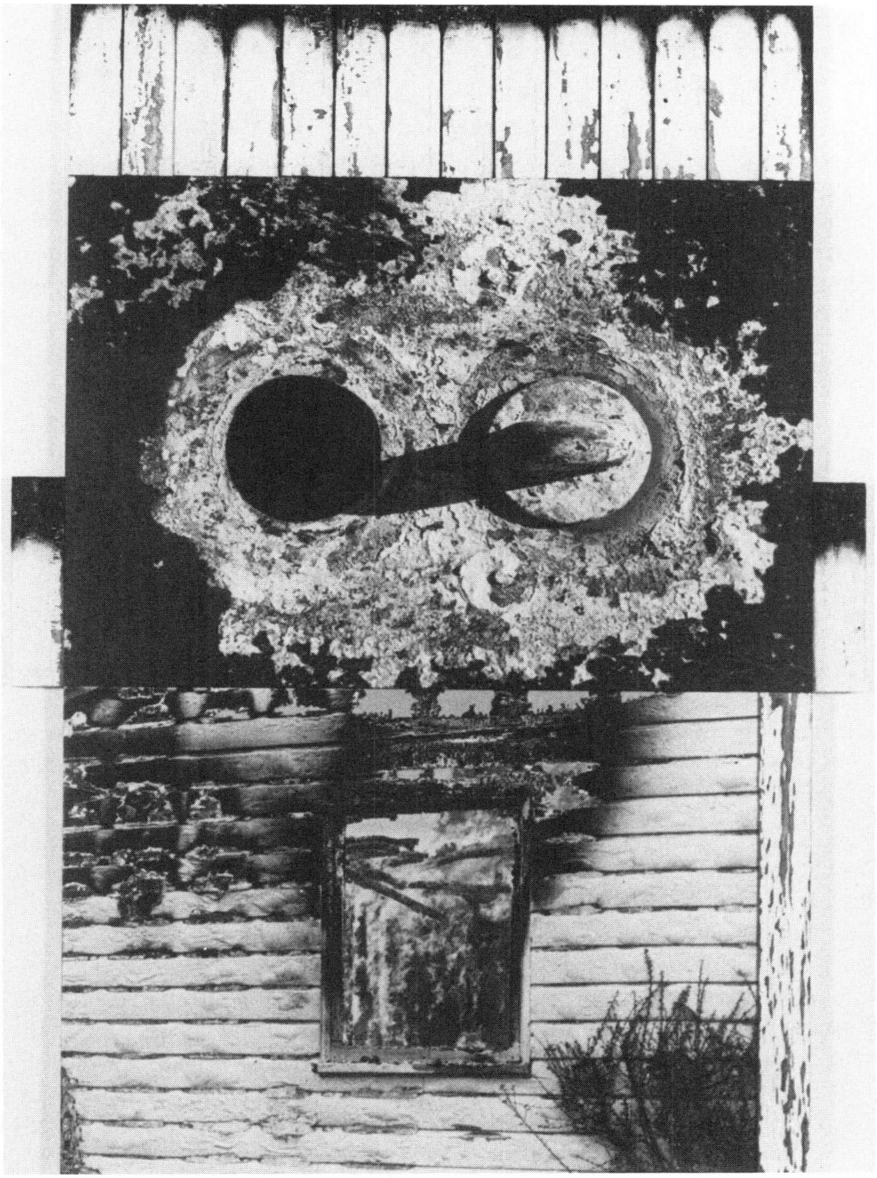

Barbara Noah, *Hold Me Close*, 1986, o/ photo-linen, burned house siding, 72 1/4 x 50 1/4 x 1 5/8.

mode of representation challenges the typical male photographic Gaze. In her approach to the documentary photograph, she constructs a female version of "reality."

Hamrick's three year project documenting the lives of the elderly threatened by the loss of low-cost housing in downtown Seattle involved careful cultivation of relationships over an extended period. The human subject is contextualized, presented in his or her environment. Hamrick used a manual roll camera, overlapping each frame slightly to create a panoramic view which is presented with the silkscreened, blown-up view of some element in the room. Mapping the room and its occupant, she simultaneously describes her own position within the room and in relation to the subject. The result is documentation without the usual voyeurism.

Hamrick used a different strategy in presenting a series of travel photographs from Nepal and India: She included a fragmented black and white panorama , but placed it beneath a deliberately grainy, and remarkably beautiful, color photograph. She then frustrates the aesthetic call of exoticism by framing each piece under glass etched with tour book phrases in Hindi or Nepali. Blocking access to these National Geographic-esque images, she makes explicit the folly of assuming we can really understand, or possess, such a different culture. In this way, she, as subject/photographer, relinquishes control over the object of her vision. Rather than enforce the vulnerability of the model through assumption of a controlling Gaze, the photographer herself becomes vulnerable to the Gaze of the world. Hamrick consciously relinquishes power — the typical cloaked stance of the male photographer — to allow the photographic subject to look back.

She did recently produce one set of images that directly represent women: a series of fruit and vegetable figures supplied with doll limbs. They seem to refer satirically to the photographs of Edward Weston, in which nude women and sensuous vegetables are often indistinguishable. In an odd way, Hamrick's vegetable women relate to the early work of the Northwest's best-known woman photographer, Marsha Burns, whose flowing nudes in the late 1970s bore a resemblance to Weston's peppers, with, if anything, even less life. Burns's nudes in blank studio settings were frequently headless as well. The black choker and the shadow of the head of a standing model (halter top undone) make her appear literally beheaded. Her mannequin quality contrasts strongly with her fully fleshed hands with deeply shadowed veins. Yet, what in the hands of Lee Friedlander might attract meanings of mingled lust and disgust is modified by Burns; the very alienation and woodenness of her nudes begins to raise questions of identity and role-playing.

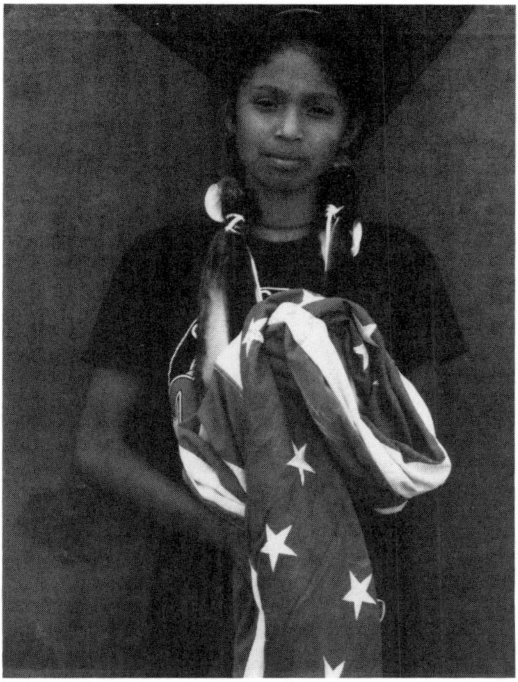

Marsha Burns, *Annie Jo*, 1991, silver print, 16 x 20.

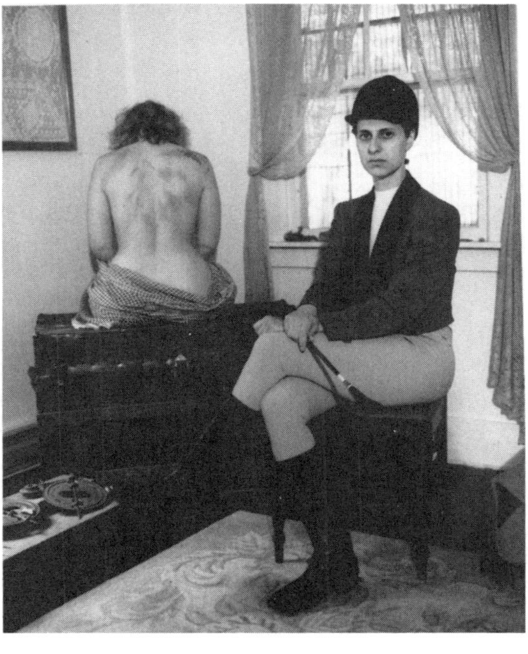

Claire Garoutte, *Untitled*, 1989, silver print, 14 x 11.

Burns has gained considerable attention over the past ten years with her photographs of alienated adolescents from Europe and the United States. Superficially, her work has continued to adhere to the traditional voyeuristic model of photography, focussing on those on the fringes of society, and yet, in her choice of subjects she has found collaboration. For these adolescents, outward appearance, their personae, is their art-form — what Burns has termed "style as a language of rejection." Rather than stealing their image, she has allowed them to speak by offering them a stage, a visual microphone.

Much of Burns's work is done with a 4 x 5 camera on type 55 Polaroid film. She has said that the "frame" left by the Polaroid process around the image acts as a window for the voyeur and a mirror for the viewer, pointing out fundamentally different ways of looking — with or without identification. It's an important difference, and one which comes into play in her more recent photographs of rodeo performers, street-kids and other "People of America."

While the street-kids hold up a deliberate mirror to society, Burns's latest photographs seem more representations of fractured identities constructed by society itself. Her photographs of young men in drag work as deliberate presentations of fractured identity created by the mirrorings of an imperfect society. There is a sense of playing with a received identity, of changing its meaning by owning it and thereby controlling its construction. This is similar to the series pursued by Claire Garoutte.

For several years, Garoutte, a 1990 MFA graduate from the University of Washington, has been documenting the lesbian S&M community in Seattle. The photos are posed, theatrical; they could be stills from a play or promotional posters for a film. Featuring riding crops and lash-marks, piercing and tattoos, stereotypes of butch and fem, they also document the trust and bonds between these women. There appears to be a different type of mirroring in the photographs. Garoutte has entered a long-term relationship with this community, and yet, unlike Diane Arbus for instance, she is producing less a voyeuristic documentation of a sub-culture than a collaborative manipulation and experimentation. Rather than acting as a keyhole to the outside, or as a mirror held up to society, the photographs function more as a mirror turned back in. The sensationalism and eroticism is narcissistic rather than voyeuristic: the subject is in control. Garoutte seems less the director of an objectifying Gaze than the tool for the self-directed Gaze of the community — a mirror on the ceiling.

Vicki Demetre, also a 1990 graduate of the University of Washington, stages photographic situations involving her own self-image. Her digital dye coupler prints touch on theory in their situations and symbolism — veils, scissors, mirrored surfaces, family dynamics, dolls and doll clothes — and yet she refuses the intellectual bait, producing imagery both clearer and more vulnerable than that of a less intuitive approach. Like Burns's alienated adolescents, the fractured mirror of Demetre's persona is her message, rendered more incisive, cutting, by her refusal to distance herself intellectually.

The use of photography to create identity through role playing or manipulation is a common ingredient for a number of young photographers.— most of whose work, while significant, is beyond the scope of this article. Jan Cook, is one such. She manipulates imagery of often nude young women to claim a self-constructed "natural" eroticism, or, by introducing images of wrenches and clothespins to an image of a woman working out, calls into question the changing nature of women's roles in society. Like Demetre, Cook seems perched on the edge of a reformulation of self.

While it is dangerous to make generalizations about gender differences or about brave new approaches to art, the traditional boundaries of photography, at least as produced by these Northwest women photographers, have become more fluid. The lens has become permeable, as it were, permitting an interchange between subject and object, objective documentation and subjective interpretation. Perhaps it is merely an increased awareness of the implications of photographic representation, or perhaps it is due to a difference in looking when the "subject" behind the lens is culturally configured as "object." If Lacanian theory holds true, this may be due to a difference in subject/object relations in men and women. When the photographic gaze implies an identification rather than a separation and objectification, voyeurism may end and the possibility of transformation begin. Whatever the cause, the work of these women photographers marks a positive trend in the contemporary art of this region.

Femform: Late Modernist Painting in the Pacific Northwest

by Matthew Kangas

INTRODUCTION

The open or "femform" — the circle, the diamond, the angled V or Y, the broken curve — is a linear configuration which appears over and over again in late modernist painting by women of the Pacific Northwest. So much so that femform will inevitably require re-examination of all regional modernist painting during the 1945-1990 period to answer a nagging question: "Were woman painters better and more imaginative than their male counterparts — Louis Bunce, Francis Celentano, Joseph Goldberg, Robert Hanson, Paul Heald, Paul Horiuchi, William Ivey, Robert C. Jones, Alden Mason, Carl Morris, Jack Portland, Charles Stokes, Milton Wilson?" For the time being, we must reach into the circle, step over the broken curve, walk into the glittering diamond.

Though it may come as a surprise to many, modernist abstraction has been the dominant art style in the Pacific Northwest since the end of World War II. Mark Tobey (1889-1976) and Morris Graves (b. 1910) were widely recognized artists from Seattle and, indeed, Tobey was even granted prior status by critic Clement Greenberg[1] as the innovator of "all-over" painting. In spite of its influence on rurally isolated male artists of the Puget Sound region, ecological "mysticism" was viewed by most highly educated women artists who moved to the area as a retrograde, sentimental direction.

The topic is a vast one, requiring a condensed discussion addressing a limited number of artists. However, one cannot overestimate the dissemination of modernist principles through regional institutions of higher learning, such as the University of Oregon, the University of Washington School of Art, Cornish Institute (now Cornish College of the Arts), Washington State University, and the University of Puget Sound. Though this essay addresses the years 1966-1993, it is important to recognize the firm standing of modernist dogma in colleges and universities during the postwar period; the high enrollment of women in such programs; the increasing migration of modernist-trained women artists to the Pacific

Northwest; and, finally, the high profiles these artists had in the rapidly expanding Seattle and Portland art scenes of the 1975-1985 period.

One might add to all this the role played by local women art historians and critics supportive of modernism, women curators at major and minor visual arts institutions such as museums, galleries, nonprofit or cooperative exhibition spaces, and women art dealers sympathetic to abstract art in Portland, Oregon, and Seattle, Washington. Today's dealers differ from their postwar predecessor Zoe Dusanne (1890?-1972)[2] who supported modernism but exhibited few women artists. Furthermore, they represent a heretofore unacknowledged network for emerging and mature women artists whose work has alluded more to mid-century international art developments than to ecological or spiritual subject matter tied to the evergreen landscape.

The spread of non-objective art may be seen, in retrospect, as not only a manifestation of educational opportunity and conditioning but a haven for the development of personal signs, a refuge for the self, and a vocabulary of image resistant to male control and traditional art historical directions.

With Abstract Expressionism finding its own female proponents during the 1950s and 1960s in Kathleen Gemberling Adkison (b. 1920) of Spokane, Washington, Viola Patterson, and Margaret Tomkins (b. 1916) and others, modernism underwent a gradual transformation as they challenged the overtly aggressive qualities of Action Painting and substituted softer brush attack and subtler palettes. Like many conscientious provincial artists, they selected aspects of an avant-garde style (largely familiar through photoreproduction), and adapted them to their own needs rather than attempting to emulate or mimic exact models.

The major women modernist painters of Oregon and Washington addressed issues of form, color, texture, canvas shape, and image. Resistant to the pull of landscape — except for early Tomkins and most of Adkison — these artists created internal landscapes reflecting encounters with varied materials and explorations of image-making powers.

The results suggest a higher level of modernist painting than has been granted up to now. This perception is rooted in the evolution of feminine forms symbolically or unconsciously representing female body parts such as breasts and vaginas. The circle, the diamond, and V-shape answer the monolithic structures of male painters and sculptors and, when taken together, form an unbroken chain of submerged private subject matter.

Three generations were at work in Portland and Seattle during the 1970s and 1980s: the First Generation, born before, during, and after World War I; the Second Generation, born before and during World War II; the Third Generation, the largest, and born after World War II but before 1955.

THE FIRST GENERATION

Patterson, Tomkins, Adkison and Mary Henry (b. 1913) comprise the First Generation of Northwest abstract woman painters. There were others, including Kerns and Morris, but these four women remained active in the 1970-80 period, capping their careers with impressive summations.

Henry received her training in a master's degree program under exiled Hungarian Constructivist Laszlo Moholy-Nagy. The teacher-student relationship was close and fruitful, formative for Henry's art, and culminating in his offer of a teaching job, which she declined.

By the mid-1960s, Henry began to exhibit her paintings again, among the first to use fluorescent paints. Her 1968 Arleigh Gallery exhibition in San Francisco was favorably reviewed in *Artforum* (October, 1969). In 1980, her shift to an isolated forest home on Whidbey Island in Washington State provided the seclusion to continue creating large multi-paneled paintings in acrylic with hard-edge Constructivist images.

At age 80, Mary Henry is the senior modernist painter in the Pacific Northwest. Her tutelage under Moholy-Nagy led to meticulous Prismacolor and graphite drawings, used as preparatory studies for large paintings in acrylic. The drawings were organized into a 1984 works-on-paper retrospective at Arthead Gallery in Seattle, one of four retrospective surveys of Henry's work since her arrival in the Puget Sound area.

She has explored femform in a variety of ways. *3 C 2 7 3* (1966), with its upright Y-shape and sharp black adjacent lines, uses a schematic female shape to create disturbing optical activity. A prior series shown in San Francisco, *On/Off* (1968), set up concentric circles executed in fluorescent paints and exhibited under "black light" tubes. Breast forms come to mind, complete with accentuated dayglo "nipples."

During the 1980s, Henry built on the encouragement of a 1976 encounter with New York School painter Jack Tworkov. It is possible that Tworkov's final paintings were influenced by Henry's graphite drawings, which he saw in her studio at the Centrum Foundation in Port Townsend, Washington: Square outlines filled with tight parallel lines appear in both artists' work of the period; Mary Henry did it first.

Passiflora Red (1985) and *Death of Sonoma* (1968-76) each extend the diamond form across a canvas diptych in each case and express a submerged sexuality not always apparent in Henry's art. An additional survey was organized by chief curator Barbara Johns for the Tacoma Art Museum in 1993.

Tomkins employed veils of pale color to approximate the marine light and kerosene lamplight in her cliffside home on Lopez Island, Washington. She moved to Seattle with her sculptor husband James FitzGerald (1910-1973) to accept an assistant professorship at the University of Washington School of Art in 1949. Trained at the University of Southern California, she explored surrealist-automatist methods as in her early work (*Anamorphosis*, 1944). Her experimentation evolved into heavily impastoed black, white, and grey canvases (*Night Passage*, 1961).

Since then, Tomkins has used a string structures suspended like a cat's cradle to "catch" light patterns that end up in her paintings. Interlocking diamonds and irregular polygons create garlands of feminine shapes around central openings which exude the light of pale blues, grays, and whites. More successful in terms of femform than her earlier, thickly painted works, these acrylic stain paintings posit awkward compositions as repositories for closely nuanced, subtle chromatics. Like Mary Henry, Tomkins works in geographic isolation. The product of this isolation is her summation paintings: innovative, individual, and in essence a rejection of male-generated art movements like Constructivism and Abstract Expressionism. Painting actively despite a temporarily disabling stroke in 1988, Tomkins has been honored with several thorough surveys, including "Margaret Tomkins, Paintings and Sculptures 1969-1978" at the Whatcom Museum of History and Art in Bellingham, Washington.

Youngest of the First Generation, Kathleen Gemberling Adkison is, after Clyfford Still, the major modernist painter to emerge from eastern Washington. She is also closer to the ecological "mysticism" of Graves and Tobey, with whom she studied privately from 1946 until 1950. Steeped in the stark geological landscape of the Spokane area, Adkison abstracts rock formations and forest vegetation into oil paintings with highly reflective surfaces, what critic Alfred Frankenstein called her "lusters and patinas."[3]

With compositions frequently pairing compressed rocks and upper horizon or "release" areas, Adkison incorporates jagged interlocking V-forms

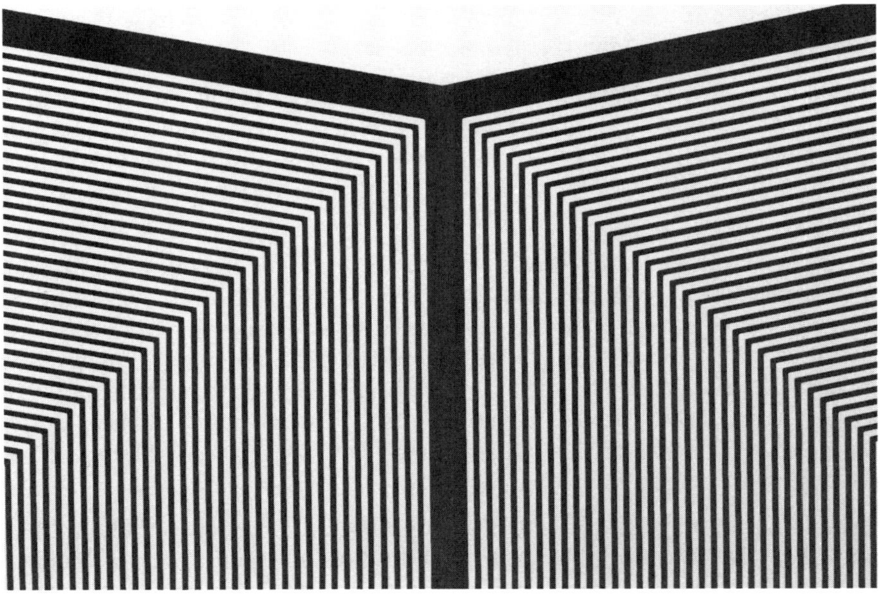

Mary Henry, ***Nexus #2***, 1965, a/c.

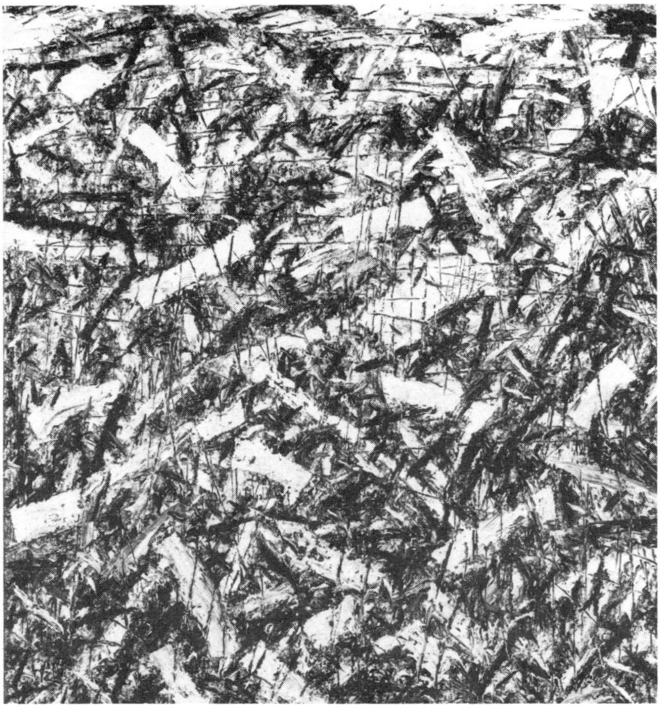

Lois Graham, ***Mooncups III***, 1985, o/c, 56 x 50. Collection of Robert Leonard, Ltd.

as well as myriad bunched circles. In this sense, a femform reading of her oeuvre is logical. *Life Skein* (1977) clearly juxtaposes a reddish descending V or Y-form against icy white walls patterned with circular, lichen-like dots. Adkison abstracts landscapes in a way which may also be read anatomically. An upright triangle in *Spring Swoll* (1979) or the deep central, cave-like recesses in the diptych *Change-Over* (1962, exhibited at the Seattle World's Fair) propose a re-examination of Adkison's art in this light. She expresses an outward world of tectonic shifts and potential earthquakes through gleaming surfaces, bright color, and a clarification of geological forms deeply concealed in Still's painting. A 1981 retrospective of Adkison's work was curated by John Olbrantz at the Bellevue Art Museum in Bellevue, Washington.

THE SECOND GENERATION: SHELTER AND SURFACE

The Second Generation of Northwest abstract painters matured within a nation of enhanced prosperity after World War II. Success was more easily achieved as the art markets in Portland and Seattle steadily grew. Well educated at respected institutions, such as Yale University (Joan Ross Bloedel, b. 1942); University of Iowa (Kay Rood, b. 1945); Stanford University (Jacqueline Barnett, b. 1935); and Sarah Lawrence College (Merrill Wagner, b. 1935), Second Generation artists settled in Seattle in the 1950-70 period. They showed regularly in Seattle's new gallery quarter, Pioneer Square.

Lois Graham (b. 1930) used open forms in her earlier work (*Light Screen*, 1976), but, gradually, aggressive mark-making took over, turning the canvas into a surface of tapestry-like "all-over" fields (*Stick Up*, 1982). Large, multi-panel paintings from eight to 15 feet long enfold the viewer in an environment of painterly stimuli. Dense veils of agitated brushwork conceal inner structures of curves as in *Neptune's Necklace* (1988), which suspends a swooping necklace-like shape within a pink, clotted surface. Graham favors violent, jabbing marks created by dragging nails through the thickly encrusted paint (*Mooncups III*, 1985). "Lois Graham: A Decade in Review," a 1985 Bellevue Art Museum exhibition, exposed the abrupt transition between light-filled, curved femforms and the later, angry and impregnable paint surfaces. Lately, her compositions remain resistant to any softening, unless one reads the thicket of tangled mark-making as an image with stern yet exhilarating actions.

Jacqueline Barnett has explored what she calls "sensual melody" in her paintings and monotypes. Using biomorphic abstraction redolent of her native New York, she brings to mind gentler, earlier tendencies in Abstract Expressionism from the 1940s and extends William Baziotes's, Adolph Gottlieb's, and Theodoros Stamos's flowing and revolving imagery into a thoroughly individual sensibility.

Moving to Seattle in 1985 after a long working relationship with Frank Lobdell and Nathan Oliveira at Stanford, she joins her work comfortably with that of the other artists under discussion here. Arguing that "women have more access to physicality than men, through the hand and sense of touch,"[4] Barnett stresses the manipulation, rubbing, of materials onto the canvas or paper surface, as a sexual analogy. An open-fingered or hand-shape, "like a woman's clitoris,"[5] repeatedly recurs in her work and is often adjacent to a wide range of other curved forms. As in *Full Endeavor* (1989), *Circulation* (1991), and *In the Forest* (1992), structure is evanescent, but apparent after extended viewings. Barnett's is an overlooked body of work, meriting greater study.

Merrill Wagner has lived in New York since 1958 but grew up in Tacoma and continued to exhibit in Seattle at Foster/White Gallery and William Traver Gallery throughout the 1970s and 1980s. Warmly praised in New York by such critics as Robert Pincus-Witten[6] and Gerrit Henry,[7] Wagner was honored in 1991 with a large-scale exhibition at Gemeentemuseum in The Hague, Netherlands. After a lifetime of hiking in the mountains, her choice of geological materials is seen in her work of the 1970s in balanced irregular-edged marble and slate wall slabs with animated Tobey-like strokes in oil pastels. Wagner's ties to the Pacific Northwest are not readily acknowledged in New York, but are evident in her debt to Tobey's mark-making, all-over composition.

By 1990, Wagner had shifted to steel sheets mounted with magnets on the wall and painted with rustoleum preservative primer paint. *Smaller Reservoir* (1991) restricts the painted area to a blue square in the left-hand corner although it crosses the line between the two vertical steel panels comprising the work's support. Wagner's femforms are enclosures, a result of surrounding unpainted areas which "shelter" the painted square. Painted and unpainted sections within each steel construction compete for status as open forms, usually ascending to the top of the metal but never departing from the harsh, material reminders of urban existence in New York.

She continues to vary support materials and, spending part of each summer in Tacoma, shifts back and forth between approaches alluding to geology (which she shares with Adkison) and those more suggestive of Color Field painting, the rise of which she witnessed first-hand.

Karen Guzak (b. 1939) and Judy Cooke (b. 1940) offer a contrast in surfaces which layer circular and angled shapes. Guzak studied at Cornish College with Charles Stokes, linking her to Tobey, who taught there in the 1930s and left a legacy of water-based media and often woozy spirituality. If there is a Tobey-influenced Cornish "look," it favors a reverse highlighting of light-over-dark and a tendency to holistic spiritual systems.

All the same, Guzak's achievement may be found in signs of subliminal feminine forms and colors. Sharing with middle-period Blaedel a palette of pinks, beiges, and metallic paints, Guzak has complicated the structure

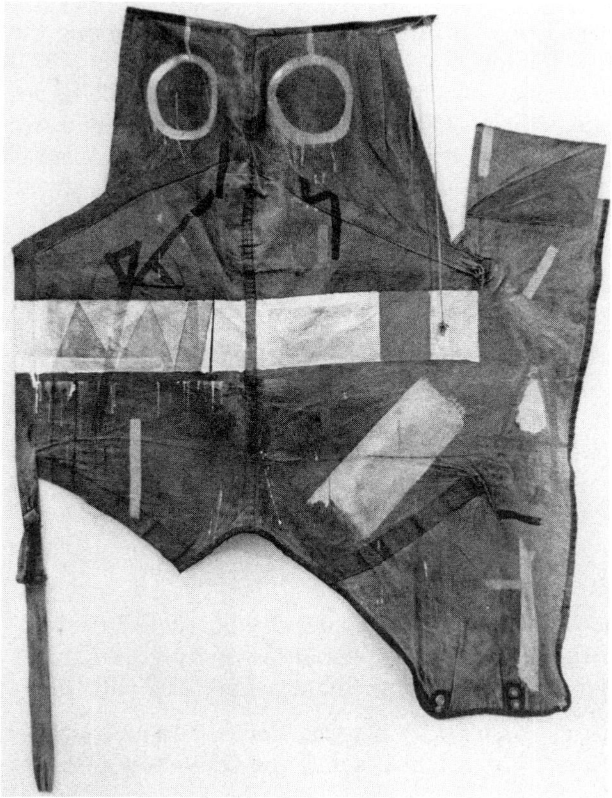

Judy Cooke, *Running Deer Left His Blanket*, 1977, tarp (old horse blanket) and acrylic, 69 x 63.

of her images by a recurrent use of circles and adjacent angles. Frequently, mandala-like compositions in her paintings and prints echo the meditative quality of Tobey, while also summoning up Grave's explorations of rising circular structures from Hindu illustrations of Tantric sex.

In *Elements VI* (1989) the illusion of contained costatic possibilities bisecting a central circle set among larger similar shapes is reinforced: liquidity of paint application inhibits any anchored physical presence of the artwork, sending it whirling into an ethereal, contemplative realm of desire.

Judy Cooke was prominently mentioned by Lucy R. Lippard in her omnibus 1976 essay, "Northwest Passage," in *Art in America*.[8] Lippard, however, did not attribute any submerged sexual content to Cooke's art nor, in general, to any of the women whose work she included in her Portland Center for the Visual Arts exhibition, "In Touch: Nature, Ritual and Sensuous Art from the Northwest."[9]

Notwithstanding, Cooke's irregular unstretched canvases are among the idiosyncratic examples of femform. *Running Deer Left His Blanket* (1977) may be a painted horse blanket, but it is also a supplanted female figure with two unmistakable breastforms in the circles at its top. Such shapes are more forthrightly sexual in related paintings like *Magic Circle* and *Women's Circle* (both 1976) and *Barrier Reef for Adrienne Rich* (1977). Works in the ensuing decades compress inverted triangles (*Laying Low*, 1990) and toy with an abstracted chastity belt (*Lock*, 1990), using copper sheeting as a reflective, rigid under-surface for rich applications of charcoal and oil paint.

Although involved in recognizable landscape imagery in the mid-1980s, Joan Ross Bloedel's art of the 1970s and early 1980s is closely tied to that of her Yale instructor Josef Albers's *Homages to the Square*. The "Silver Fox" series sets two squares-within-squares side by side and layers them with a cosmetic counter-palette of pinks, beiges, reds, and purples beneath washes of water-based metallic paints. Shimmering and evocative, Bloedel's formal explorations are inviting areas which provide visual resting places beneath the assault of animated mark-making.

In recent exhibitions at Grover/Thurston Gallery in Seattle, she has returned to shapes subliminally suggestive of female anatomy: cones, shells, diamonds, and vine-like lines are redolent of natural and seasonal rebirth.

Sharing a printmaking background with Blaedel, Cooke, and Guzak, Kay Rood (b. 1945) studied under Mauricio Lasansky at University of Iowa.

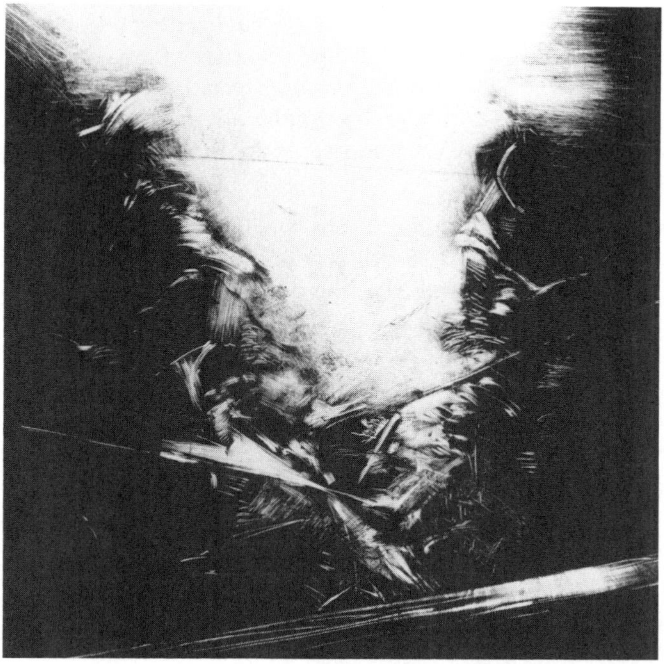

Kay Rood, *Moment V*, 1983, monotype/drypoint, 16 x 16.

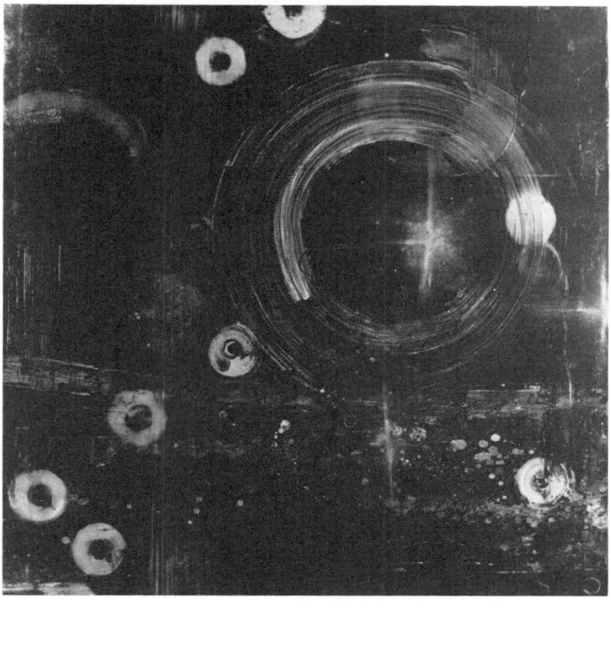

Malei Young, *Locua Amoneus I*, 1992, o/c, 40 x 40.

During the late 1970s and early 1980s, her imagery vacillates between abstracted female torsos and cave-like landscapes. Master of the sensuous surface, Rood is placed by many years of life studies closest to the realistic figurative femform artists discussed here. Especially adept at monotypes, she has developed an important oeuvre honored at the Whatcom Museum of History and Art in 1992.

Black Phase II (1980) sets two women's torsos beside one another as a departure point for developing an extraordinary range of strokes. *Vestige I* (1984) returns to the abstracted figure, recalling Francis Bacon. It operates as a palimpsest for an extravagant investigation of curved and straight lines, smooth and cluttered surfaces.

THE THIRD GENERATION: COMPLETING THE CIRCLE

Five Seattle painters born after World War II: Margaret Moorman (b. 1947), Mary Ann Peters (b. 1949), Linda Beaumont (b. 1950), Lisa Buchanan (b. 1951), and Malei Young (b. 1964) affirm the continuation of femform imagery while developing completely individual approaches to the challenge of waning modernism.

In spite of intervening stylistic trends after Abstract Expressionism, such as Minimalism, Pop Art, and Neo-Expressionism, an attenuated modernist abstraction has prevailed as the dominant style in Pacific Northwest art. The best artists of the period, male or female, have been abstract painters. Modernism arrived late in the Northwest, but women in the arts, advanced art schools, and a burgeoning gallery system in Seattle and Portland nurtured abstraction in the baby-boom generation.

It is worth concluding this investigation into gender-related abstract imagery with a brief examination of five women who add a sustaining energy to regional modernism when elsewhere it is believed to be played out or passé.

Under the age of 46, these artists have already created a substantial achievement. Much scholarship is needed to further chronicle and analyze the evolution of their art. Femform is but one key to what they have shared.

In opposition to the bright, cosmetic-counter colors of the Second Generation, the Third Generation painters prefer darker, more subdued and mysterious tones. Or, if they used an illusory natural light à la Tomkins, as was the case with Moorman, it resides in faint grays, blues, and browns.

Margaret Moorman left Seattle in the mid-1970s for New York. After a tragic studio fire, she turned to art criticism and is now an editor at *ARTnews*. Her Seattle paintings remain a small and glowing light of enduring strength. With immaculately brushed surfaces, balance and proportion, Moorman's paintings echoed Albers's *Homage to the Square* series. Unlike Bloedel, Moorman eschewed visibly animated strokes. Broad areas of close-value colors were juxtaposed against each other and appear as centralized, nested "boxes." Moorman's brushed surfaces are drier and more economical in paint application than Bloedel's or Graham's.

Also preoccupied with the subtleties of surface treatment is another University of Washington graduate, Mary Ann Peters. Ceaselessly innovative with regard to imagery and canvas shape, Peters parlayed her printmaking expertise gained under Bruce McCurdy and Dick Dunlap at University of California-Santa Barbara and Bill Ritchie of the U.W, into an exploration of inky blacks, grays, whites, and silvers along with an impressive range of femform imagery. Antoni Tapies is another crucial influence. The smoky, Spanish moods of Tapies are transformed into a succession of paintings on muslin-backed paper or plaster which allude to Mediterranean architecture and, for our purposes, circles (*Echo — Autumn's Edge*, 1978), broken curves (*Reunion*, 1970), and inverted and truncated triangles (*Madonna Negra: Ornamenta*, both 1988).

Site Unseen (Montage from Mind's Eye) (1980) was a three-dimensional painted floor installation at the Henry Art Gallery. It literalized femform: a meandering, labyrinthine path of no certain destination, doubling back in on itself. In retrospect, it is significant for physicalizing the gender-related imagery in her paintings.[10]

By decade's end, Peters evolved an extraordinarily impressive range of shapes: shells, cones, stairsteps, overlapping circles. These shapes, combined with a masterful manipulation of dark and light (*Andaluz*, 1989), resonate with a smoldering intensity and *duende*.

At first an openly figurative painter, Linda Beaumont is abstract in her best work. After a 1986 trip to India, she used thicker paint, encaustic, metallic tape and, like Peters, a sensuous darkness. *Burning Ghat* (1987) echoes the shelter or enclosure forms of Merrill Wagner, but, with its intersecting lines, suggests tension, conflict, and troubling entanglements. One looks into the surface of a Beaumont canvas as if into the mouth of a dangerous cave. Doubt, correction, underpainting, and repainting are crucial to Beaumont. When they coalesce into an aesthetic totality, the effect is peculiarly disturbing and satisfying.

Lisa Buchanan, also dependent upon layering, correction, and *pentimenti*, has found an audience in New York. Buchanan's painting sets unusually tight limits with many recent works in a range limited to green and red. The inverted and truncated triangles emerge slowly out of a heavily worked surface and assemble themselves into oblique shelter or enclosure shapes. Their inviting character suggests indeterminate nesting places and conveys a vague sense of inhabited nature. Buchanan's debt to early Abstract Expressionism matches Barnett's and, with Tomkins, the three comprise the organic, landscape wing of femform abstraction.

Closer to the New Yorkers of the 1940s (and Barnett), Buchanan uses the private studio strategies of attack and correction to construct a sequence of paintings which deepen with time in potential for interpretation.

Finally, Malei Young, a Seattle native resident in the Chicago area, had her second solo exhibition in August, 1992. The entire exhibition was based on the circle. She writes:

> "The circle remains a constant throughout history, symbolically representing the nature of the physical world . . . it is nature's pattern and we are innately part of her network of numerous cycles."[11]

Locua Amoneus I (1992) forms a pendant to Guzak's *Elements VI* (1989). Its large central circle ascends and accompanies smaller "moons," merging the universal, transcendent imagery of Tobey with the Third Generation palette of somber colors.

Strongly formal, frontal, and rooted in geometry, Malei Young and her older colleagues balance external and internal worlds with paint, process, and private iconographies. That their paintings elicit such interpretations is a tribute to the considerable intellectual and painterly abilities of Northwest women. It is also proof that late modernism remains viable to artists addressing an internal reality in line with its original impulses.

NOTES:

[1] Clement Greenberg, "Perceptions and Judgements, 1939-1944," Volume I *The Collected Essays and Criticism*, edited by John O'Brian, Chicago: The University of Chicago Press, 1986, pp. 205-6.

[2] Matthew Kangas, "Merchants, Mavens, and Money: A History of Art Dealers in Seattle," *ARTSline*, October, 1986, pp. 11-27.

[3] Alfred Frankenstein, "Spotlight on New Galleries," *San Francisco Chronicle*, October 25, 1966.

[4] Conversation with author, September 23, 1992.

[5] Ibid.

[6] Robert Pincus-Witten, review of 55 Mercer Gallery [NYC] show, *Artforum*, February, 1972.

[7] Gerrit Henry, "Merrill Wagner at John Gibson," *Art in America*, September, 1986, p. 138.

[8] Lucy R. Lippard, "Northwest Passage," *Art in America*, October, 1976, p. 60.

[9] Lucy R. Lippard, "In Touch: Nature, Ritual and Sensuous Art from the Northwest," Portland Center for the Visual Arts, 1976.

[10] Matthew Kangas, "Notes on Recent Installation Art III," *and/or Notes*, July, 1980, pp .20-22.

[11] Malei Young, artist's statement, Friesen Gallery, Seattle, August, 1992.

Women Active in the Northwest Art Scene of 1975-1985:

Art historians: Laura Brunsman, Rachael Griffin, Martha Kingsbury, Erika Michael.

Art critics: Delores Tarzan Ament, Beth Fagan, Regina Hackett, Ann Faber, Sue Ann Kendall, Thelma Lehmann, Anne G. Todd, Mayumi Tsutakawa (newspaper critics in Seattle and Portland).

Museum curators: Sarah Clark-Langager, Mary Clure, Polly Eyerly, Rachael Griffin, Vicki Halper, LaMar Harrington, Barbara Johns, Beth Sellars.

Alternative space curators: Mary Beebe, Anne Focke, Terri Hopkins, Nancy Weymouth Halbrooks, Kathryn Marczuk, Tracy Savage.

Art dealers: Linda Farris, Andrea Friesen, Diane Gilson, Susan Grover, Lisa Harris, Linda Hodges, and Lynn McAllister in Seattle; Anne Hughes, Elizabeth Leach, Laura Russo, and Arlene Schnitzer in Portland.

Diversity in Oregon: Women's Art After 1970

by Lois Allan

Until cancer ended her life in 1987, LaVerne Krause was a forceful and colorful figure in advancing Oregon's slow recognition of its women artists. Born in 1924, she came of age artistically just after World War II, a time when home-making was idealized and "woman artist" was a term of condescension. As with many women of her era, for many years artmaking had to be subordinated to caring for family and home. However, personal problems and cultural restrictions failed to squelch her determination to study (at the University of Oregon and the Museum Art School, now the Pacific Northwest College of Art) and to persevere as an artist. Beginning in the 1950s, she was showing regularly and active in Oregon's art community. She also helped organize the Oregon chapter of Artists Equity, of which she later became president.

By the early 1970s, as the feminist movement was gathering momentum nationally, Krause was in her late 40s. Now freed from domesticity by divorce and nearly grown children, she became a full professor at the University of Oregon, exhibiting throughout the Northwest. Although never a self-proclaimed feminist, she was certainly a force for change, attending meetings and events dramatically dressed, always with a large hat, speaking out on issues of art and education.

Krause's roots in Oregon, where she lived all her life, are the basis for the expressionistic landscape paintings, watercolors, and prints that comprise her best work. An exceptional colorist, she transformed her immediate environment into polychromatic amalgamations of light, space, and form, evocations of a place, rather than descriptions. A major retrospective at the University of Oregon Museum in the fall of 1992 with an informative catalogue provided the first comprehensive exposition of her work, her contributions to the University's development, and her life.

Painting is, historically, the medium of choice for most Oregon artists and, although its dominance is now challenged by newer art forms, pure painting remains both strong and diverse. Sally Haley, a Yale graduate who settled in Portland in 1947 and whose oeuvre stretches back to the 1930s, continues to create elegant still lifes in which humble objects from kitchen and garden are presented singly and centrally in austere, geometrically composed paintings that re-invent the style of mid-century hard-edge abstraction.

The generation of painters who came into maturity in the late '70s and early '80s, ready to challenge male dominance in the field, includes three artists of quite different styles: Lucinda Parker, Laura Ross-Paul, and Phyllis Yes. Of the three, Yes alone deals overtly with issues of femininity and gender identification; Ross-Paul is interested in the psychology of relationships and Parker uses shapes and colors that have primordial and archetypal associations.

An abstract painter, Lucinda Parker is known for-slashing, swirling, gestural brushstrokes, as arm and body-driven as those by the renowned Abstract Expressionist painters of the post-World War II New York School. Her completely abstract, flat quadrant paintings of the '70s were concerned solely with visual impact, but in the ensuing years she has moved toward both volume and content. Always maintaining a tension between figure and ground, she now uses simplified, symbolic images, such as a snake or fish — and sometimes, a word — that twist and turn upon themselves within a maelstrom of brushstrokes.

Perhaps because Laura Ross-Paul draws on her own experience as wife and mother, her surreal, expressionistic paintings typically address relationships and a search for psychological wholeness. Landscape and water, especially water, a metaphor for the unconscious, form the contextual setting for mysterious figures who move in or on the water. The "stories" suggested are never clear. Their dream-like quality is enhanced by unnatural color and non-specificity of the figures as well as the setting.

Both Parker and Ross-Paul represent a long-held view of Oregon artists as introspective and "painterly," more interested in nature or a particular aesthetic than in engaging the outer, active world of politics and social criticism. Phyllis Yes is an exception. Her painting has the smooth, impersonal surface and precise rendition of images one associates with commercial art, and her primary themes are a questioning of sex roles and gender identification. A recent series, "Mixed Metaphors," depicted place settings of china, crystal, and silver as might be seen in a bridal ad, placed with flower arrangements on a crisp tablecloth. In each painting one piece of flatware has been replaced by a "man's" tool, a wrench, for example.

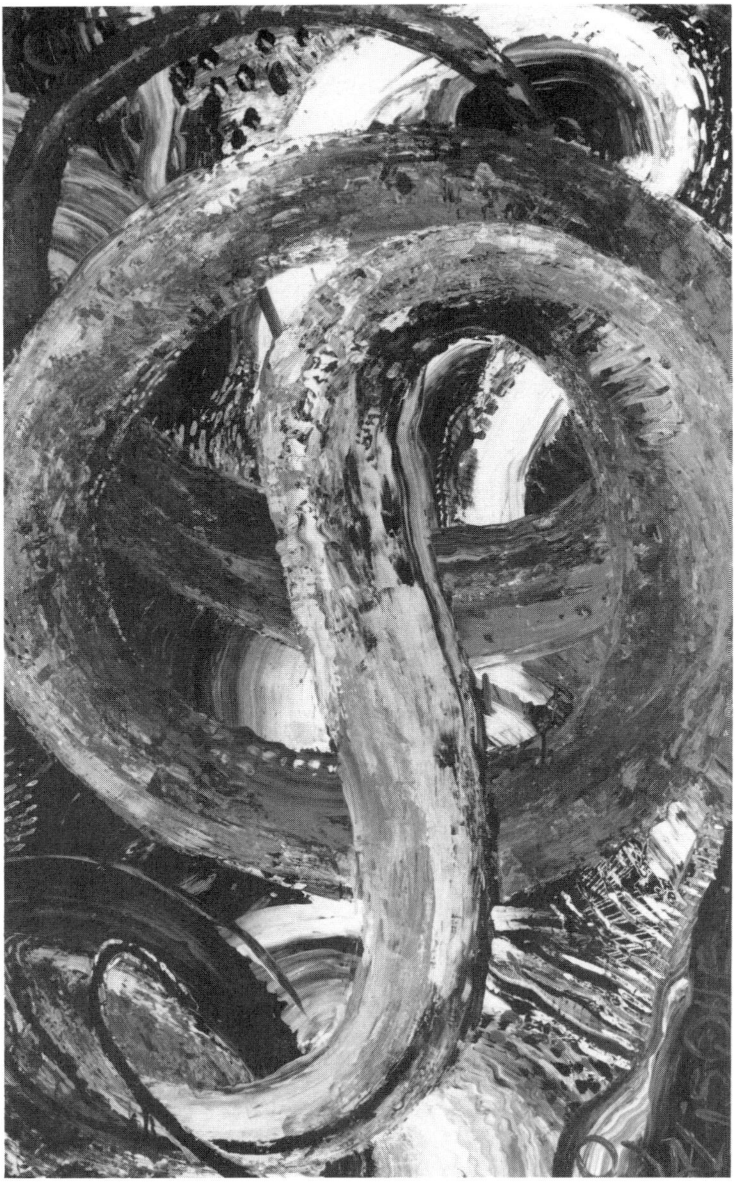

Lucinda Parker, *Boa Odalisque*, 1990,
a/c, 79 x 48.

Although she is primarily a painter, Yes might also be described as a multimedia artist who uses materials best suited to her project. She attracted national attention in 1984 with her use of lace to cover what she refers to as "men's toys," including a pistol and a Porsche sports car *(Por/She)*. Her "Honored Woman" series, clay body casts of female torsos, have decorations simulating military honors. An art professor at Lewis and Clark College, Yes has researched culturally related gender issues, which she addresses in videos, lectures, and public symposia.

Almost all the many sculptures, installations, drawings, and artists' books created by Christine Bourdette relate in some way to the human body. She, too, is a product of the 1970s, the era of minimalism and conceptualism, which in Portland was more heard of than seen. As a college-trained artist, she, like her colleagues, was aware of these trends, but by inclination and no doubt the influence of her Oregon surroundings was drawn to figuration, which soon led to strange, humanoid creatures of unfinished wood, clay, and metal. In the pluralism of the 1980s, when figuration again was *au courant*, Bourdette established a regional reputation for dramatically eccentric figures of metaphoric meanings. The figures in her 1987 series, "Squatting Melissas," based on her travels in Asia, convey various social, biological (including childbirth), and political implications of a posture common in much of the world but disdained in the chair-sitting developed nations. In 1991 she showed plywood constructions of rough-hewn, part-human, part-vehicle forms. Dilapidated in appearance, they seemed to be abandoned artifacts of another, very strange, culture.

As artists and critics of color, feminists, and their allies began actively to question and re-position art's relationship to the dominant culture, Kay Slusarenko contributed to the discourse with installations that subverted conventional notions of art as precious or exclusive. A formidable collector of mid-century, everyday domestic objects that, in her work, become cultural artifacts — lucite purses, plastic figurines and toys, souvenir items, handkerchiefs — she assembles dazzling displays of American middle-class popular culture. While these mundane articles, especially when presented in quantity, are amusingly historical, they also pose serious questions of authorship, context, value, and categories of taste like "kitsch" and "fine art."

As the organizer in 1978 and chair of the Marylhurst College Art Department, Slusarenko launched a program and faculty that have injected welcome dynamism into Portland's art community. Some of the strongest, most idiosyncratic emerging artists of the area, including sculptor and

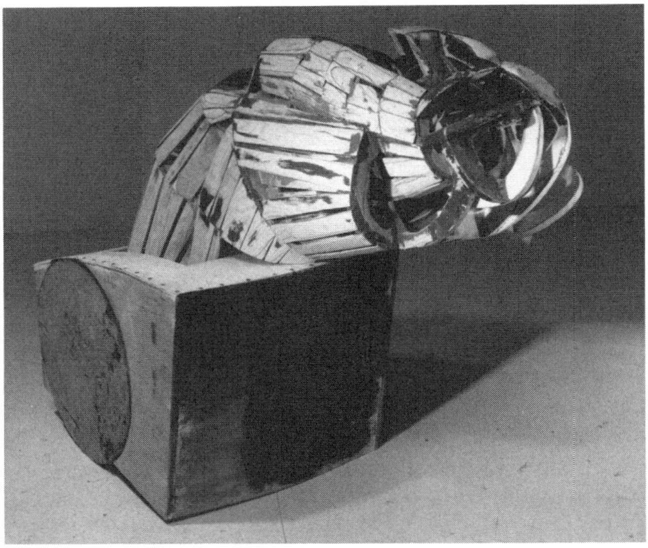

Christine Bourdette, *Untitled*, 1991, mixed media, 38 x 44 x 30. Courtesy of Jamison Thomas Gallery.

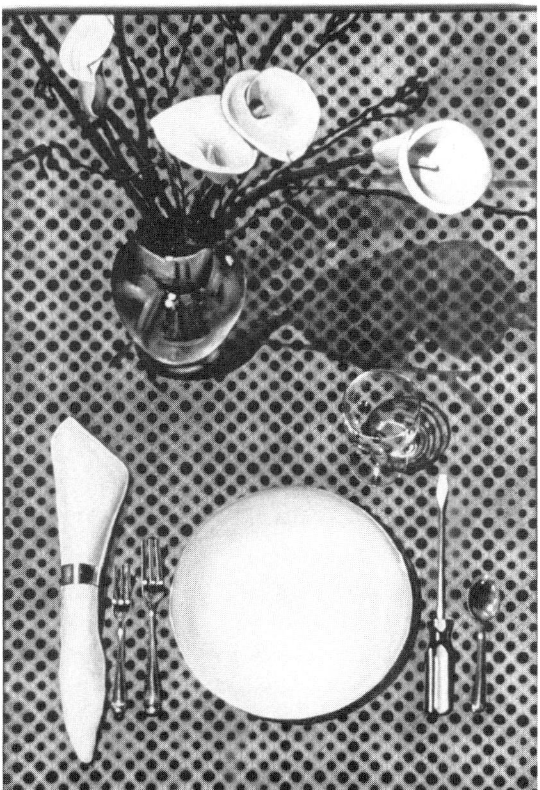

Phyllis Yes, *Mixed Metaphor #5*, 1990, a/c, 24 x 36.

installation artist Carolyn King, are graduates. The Marylhurst Art Gym, a gallery converted from a gymnasium, consistently mounts exhibitions (under the direction of Terri Hopkins) noted for a strong curatorial point of view and for directing attention to non-commercial art, art often far outside the mainstream.

Weaving, once considered strictly within the domain of women's craft, now commands a respect formerly reserved for painting and sculpture, thanks to such artists as Judith Poxson Fawkes. A major exhibition of her linen tapestries at the Laura Russo Gallery in Portland in fall, 1992, attested to the expressive potential of the medium as well as her command of both craft and art. These extraordinarily precise, axonometric views of peopleless Italian Renaissance towns, buildings, arcades, steps, columns, and their shadows formed by straight and diagonal lines, give the appearance of geometrical design. Although the tapestries refer obliquely to de Chirico's paintings of empty streets, Fawkes's emphasis is on the order and beauty of classical architecture, not on portentous dreams.

Printmaking has for many years been a strong pulse in the Northwest, and in 1981 it brought Eastern artists and printers Vicki Vanderslice and Myrna Burks to Portland to open a lithography studio and shop, North Light Editions. In this collaborative environment, artist-clients profited from the printers' artistic as well as technical expertise. When in 1987, Burks developed back trouble from handling the heavy stones, the workshop limited its production to monoprints and monotypes created through intensive inter-active work with artists, often prominent painters eager to explore the possibilities of monotypes. In 1990 the partnership dissolved and North Light Editions closed. Myrna Burks relocated to New York where she continues to create abstract prints and collages, exhibiting both there and in Portland. Vicki Vanderslice maintains a studio in Portland where she produces her own work and assists artists making monotypes.

At the University of Oregon, professor, printmaker, and papermaker Margaret Prentice has devised a printing technique in which colored pulp made with a base of unbleached abaca fiber becomes an integral part of the design impressed on it by the etching press. Prints in a recent series, based on a river and canyon trip in Utah, have the appearance of weathered rock surfaces embedded with petroglyphic markings. Prentice was a co-founder in 1971 of Twinrocker Handmade Paper in Brookston, Indiana, which still produces custom sheets. She left the company in 1986 to concentrate on studio work and teaching at the University of Oregon.

Photographic art, like printmaking, has been advanced in Oregon through the efforts of a woman, in this case, Ann Hughes. In 1975 she and four friends (Craig Hickman, Terry Toedtemeier, Christopher Rauschenberg, and Robert DiFranco) started Blue Sky Gallery in the storefront that was her studio at the time. In those days it was called an alternative space and, although now in a much larger space, it continues to be one of the few non-profit, non-commercial exhibition spaces in the country for photographic art. The gallery brings in exhibitions of work by nationally-and internationally-recognized contemporary photographers and also sponsors lectures, shows local work and, in general, provides visibility and support for local photographer members. Although Hughes is no longer active in Blue Sky, she continues to make provocative photographs, often large color prints of her immediate environment, or "still lifes," as she refers to them. Usually of interiors, sometimes of landscape, and always full of texture and detail, they pull viewers into an inner world of memory and sensuality.

As Oregonians become more sensitive to the history and importance of Native American culture in the state, art by contemporary tribal artists takes on social as well as aesthetic importance. Lillian Pitt, who is a Yakima and member of the Confederated Tribes of Warm Springs, makes highly stylized masks, many based on specific Indian myths. Using clay, sticks, shells, leather fringe, and other decorative objects, she has developed a signature style that fuses energized references to her native culture with its aesthetic tradition.

In contrast to the specificity of Pitt's art, Helen Lessick's is inspired by international postmodern theory in literature and philosophy. A conceptual artist who doesn't mind using old-fashioned pastels or oils when an idea demands it, she is known for her artist's books in which form, images, and text are signifiers of cultural encoding as well as an implied subject. When the books, in her words, "needed a place to be read," she conceived the series of houses called "A Calendar of Habitations." Relating to the seasons and natural elements, and now numbering six, these are very simple, iconic house shapes large enough to be entered. They are sites of the artist's performances, and in one instance (*House for Summer/Birch Tree House* in Portland's Hoyt Arboretum) a site also for hikers' "performances" (resting and picnicking) as the "house" is permanent, shaped by living birch trees pruned to house form. Meant to decompose, *House for Autumn/ Harvest House,* constructed of hay bales on Sauvie Island at the confluence of the Willamette and Columbia Rivers, celebrated the 1991 autumn equinox.

Lessick's work is representative of the shift toward multimedia, cross-disciplinary, and temporal art that has so altered the scope, the structure, and even the meaning of art in the last quarter of the 20th century. Laurie

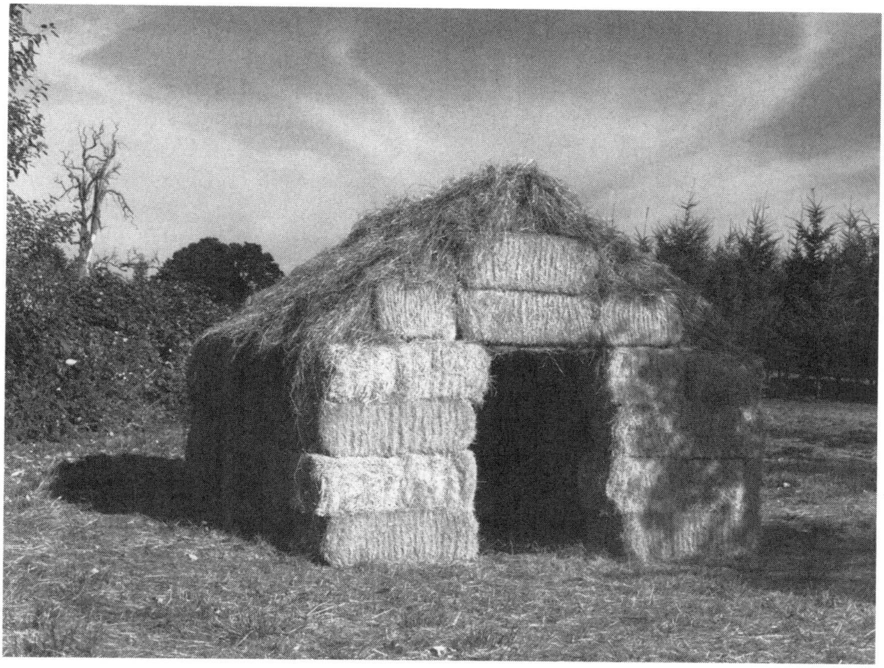

Helen Lessick, *House for Autumn*, 1991, outdoor installation, Sauvie Island, Oregon.

Judith Poxson Fawkes, *Campanile, Capella and Cloister*, 1992, linen tapestry, 44 x 79. Courtesy of the Laura Russo Gallery, Inc.

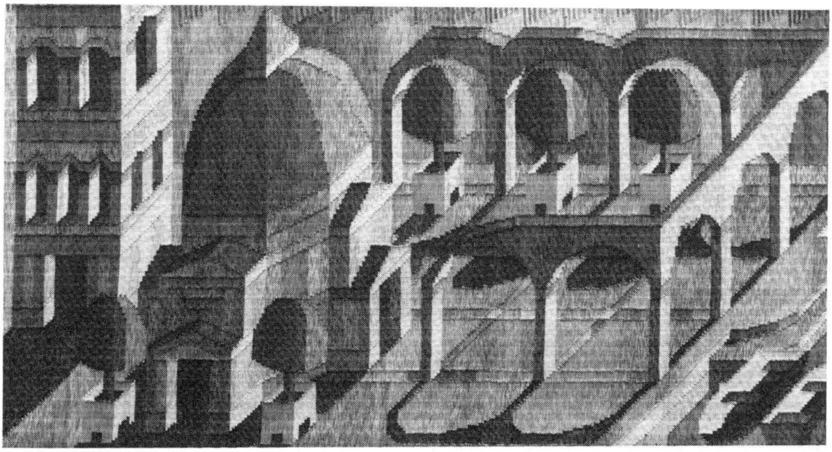

Anderson, one of the pioneers in this movement, influenced the formation of a Portland performance group, The Girl Artists, in 1981. The five women (Char Breshgold, Kathy Clark, Cristina DeGennaro, Susan Martin, and Lisa Siegel) decided to collaborate when they learned, while participating in a group show, that each was or had been a waitress. From that discovery *Split Shift Cafe* came into being. The gallery Outer Space was transformed into a full-size roadside cafe right down to foam rubber French fries, with the audience seated at tables or at the counter. Critic Ted Bunker of the *Seattle Post-Intelligence* wrote that the performance was a "satirical, touching, scathingly accurate piece about the lives, the roles, of service workers, whether male or female."

Subsequent productions, five in all before the group disbanded in 1987, also dealt with issues from the women's personal experiences — shopping, the effect of TV on adolescents, neighborhood life — which struck a responsive chord in audiences in Seattle, San Francisco, and Los Angeles, as well as Portland.

Surprisingly, the success of The Girl Artists did not generate a flowering of performance art in Portland. Susan Banyas maintains Dream's Well studio for her own and other artists' individual performances, but it was not until 1992 that a local artist undertook a major collaborative production. Kristy Edmonds, a young video artist, wrote, produced, and directed *Partitio,* her first major work. It was an auspicious debut; performance, film, soundtrack, photography, and props and sets by some of Portland's best sculptors created a powerful presentation of Edmonds's poetic exposition of American attitudes toward and treatment of helpless, expiring old people. Motivated by visits with a dying great-grandmother in a nursing home, Edmonds transmogrified personal experience into a darkly dramatic statement, one that might easily have dissolved into sentimentality or melodrama, but instead was intellectually challenging as well as emotionally affecting.

Edmunds exemplifies the distance travelled by Oregon's women artists since the time of LaVerne Krause. In their attitudes and in their work, women today are spirited, engaged, and willing to take risks — a good omen for art in the 21st century.

BIBLIOGRAPHY:

LaVerne Krause: Painter and Printmaker (1924-1987) catalogue essays by Karie Nicolson, Ken Paul, Darcia Krause, Eugene: University of Oregon, 1991.

Craft Roots and Industrial Collage

by Regina Hackett

Chaos may not be, as Henry Miller once claimed, the score on which reality is written, but over the last two decades it has become a given in visual arts. No safety net of theoretical imperatives holds past a season or two, and no single chain exists on which artists must forge a link.

Aesthetic chaos (better known as pluralism) has its drawbacks (fads, unstable market values, enervating uncertainty), but few deny that it has been good for women, including women living outside the country's cultural strongholds. If there no longer is a prescribed set of right times and places, key people and essential notions, then we're all making this up as we go along, and a wide range of visual art realities have a chance of being considered.

Contemporary art's open options have led to heady developments in the Northwest, especially in sculpture, never considered the region's strong suit, beyond the Northwest Coast Native American carving traditions.

Women are at the forefront of the region's recent claim to significance through their sculpture, and some of the most interesting are working in what can be called a craft roots movement — Sherry Markovitz, Barbara Noah, Marita Dingus, Alison "Slow" Loris — or industrial collage — Deborah Butterfield, Sheila Klein, Claudia Fitch, Ross Palmer Beecher, Amanda Fin.

Sherry Markovitz was born and raised in Chicago and graduated from the University of Washington in printmaking in 1975. If she'd stayed in Chicago, her work would have been seen as a new twist on the city's strong tradition of eccentric figuration. In Seattle, her first exhibit of paintings at the Linda Farris Gallery was a shock.

Here were portraits of lambs, donkeys and elephants in gouache and egg tempera on rice paper mounted on linen: sober, serious presences in deep, dirty, dark colors, blue on rose fields, wooly whites on stained pinks. To counter her pastel tonalities, she battered their surfaces, dragging these large paintings outside and washing them down with a garden hose. As Seattle Art Museum assistant curator Vicki Halper noted, the "resulting crinkled, peeling, scarred and torn surface" was then "darned, patched and painted — lovingly tended."[1] Stitched into the surface were beads and sequins, Markovitz's first tribute to the world community of women's handiwork.

In 1980, on impulse, she bought a set of fiberglass taxidermy forms. By the following year, working with the taxidermy bases, she had begun her bead, shell and sequin-encrusted papier-mâché menage. Animal heads associated with hunter's lodges and cowboy bars became life forces instead of kill counts.

Markovitz has moved from painting to sculpture over the years, working slowly, exhibiting infrequently. A recent solo show at the Mint Museum of Art in North Carolina (August-October,1992) featured a new foray into organic abstraction: tightly beaded, dangling orbs and swelling protuberances. Their polymorphous sensuality evokes Louise Bourgeois without falling under her large shadow. They are goofy, and yet seriously, lovingly crafted, bead by bead, row on radiant row, with paint for high-tone highlight.

Barbara Noah, born in Seattle, got her first art lessons as a child in the early 1960s watching "Learn to Draw" on TV.[2] Although Noah admits the show was "cornporn," it enabled her to teach her sixth grade class the secrets of Renaissance perspective, light and shadow.

A middle child with two sisters, Noah grew up making things with the females in her family. Her mother still has a number of ash trays encrusted with sea shells, driftwood planters and collages. Noah said her mother favored driftwood that looked like something, a Neanderthal head maybe, or an owl. This spirit of middle-class, white, American female hobbyist decor haunts Noah's work. She uses it as a joke and real deal, a touchstone and homage to her upbringing.

Not that she is by any stretch a folk artist. She brings a quality of industrial, technical precision to her work, an impersonal delivery for her highly personal themes. She's a master of everyday embarrassments and night time fears, celestial longings and industrial anonymities, dumb-smart, wise-cracking wit, the shifting layers of reality and illusion.

After graduating from Mills College in Oakland with a B.A. and MFA from Pratt Institute in Brooklyn, New York, Noah had her first solo show in Seattle at the Linda Farris Gallery in 1979.

The core of her work continues to be enlarged black and white photographs on linen collaged with paint and a variety of objects: rods, lights, sound boxes, window sills, bowling balls, even a flocked deer. She finds faces in the cracks of a wall, daubs eyes onto the smoke funnels of an exploding volcano, uses the three-finger holes in bowling balls as two eyes and mouth saying "oh" (as in her 1982 installation at Artists Space, New York, "Bowling for Dollars") Lately she has been finding her faces in nature: fire, luridly colored on photo linen, the movement of planets, streams of sperm assaulting an egg, stones dropping into water.

Marita Dingus was born in Auburn, WA., graduated with a BFA from Tyler School of Art in Philadelphia in 1980 and MFA from San Jose State University in 1985.

Her work reflects what David Hammons once called the classic Afro-American aesthetic. It seeks to make-do instead of make-nice, using every scrap with an unerring rough grace and animating the proportions by avoiding symmetry. Her figures come from plastic tubes, sheets and bottles, old hair ribbons and barrettes, baby-bottle nipples, buttons, wire, tape and rope. They nod in the direction of the Caribbean carnival tradition, but bear Dingus's distinct visual stamp. They are characters out of her own play, increasingly expressing a wide range of spiritual and psychic states.

Alison "Slow" Loris flunked out of Barnard College on a full scholarship in 1969 and made her way to Seattle a few years later. At 21, she already had the first of her two children and was well on the way to exploring her life's theme, the poverty-ridden, decorative detritus that adorns and clutters the lives of urban single mothers.

Her first notable effort was a series of delicate collages on bus transfer passes, using color Xerox. In the late 1970s through the mid-1980s she produced a series of installations, first at the now-defunct Rosco Louie Gallery, then at various cafés and the Center on Contemporary Art. They were for her a visual stream-of-consciousness, a collection of worn-out feminine touches honored for the noble effort they represent, decorations born of impoverishment. Faded and stained floral wallpaper, spent fabrics, and torn up carpets had a valiant air, lovely in their ruin and lovely because they had been saved, passed down and used up. Since the late 1980s she has been making functional ware from old fabrics ("quilted into submission," she says) and selling them at the Pike Place Market.

Deborah Butterfield's work ignores the most basic modernist imperative, to make it new. In a century where innovation is prized above all else, she works a single vein, and an old vein at that.

Butterfield, who graduated with an MFA from the University of California at Davis in 1975 and lives in Bozeman, Montana, makes horses. She has made them from mud and sticks, wire and old fence posts, metal scraps and most recently cast bronze. Lean as rakes, her hollow, ravaged horses convey a poised sort of attention, blunt heads lifted, or they are clattering form, splayed on the floor. When they are steel, they tend to be pulverized steel, colors faded and dusted with rust. Butterfield's horses are not exercises in nostalgia. Their grace comes from the ravaging force of their material.

Self-taught sculptor Sheila Klein lived in the Northwest from the early 1970s to the mid-1980s. After eight years in Los Angeles, she is currently contemplating a move back up the coast, some place outside Seattle in a rural setting.

Following Claes Oldenburg, who enlarged the scale of common objects to charge their form with new meaning, Klein makes jewelry as monumental sculpture and engineering feat. She is interested in the underpinnings of all built things, the architecture of adornment, making eyelashes out of garden rakes and necklaces out of painted Jello-molds, glass saucers, color reflector discs and butter dishes.

Her massive "ring" of blinking traffic lights (ruby, topaz, and emerald) sits on a walkway in Los Angeles's Union Station. A 15-foot, "commemorative ground ring" is sited in the yard of the Chicago Historical Society, ornamented with "quotes" from Chicago's most famous architectural landmarks. She is currently working on a public project for South Los Angeles with recycled fire hydrants, parking bumps, lamp posts, and benches.

Operating from what she calls her "femme tech" premises,[3] Klein dissolves distinctions between elegant and tacky, domestic and industrial, decorative and essential form.

Claudia Fitch, born in Seattle, received her BFA from the University of Washington in painting in 1975 and an MFA from Tyler School of Art in 1979, and spent the next decade moving to Philadelphia, Rome, and New York.

She returned to the Northwest in 1989 and made her presence felt the following year with a show at what is now Fuel Gallery. Fitch is best known for the sculptural qualities she abstracts from formal gardens and warps through Pop cartoon time, making work that's skeletal and vaguely humanoid, with lavish grills and latticed edges.

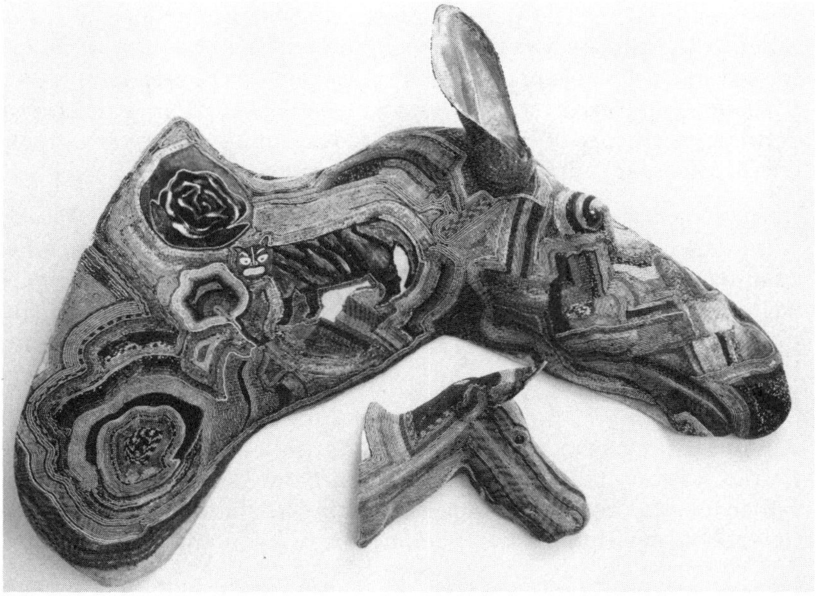

Sherry Markovitz, *Moose Landscape*, 1985-1989, beads, papier mâché, oil paint, 42 x 21 x 7 1/2 (mama); 13 x 9 x 3 (baby). Collection of University Hospital, University of Washington.

Amanda Fin, *Language*, 1992, glass, steel, ink, and water, 5 x 10 x 5. Courtesy of Fuel Gallery, Seattle.

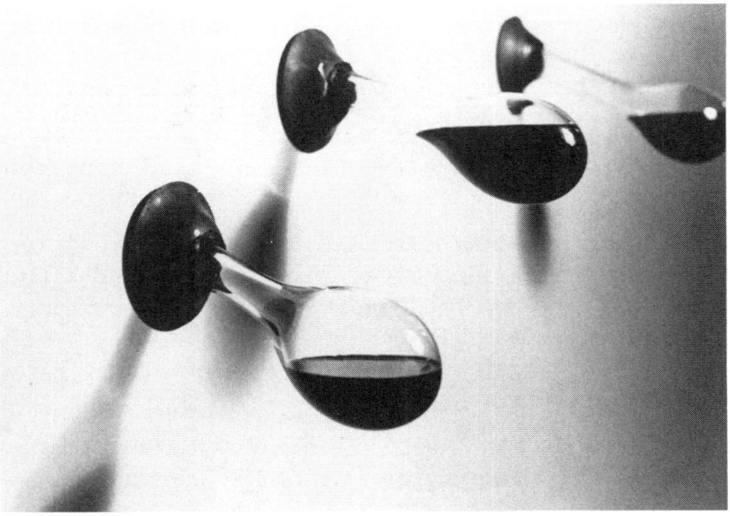

She uses welded steel painted black, styrofoam, and plastic. Critic Lyn Smallwood said of her 1990, installation-style exhibition at Fuel that it looked like a "skewed stage set, or a garden on the outskirts of Wonderland, or a department store somewhere between St. Rémy and Auschwitz. Among the virtues of Fitch's work are its moving and multifarious references. Meaning is fluid, and far from comforting."[4]

Ross Palmer Beecher quilts with recycled tin, nails, and wood. Trained as a printmaker and painter at the Rhode Island School of Design, where she graduated with a BFA in 1975, she has lived in Seattle for 15 years. She's a strikingly solitary artist, working from sources she found early: American quilt-makers and backwoods whittlers; traveling puppet and Punch and Judy shows; 19th-century East-Coast American signage and advertisements.

Although she has an obvious affinity for folk art, her work doesn't look pseudo-folk or fake primitive. She's clearly inhabiting her own experience rather than taking a conscious step backwards into an idealized, simpler time. She has visual muscle, with clear figuration and a bold color sense.

Beecher's working methods have remained consistent. She punches patterned designs on tin surfaces and paints them, sometimes adding collage elements for decorative effect, such as buttons, knobs, radio parts, reflector lights. Her quilted tin assemblages tend to be shaped, into coffins, for example, or hearts, flags, old-fashioned stage sets. She also likes panels, long and lean, and doesn't work large — her work is not more than several feet at its tallest or widest point. She is drawn to narrative, or at least the sensation of narrative, the feeling that whole stories lurk on her surfaces and the figures found there are merely pausing, mid-tale, to catch their breath.

Amanda Fin moved to Seattle in 1989, several years after graduating with a BFA in sculpture from the State University of New York in Purchase, NY.

Her first local efforts showed up in the part of the city's downtown known as the Denny Regrade, once full of cheap artists' housing and studio spaces but rapidly declining into upscale high rises and office buildings. An earlier generation of Seattle artists, including Buster Simpson and Carl Smool, had tried to save the neighborhood, and won some concessions, but were outmaneuvered by money interests.

Participating in the "Civilization Project" organized by freelance curator Helen Slade, Fin issued a new and startling notice. Her shark fin outlines (an obvious play on her name) appeared on the area's many land-use

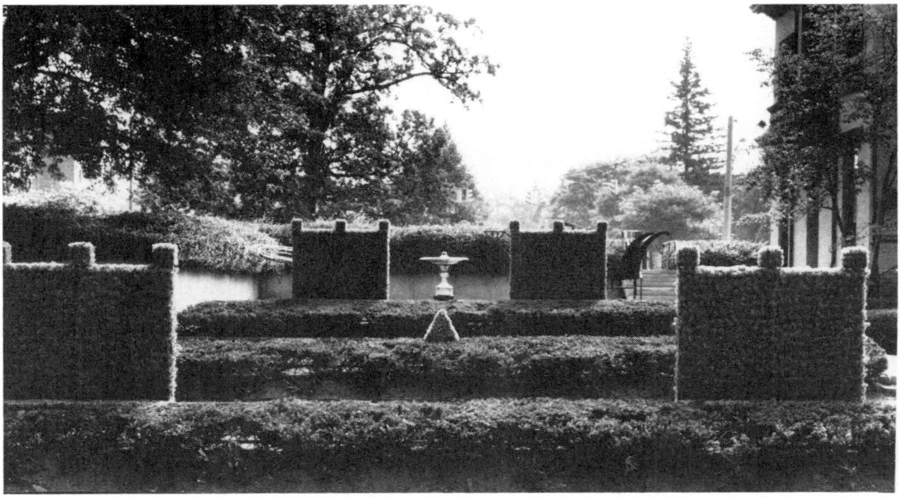

Claudia Fitch, ***The Victorian Hedge, A Garden for the Mohawk Valley***, 1989. garden installation, Munson-Williams Proctor Institute Art Museum, co-sponsored by Sculpture Space, Utica, New York.

Sheila Klein, *Commemorative Ground Ring*, 1989, sculpture installation.

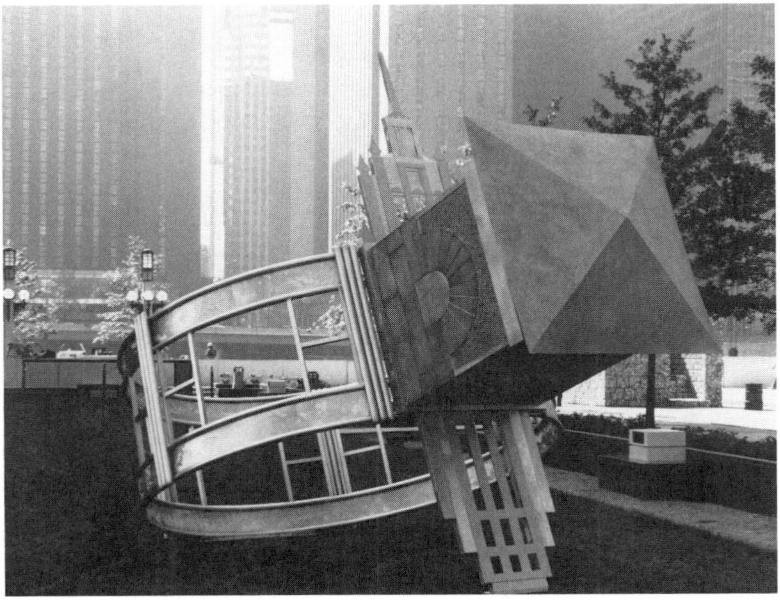

planning signs, indicating development. Unlike earlier artists, she wasn't trying to prevent the inevitable; she was, by the simplest of means, changing the frame of public signs to evoke their underlying meaning.

In her gallery and museum sculpture (Seattle's Fuel, Portland's Elizabeth Leach, the University of Washington's Henry Art Gallery) she layers meaning in a subtler way. Working in bronze, wax, welded steel, rubber, glass, marble dust and paint, she gives vaguely industrial forms intimate new identities. Welded steel plates look like duck's bills. Toilet floats, smeared in wax, look like fruit. Her long steel rods have pinhead protuberances at their tops, like light posts with tiny bulbs, or cue sticks with their own billiards affixed to the tips. She makes periscopes for Krazy Kat, had he been a scientist or in the Navy.

Fin's work has some of the charm of early Eva Hesse, that master of ugly-comic industrial castoffs. A sense of narrative hangs over her shows, as if her dark and dopey sculptures were talking to each other.

Bertolt Brecht once wrote that "women . . . are not well directed, can't be sharply enough distinguished one from another, nor is their story carefully enough composed."[5] The artists considered here compose their stories with supreme care. They don't need to be lumped together by someone who fails to note the distance between Markovitz's purity and Fin's rowdy humor.

If, however, assemblage is what Louise Bourgeois called "a coming to terms with things,"[6] then that is what these artists have in common. They mark their own time, raise their own questions and come to terms with material worlds of their own making.

NOTES:

[1] Vicki Halper, "Sherry Markovitz," exhibition catalogue essay for *Documents Northwest* series, Seattle Art Museum, April 30-May 31, 1987.

[2] All personal information about and quotes from the artists given to the writer, except as otherwise noted.

[3] Sheila Klein, quoted in *50 Northwest Artists*, by Bruce Guenther, San Francisco: Chronicle Books, 1983.

[4] Lyn Smallwood, "The Edge of Wonderland," *The Seattle Weekly*, March 28, 1990.

[5] Michael Wood, "Taking Brecht's Measure," *The New York Review of Books*, May 15, 1980, p. 18.

[6] Robert Storr, "Louise Bourgeois: The Matter at Hand," *Journal of Art*, December, 1990, p. 10.

Postmodernist Developments in Puget Sound and Contemporary Alternative Venues

by Pam Keeley

This essay looks at ways in which several Northwest women artists and exhibitions reflect central characteristics of postmodern aesthetics and issues. In place of the individual heroics of the modern era, the installation, video, and performance work of these artists moves toward an emphasis on collaboration and community action.

Do these approaches suggest a new humility with regard to the importance of the individual, or do they also express the dissolution of older ideas about subjectivity altogether? What questions must still be raised in terms of women's socialization to work, individually or in groups?

As theorist Fredric Jameson has noted, the poststructuralist notion of the dissolution of the unique self has created an aesthetic dilemma and, "it is no longer clear what artists and writers of the present period are supposed to be doing."[1] Do current investigations by women artists, many of whom tend toward collaboration, reflect questions of the social self in dilemma? Or do these diverse activities reflect movement toward the fundamental paradigm shift called for by theorist Suzi Gablik?[2] Perhaps our real hopes lie in finding the ability to live free of paradigms altogether, as proposed by social historian Morris Berman.[3]

True to the eclectic nature of postmodernism, many of the more established artists discussed here address a variety of themes through a wide range of materials and media. The strongest commonality emerges from an individual propensity to work collaboratively, as part of a public art team, and to refuse specialization. The artists featured in this overview are predominantly white, educated middle class and middle-aged women. Their work tends to take a reflective and wide-angle approach that may not always look "feminist," but arises from philosophies strongly connected to individual feminist values.

While many Northwest women artists continue to participate in conventional gallery and museum venues, they also extend the exhibition space to shopping malls, public thoroughfares, and other non-traditional sites for art. What significance does the current shift from private to public patronage have? What happens when art enters the arterials of consumer culture? These and other critical questions must be asked as we consider the increasingly complex visions and strategies undertaken by contemporary artists. Sometimes the questions themselves become the art.

For over 20 years Gloria Bornstein has used sculpture, performance, video, and installation to dislodge control of representation from patriarchal structures and re-focus the public eye on Other points of view. Among the topics Bornstein has explored are censorship, the rights of prostitutes — as brought out by the unsolved Green River murders — homelessness, and the myth of home.

As part of "In Public: Seattle 1991," a series of public artworks and events sponsored by the Seattle Arts Commission, Bornstein and her collaborator Donald Fels created an interactive installation along the downtown waterfront. In *Shore Viewpoints* and *Voice Library*, they placed signboards that offered revisionist text and questions, such as "What happens when the government holds land in public trust?" alongside "official" historical markers and regulatory signs. The *Voice Library* provided a telephone line where callers could register responses and listen to the recorded messages of others.

Bornstein's early work involved identity-oriented collaboration with another Seattle pioneer in video and performance art, Annie Grosshans, the co-owner, with Laura Millin, of Art In Form, a now-defunct art bookstore and showcase for artists' books and window installations. Grosshans currently focuses on text-based video art and describes herself as "on the outside of the outside." In 1976, the performance *Public Document* by Bornstein, Grosshans, and Danae Willson (part of Northwest Projects juried by Lucy Lippard) counted among the many feminist projects by artists in the '70s and '80s working out of and/or and 911.[4] Several later 911 installation projects moved beyond the confines of the center itself with innovative programs, such as "Homes for Art" of the late-'80s, where site-specific works were made on the property of private homes throughout Seattle. For example, Bornstein's "home" dealt with the myth of home and family. Actively working as a psychotherapist, Bornstein continues to layer socio-political questionings in her work with identity and gender, excavating difficult issues like incest and the holocaust.

Susan Sagawa is also an installation artist and, like Bornstein, concerned with cultural intersections. Currently an associate curator at the Bellevue

Art Museum, Sagawa served as acting director of 911 in the last months before its formal transition to a media arts center in 1983. Following a news article about the encroachment of downtown developers on Seattle's International District, a major hub for Asian communities in the Pacific Northwest, Sagawa responded with an installation, *If a Pigeon Could Talk*.(1988). In this piece, Sagawa (born in Britain and married to a Japanese-American) combined Western materials with an Eastern aesthetic to focus on the changes imposed on a community without the participation of its members. The installation, done at the Wing Luke Asian Museum, included a pigeon as a symbol of the living, yet voiceless Asian community. The bird, provided by a Chinese pet-shop owner in a nearby alleyway, was quickly adopted by district residents who took up its care for the duration of the exhibition. Fears that Sagawa's piece might spark controversy in the business community were allayed after a preview was hastily arranged for local Japanese businessmen, who, on opening night, sent Sagawa a large bouquet of flowers.

While pieces like *Shore Viewpoints* and *If a Pigeon Could Talk*, don't provide immediate solutions to the problems they identify, they nonetheless propose a model of shared social responsibility and gnaw at the blindness and isolationism of dominant Western culture.

Although initial installations by Seattle artist Beliz Brother were often found in conventional museum settings, her work as a scenic and lighting designer has taken place across a wide variety of performance sites. Like forerunner Doris Totten Chase, Brother has investigated the importance of light and space as integral components of performance art. In the '80s, working with choreographers Llory Wilson and Pat Graney, Brother pulled emotional themes through filters of metaphor and abstraction, creating austere, yet highly evocative performance sets.

During the same period she participated in various 911 projects and received several commissions from Seattle and King County for public art works. In 1991 Brother and Mary Ann Peters, also a key figure in Northwest installation art, curatorial work, and arts organizations, collaborated on a solarium designed for the Bailey-Boushay AIDS Housing Project. Another public art project that Brother is involved in (due for completion in 1995) is an interactive courtyard garden for Harborview Medical Center in Seattle. Coinciding with the Gulf War, Brother installed a large-scale piece, *COUNT*, at the Center on Contemporary Art, which included a monumental moving wall made out of 400,000 body-bag tags.

Brother's most recent piece is a formidable example of how art can literally move into the mainstream, comfort, and perhaps renew, our souls. As with Sagawa, a newspaper item served as catalyst for Brother's performance piece. She read the story of Vedran Smailovic, a cellist with the Sarajevo Opera, who played for 22 days amid gunfire in front of a bakery to commemorate the deaths of 22 people killed by Serbian mortars while standing in a breadline there. Brother organized a series of site-varying cello performances throughout Seattle, including one on a ferry boat, all of which became like mobile grief units. For 22 successive days, volunteer cellists played parts of Albinoni's Adagio for Strings, as Smailovic had

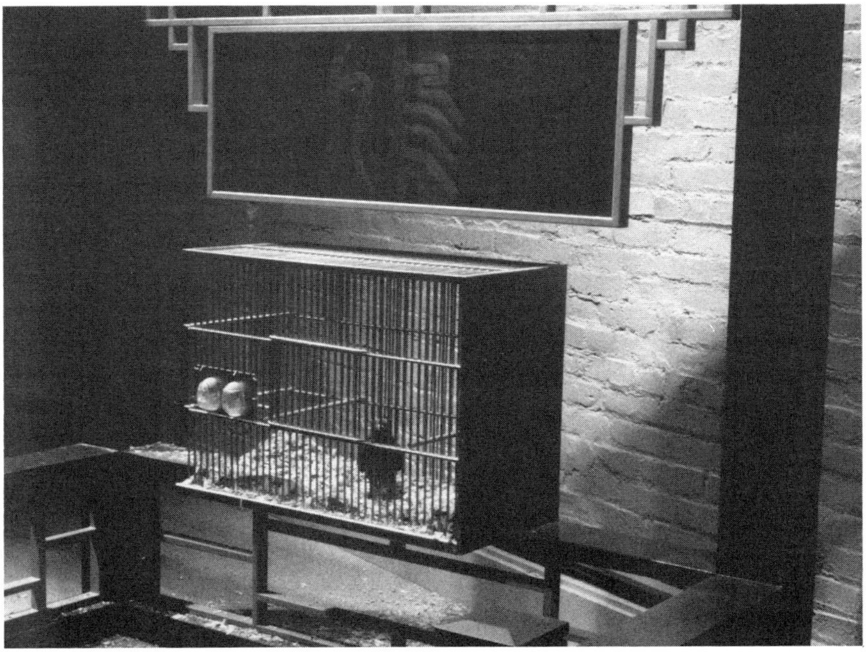

Susan Sagawa, *If a Pigeon Could Talk*, 1988, installation, Wing Luke Asian Museum, International District, Seattle.

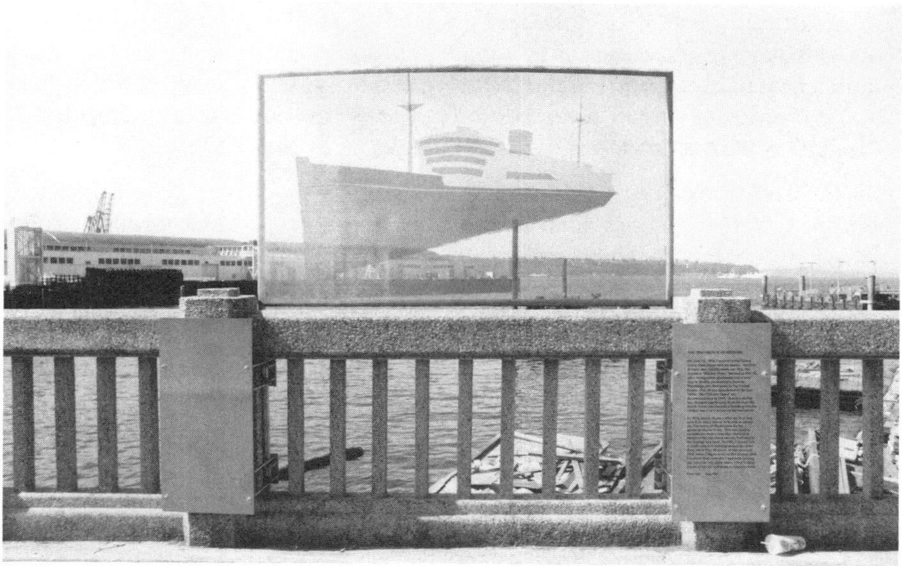

Norie Sato, *Transience of Memory*, 1991, Seattle Waterfront, part of "In Public: Seattle 1991," sponsored by the Seattle Arts Commission.

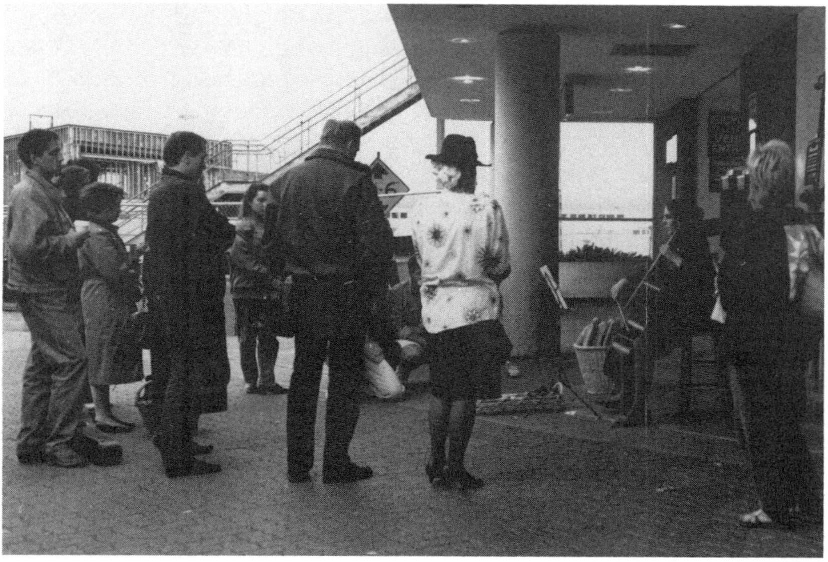

Beliz Brother, *22 Adagio*, 1992, sculpture installation and 22 cello performances at public places in Seattle.

done, drawing small crowds, and eventually a following of former Yugoslavian natives. In contrast to the individual performances, Brother created a small installation in the window of a downscale music shop: in this static memorial a wall of empty bread pans served as a backdrop for a "fallen" cello case covered by a heavy layer of flour.

At the end of one performance a woman from the crowd gave Brother a bouquet of rosemary, which she said is the plant of remembrance, from her grandmother's garden in Croatia.

Although Bornstein, Sagawa, and Brother have all incorporated video — produced by themselves or in collaboration with videographers — into larger works, Japanese-American Norie Sato reverses the arrangement, making video her primary focus even when it appears in the context of an installation. For Sato, the medium of video is materially and conceptually closest to the heart of her interests, the place where form is determined by elusive and transient images, where the non-physical paradoxically becomes physical.

Sato's videos sometimes include specific imagery; at other times her screens are filled with nonspecific, abstract electronic pulses, interference patterns, and ghost images. Her audio tracks may incorporate "identifiable" sounds, such as surf, but they also include voices, sirens, and other known sounds recorded at extremely low volumes so that they verge on unrecognizability and fall into the realm of white noise or barely discernible whispers from "ghosts." In her sculpture and installations, Sato has worked consistently with glass, a physical complement to her video elements that ties in conceptually with her questions about illusion, memory, and edges. Having worked as an arts organizer, in the '70s doing video and installation programming at and/or and 911, as well as working with the Western States Art Federation of the National Endowment for the Arts, Sato is currently a collaborator on three artist-design teams for public art projects in Seattle, Portland, and Dallas.

Since the early 1980s, many Seattle women artists have increasingly turned toward video and film to explore gender-related issues. Videographer Heather Oaksen, who teaches at Cornish College of the Arts in Seattle, explores gender and issue-related subjects in loosely narrative forms. She is an active part of a broad network of Northwest women in video and film whose experimental and documentary works focus on semiotics, deconstruction, a variety of socio-political topics, and music video.[5]

What about women working "outside of the outside?" More confrontational, overtly feminist work along these lines is beginning to develop in places like Olympia, Washington. There, younger women are forming "girl-bands," staging performances — parading down main street — and making gender and identity-related art heavily inflected with postmodern strategies of irony and cynicism. Exhibitions such as "CounterPositions," a group of installations in a run-down, former Seattle hotel by recent University of Washington MFA graduates Ruth Marie Tomlinson, Linda Helander, Edith Carson, Ingrid Lahti, Amy Hamblin, Brandon Zebold, and Harriet Sanderson, addressed social degeneration and life in suspension. *Piercings,* a one-night performance/installation where twelve women (who do not define themselves as artists) confronted their audience with their passive, immobilized, needle-ridden bodies as an art exhibition. These are all examples of ongoing questioning and explorations of identity and power structures.

The artists highlighted here represent only a handful of the many Northwest women working in alternative venues. Even the question of what "alternative" means is shifting: are we talking about alternative art forms, alternative structures to conventional institutions of art, or both? Because many forms of video, installation, and performance have been absorbed in sanctioned art institutions, by the mid-'70s, categorizing them as alternative began to feel archaic, and may no longer be appropriate, even in the Northwest. Yet their relative newness within the transitional and still-evolving eras of late-modern and early-postmodern art, and their relative freedom from the constrictions of male-dominated traditional forms makes these areas more open and obvious territories for exploration by women. Picking new ways through this landscape of postmodern ideological debris requires teamwork and the courage to experiment individually. Tough questions meet complex answers. Often with nothing more to go on than an impulse from the soul, Northwest women artists are working to make a positive difference in the world.

NOTES:

[1] Fredric Jameson, "Postmodernism and Consumer Society," in *Postmodernism and Its Discontents,* ed. E. Ann Kaplan. New York: 198: 17.

[2] Suzi Gablik, *The Reenchantment of Art* , London and New York: Thames and Hudson, 1991.

[3] Morris Berman, *Coming to Our Senses,* New York: Simon and Schuster, 1989.

[4] See Robin Reidy's extensive history of 911 Media Arts Center (formerly 911 Contemporary Arts Center) published serially in volumes of 911's Newsletter in 1991. (Reidy was Executive Director of 911 Media Arts Center in Seattle.)

[5] See Robin Reidy's extensive resource list, *Our Images Our Selves,* Seattle: 911 Media Arts Center, 1992.

Part V:
Feminist Spin-Offs: 1970 through the Present

The opportunities arising with the women's art movement of the late 1960s and early '70s have been significant for contemporary women; feminist spin-offs are highlighted in this section. Artist/curator Nancy Weymouth Halbrooks discusses her involvement in the influential Women Artists Group (WAG), as well as other feminist offshoots. Another active presence in Puget Sound, the Seattle Women's Caucus for the Arts, is chronicled by artist Ann T. Rosenthal. Feminist developments in Eastern Washington are surveyed by artist and educator Jo Hockenhull. An overview of feminist developments in the Vancouver, B.C. art community by writer and publisher Caffyn Kelley focuses on women of color and cultural diversity. A conversation with Anne Focke, founder of the alternative artists organization, and/or, recaptures the evolution of early 1970s feminist activities in the Northwest.

The focus is on the most influential women artists' organizations, since it is impossible to address all the many small groups or individual activities. One example is the eleven-member Fremont Artist-Mother Co-op, founded by painter Terry Furchgott and Frankie Kennedy, in which nine members shared child care, studio space and exhibitions in Seattle in the early 1980s. The numerous other activities of women artists of the 1970s and '80s who drew inspiration from feminist art and worked to expand opportunities for women by involvement in alternative venues are also difficult to address individually. One example is artist and educator Kathleen Rabel's role in MULTICOM, a group of four artists (Rabel, Stephen Hazel, Bill Ritchie, and Keith Achepol) who saw artists' roles as beyond gender; by functioning interchangeably they opened up issues of androgyny.

This final section explores how feminist artists have been vital forces working within — or at the fringes of — the Northwest contemporary art scene.

Roots and Offshoots: Women Artists' Groups and Feminist Art, 1970s and Early '80s

by Nancy Weymouth Halbrooks

The meeting room was packed with women. I felt hot and heady, and, although just 23 years old, I knew it was a remarkable moment. It was the 1977 annual meeting of Women Artists Group of the Northwest (WAG). The first of its kind in Seattle, WAG began meeting in 1976: all women, all artists. By 1977, attendance was well over 400. It felt like thousands. The energy was contagious and a sense of movement, something larger than one's self, was in the air.

I focus in this essay on Puget Sound-based women's art groups of the 1970s and '80s that grew out of the national women's movement of the '70s. An important facet of discussion is how emerging lesbian artists' groups experience issues of isolation and integrate their lives as artists with their artwork.

During the '70s it was clear that few alternatives to mainstream galleries and museums existed for women artists. One of the first women-only spaces was the Women's Cultural Center at the University YWCA, founded by Sibyl James, a Seattle poet on a CETA Artist-in-the-City grant from the Seattle Arts Commission and the City of Seattle. Created in the late 1970s, the Cunningham Gallery at the University of Washington continues its commitment to exhibiting Northwest women artists. Two other alternative women's exhibition spaces were an informal gallery at Innerspace Café attached to It's About Time (a now defunct women's bookstore), as well as an off-and-on-again exhibition program at the Lesbian Resource Center.

These venues have historically been linked to women's groups. All depended on a larger support system to survive — they were not created as independent galleries — whereas the women's groups I focus on here struggled to be independent of any other structure.

In the early 1970s, Seattle women artists began to meet to share slides of work and establish informal support groups. These early meetings were loosely structured by behind-the-scenes efforts of arts organizer Anne Focke (who founded alternative arts organization and/or), as well as others like Mary Avery and Cathy Hillenbrand.

In 1975 a group of 20 to 30 women artists within the context of and/or formed WAG. These meetings were held in homes, cafés, restaurants, bars and at and/or. Part of the impetus to become officially incorporated was the goal of bringing artist Judy Chicago to the Northwest area. The group raised money with an art auction and Chicago came to Seattle, did an installation at and/or, talked, and met with artists. Money left over from their successful auction launched the group, which soon became a substantial entity, with a peak membership of around 450 before its demise in 1981.

As such, WAG grew out of a larger context of women artists throughout the country who were organizing and teaching women art students in innovative feminist programs. Through such projects as Womanhouse (1972), a project at California Institute of the Arts, the Feminist Studio Workshops at the Woman's Building in Los Angeles (1973), as well as organizations in Boston, Miami and New York, women artists began working together. A network of these groups called West East Coast Bag (WEB) linked the groups from coast to coast with a slide registry and newsletter. By 1972, a directory identified more than 27 women's art organizations.

WAG thrived for several years, attaining its not-for-profit incorporation in 1976. Official founders were Mary Avery, Cathy Hillenbrand, Judy Kleinberg and Bonita Corliss; others involved in initial organizing were Susan MacLeod, Christine Ziemnik, Marya Roland, Jan Nelson, Anita Fisk, Wendy Brawer, Judith Starbuck and Christi Norman.

WAG was non-hierarchical; board members were elected from the membership at large and positions were titles in name only. As an organic, member-oriented group, it was dynamic and at times chaotic — I remember noisy, crowded meetings. WAG brought several visiting artists and critics to the region, including Deborah Remington, Jackie Winsor, Miriam Schapiro, Judy Chicago and Lucy Lippard. Group exhibitions were organized with shows such as "EAT ART" (edible art), "Circle Show," and "6 over 50" (6 women over the age of 50: Dorothy Rising, Lizel Salzer, Ramona Solberg, Alma Penberthy, Flora Correa and Alette Skille). For several years WAG produced an informative and well-designed monthly

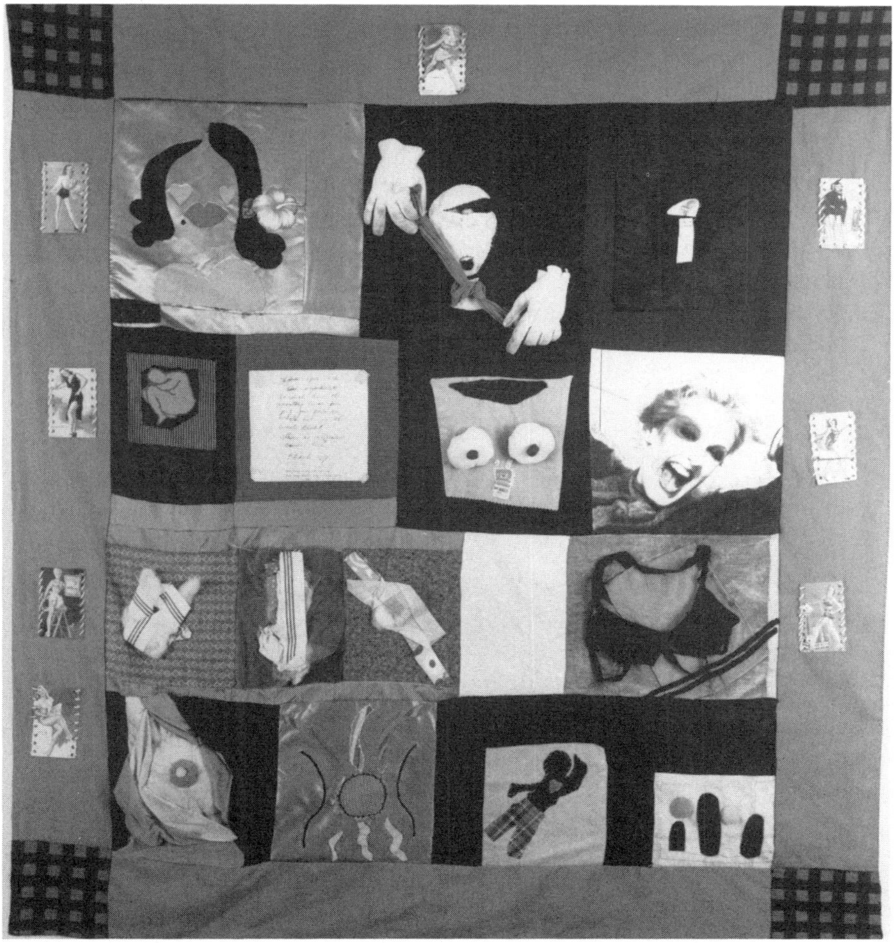

Feminist Art Project, ***The Curse, A Quilt on Misogyny***, 1979, mixed media, 70 x 64.

member's newsletter with an extensive calendar of events.

Perusing the WAG membership roster and newsletters, one finds an impressive range of artists: Francie Allen, Maryann Ariizumi, Gloria Bornstein, Carola Burroughs, Beliz Brother, Doris Totten Chase, Ginny Conrow, Katie Dike (Anthony), Lynn DiNino, Catherine Fallingwater, Karen Guzak, Joanne Hammer, Anne Hauberg, Nadine Haynes, Joyce Izumi, Sibyl James, Diane Katsiaficas, Janet Laurel, Mary Jeanne Linford, Lucy Liu, Susan Lytle, Sherry Markovitz, Gene Gentry McMahon, Laura Millin, Diane Neumaier, Carol Orlock, Charlene Rosser, Virginia Paquette, Mary Ann Peters, Isabel Sim-Hamilton, Barbara Swift, Karen Strawhat, LaDeane Tate, Sarah Teofanov, Barbara Tomash, Bea Vogel, Kris Wheeler, Barbara Wilson, Peggy Zehring, and many, many more.

Controversy eventually arose over issues of feminism and male membership. The arts community of the time did not appear to welcome lesbian and feminist artists. There were mixed feelings about maintaining a women-only membership. WAG eventually died in 1981.

In 1978, WAG members Jo Goodwin, Paula Lumbard, Viviane Clarac, Alexandra Stone and Bonnie Sundance attended either the year long or summer intensive Feminist Studio Workshop at the L.A. Woman's Building. Out of this exchange Clarac and I created the Feminist Art Project (FAP) in 1978. Clarac decided to model FAP on the structure of the Lesbian Art Project founded by art historian Arlene Raven at the Feminist Studio Workshop.

We invited several women we had worked with in WAG and other groups, and formed a collective of 12 women. We met for a year, twice a month in community meetings and consciousness-raising groups. Where WAG was event oriented, FAP was process oriented. We struggled to integrate intellect and feeling: politics pushed into process. FAP produced several projects including a misogyny quilt which was exhibited at a local quilt show. FAP also demonstrated against the Seattle Art Museum's cancellation of Judy Chicago's Dinner Party in 1979. FAP operated as a collective for a year, opened to new members and died in its second year as a result of unresolved internal strife.

Though short-lived, FAP was a remarkable experiment. I believe it deeply and positively affected all its initial twelve members: Deborah Rountry, Jan Nelson, Edith Fairhall, Ginnie Bauman, Nancy W. Halbrooks, Margaret Elmer, Doris Brevoort, Alexandra Stone, Betty Swift, Becky Wall, Gretchen Frederick and Viviane Clarac.

In the early 1980s, when the Reagan years descended, WAG died, and/or's exhibition space closed, and 911 Contemporary Arts Center was established as the Center of Contemporary Art (COCA), I began dreaming of a non-profit organization that would combine the best of FAP and WAG. In spite of the difficult political climate, or perhaps because of it, Stepping Stone was incorporated as a non-profit organization in 1981. Our first event was a slide lecture by Jacqueline Morreau of the British exhibition, "Women's Images of Men." We ran into problems almost immediately. Money was tight everywhere, the CETA grants program was gone, and general apathy was upon the women's arts community.

Stepping Stone's focus was to create an umbrella for women artists' projects and productions — an attempt to combine the events-orientation of WAG with the philosophical process of FAP. The board remained small with members Tisha Ranfone, Carol Tiebot, Patt Cranage and myself. We produced several events: a month-long juried exhibition entitled "In Our Own Image, Women's Images of Women" and "Women's Voices and Visions," classes for women artists and writers. Women's Voices, a series of writing workshops taught by Pesha Gertler, a Seattle poet, operated independently for several years. Stepping Stone dissolved in 1985. It was an idea that worked, but economically and spiritually it came at the wrong time.

In contrast to the organized groups of women artists like WAG or FAP, lesbian artists have worked in greater isolation. Not all art made by lesbians is clearly identified and it overlaps into other communities — feminist art, women's art, other political arenas — and is as diverse in media and approach as any other group's work. Yet it is created within a sub culture, a place of difference. Recently, lesbian-artist support groups have been emerging in the Northwest. This network helps to counter the fear and risk for many lesbian artists in revealing their identity to the larger community which has contributed to their isolation and invisibility.

In a recent gathering of lesbian artists it was agreed that there is little economic power in being a lesbian artist. In discussing visibility or invisibility, the group felt a lack of identity — not knowing who they were in either the lesbian community or the arts community. Questions have started to form. How does that invisibility protect? How does it de-power? How does it isolate lesbian artists from each other? The need for identity might be more important to us to find community, to feel less isolated within our communities, than to identify us to the exterior world.

Perhaps the emerging lesbian support groups springing up in the Northwest will allow lesbian artists to raise issues of culture and sexuality, to integrate political choices into their art and their communities. In San Francisco an organization, LVA (Lesbian Visual Artists), sends out newsletters, maintains a slide registry and produces shows. In Oregon there is a Southern Oregon lesbian artists support group, and in Portland and Eugene there are lesbian support groups started within the last year.

Lesbian artists, like all women artists, reflect different points of view as well as create diverse work, but a striking consistency is their integration of politics, lesbian identity, and art.

Over the years, Kate Anthony's work has evolved to an interest in realism. For a time she painted the Seattle lesbian bar scene from an insider view. The paintings, warm and playful in tone, have a quality of realism and affection for the milieu.The subject matter is not deviant, nor does it reflect a seedy, titillating view — such as voyeuristic mainstream movies depicting lesbian subculture. The paintings reflect a community; women spill around each other, smoke rises, there is a sense of activity in a place of safety.

In a series of "Broken Hearted Butch Madonnas" Portland, Oregon, artist Sierra Lonepine Briano explores issues of female archetypes and role models modeled on historic images of Madonnas. She plays with stereotypes of butch and femme, or strong women feeling the blues, creating what she calls "Dycons." Briano's work is funny and powerful, and somehow her brazenness leads to acceptance, not animosity. Challenging the myth of large, butchy women as stoic and unfeeling, she inserts tenderness into the scene, balancing strength and gentleness in her "bull dyke."The crudely applied paint portrays a vulnerable and revealing self.

Tracy Kachtick-Anders's art reflects a political interest and methodology. She works primarily within her political affiliations in the Seattle Lesbian/Gay community and the group Heart to Art to empower people affected by Aids through a series of creative arts workshops, exhibitions, and projects such as murals. Themes include Aids, homeless people and gay / lesbian issues. There is little separation between the political activity and art-making. Kachtick-Anders paints with acrylics on inexpensive support materials, then photographs the paintings to create cards, an affordable and accessible means of communicating her message and sharing her images. Gender roles float in an androgynous mix, some female forms seem at times masculine, some male forms have a sense of femininity. This

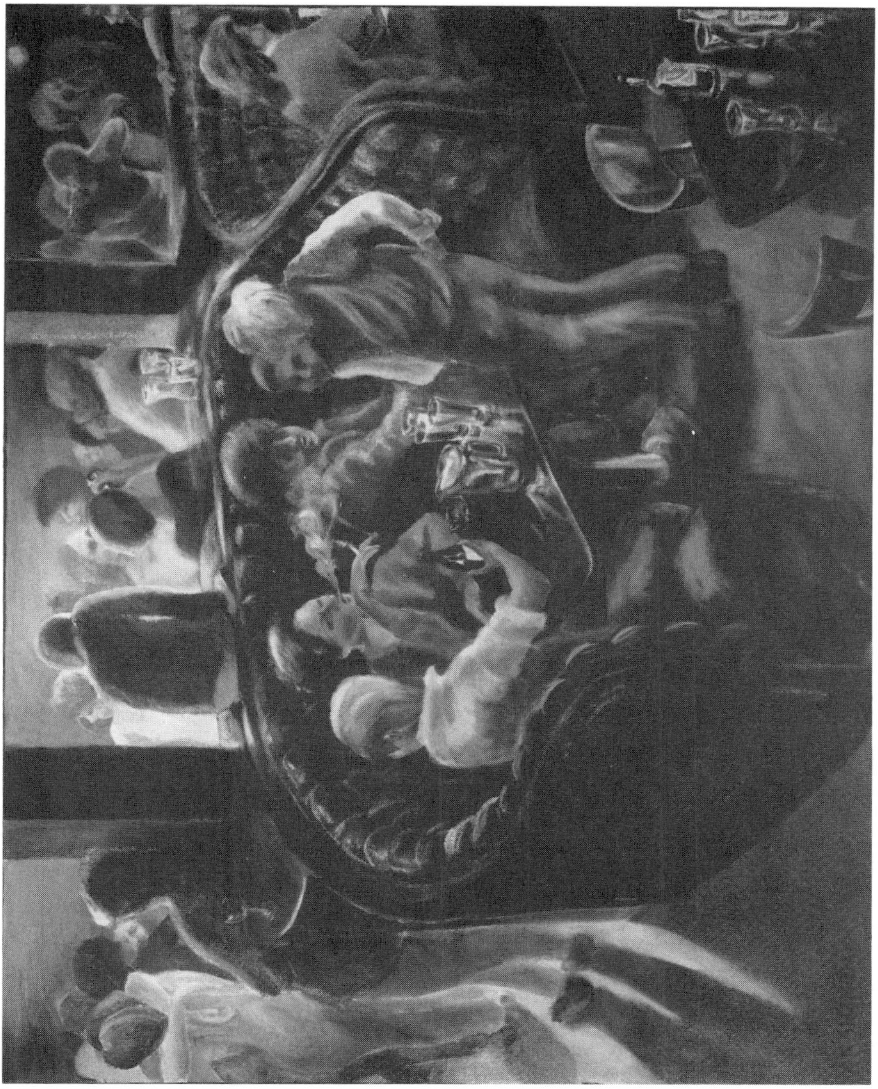

Kate Anthony, *Sappho's*, 1987, o/c, 29 x 24.

The WomEN ArtiSts grouP News

©women artists group of the northwest 1977

Volume Three Number THREE 1977

April

P. O. BOX 9462
SEATTLE 98109

*EVENT SPONSORED BY WOMEN ARTISTS GROUP

1 APRIL isy BOUKIR

@ 8pm @ Hammondball Studios @ 1100 Post (@ Spring near Waterfront) @ $2 @ 624-9397 or for questions, call Cathy @ 325-3048
Hammond Ball Productions presents Nancy Graves' Camel Movie, "Isy Boukir." Nancy Graves is a sculptor known as the Camel Lady; she is totally fascinated with camels. This 16-minute film made in 1971 is being shown with 4 others as part of an ongoing series on avant-garde films shown the first Friday of each month.

2 APRIL WOMYN'S LAnd PROJECT

@ 10am @ 206 12th Ave NE Patty @ 324-6292, Amy @ 632-0530, Rose @ 523-2055
A meeting for womyn interested in land (for retreats, workshops, living, healing, etc.). We will also spend 23 & 24 April on Vashon to talk in more detail.

* 5 April PORK out at THE ATLAS

@ 6pm @ The Atlas Cafe @ 424 Maynard S. (China Town) @ 623-0913
General celebration of our accomplishments to date. Frivolity and food. Questions? Call Christine @ 682-5947.

6 apRIL AN OpeNING

@ 5pm-8pm @ The Artists @ 919 East Pike Street @ 322-9197 or 723-5780
The Artists Gallery invites you to the gala opening of the Fourth Annual Seward Park Art Studio Faculty Exhibition. Show runs thru 30 April; regular hours Wed, Fri, Sat noon-6pm, Thursday 1pm-9:30pm, Sundays noon-6pm, or by appointment.

7 April an OPENING

@ 6pm-8pm @ Polly Friedlander Gallery @ 89 Yesler Way @ 682-8900
The reception for a showing of recent works by Miro Fitzgerald, including a performance, "Amalgam" at 7:30pm. Show runs thru 26 April; Mon-Sat 10am-5pm.

* 11 april GENERAL MEMBERSHIP MeetiNG

Doors open @ 6:30, meeting starts prompt @ 7:30pm @ UW Ethnic Cultural Center "The Chicano Room" @ 3931 Brooklyn Ave NE Questions: Mary @ 329-5162
Please bring cup, refreshments, writing tools. Critique & feedback on W.A.G. programs: newsletter, roster, guest artist series. Discussion of Draft for Committees (see p. 4). Evaluation & clarification of programs & purposes. Followed by a primordial jam led by Elizabeth Franko (1-582-3761). Bring an "instrument" to play--a wooden spoon, a little bell--to make noise, to express yourself. Wear a costume or something that introduces you or tells something about you. Bring some spare change & spare the treasury (room rental $8). Mtg ends 10pm; close 11p

* 12 APRil WRITER's POTluck

@ 6pm @ Pati McCoy's @ 134 NE 61st Pati @ 522-6212 or Viviane @ 522-9435
A gathering for women who write words: poems, journals, short stories, and ??? and who are tired of being closet writers. Bring a pie, casserole, bread, beverage, plate & cup, and your ideas and feelings about projects for W.A.G. writers.

* 13 april PLANNiNG to PLAN

@ 6:30-9:30pm @ The Factory of Visual Art @ 4649 Sunnyside North (wallingford)
W.A.G. begins to plan a group show(s). (See article, page 6) The subject is wide open and there will be LOTS of ideas. Bring a cup/refreshments and a sense of humor, plus a piece of your own work and we will hang the first "symbolic" show, celebrating its opening & closing that same nite. Questions: Sue @ 329-3644.

14/15 april PuBlic DoCUMENT

@ 8:30pm @ and/or @ 1525 Tenth Avenue @ 324-5880
Gloria Bornstein, in collaboration with Annie Grosshans and Danae Willson, will present her NW Projects performance, "Public Document."

WAG Newsletter. 1977, front page.

androgyny parallels her involvement in a community where men and women associate for common causes — to fight aids and work for gay/lesbian rights.

WAG, FAP and Stepping Stone are not failures because they ended; they were amazing experiments. At a meeting about the creation of a women's building in Seattle — a dream never realized here — former WAG member Nelleke Langhout-Nix handed me a membership form to sign to create the first chapter of the Women's Caucus for Art in the Northwest. Collective energies that held the early groups together eventually became exhausted, but regenerated energies do sometimes spring forth, as in the Seattle Women's Caucus for the Arts (SWCA). WAG is still the model for women artists groups and activities in the Northwest.

For years I thought a lasting, permanent women's art organization was needed in the Northwest. In reflection, I believe each generation will produce a variation that suits its time as the need arises. Meanwhile we document and preserve the memory of this evolving process.

BIBLIOGRAPHY:

Nicolas A. Moufarrege, "Lavender: On Homosexuality and Art," *Arts Magazine*, October 1982: 84.

Gylbert Coker, "Harmony Hammond," *Arts Magazine* April 1984: 2.

Judy Collischan Van Wagner, "Harmony Hammond's Painted Spirits," *Arts Magazine*, Jan. 1987: 22.

Harmony Hammond, "Wrappings, Essays on Feminism, Art and the Martial Arts," Time and Space Limited Press (TSL), c 1984.

LVA, *Lesbian Visual Artists Newsletter*, Summer 1992, San Francisco CA.

Thanks to Matthew Stadler and Francis McCue for editorial assistance and to Sally Schuh for encouragement and research help. Thanks also to all the lesbian artists who attended gatherings at my home during research for this essay.

The 1980s: Seattle Women's Caucus for Art

by Ann T. Rosenthal

In 1992, two decades after the beginning of the women's art movement and the founding of the Women's Caucus for Art (WCA), the art world still reflects the inequities of the larger society, although, in Seattle, women artists fare better than elsewhere. We are well represented in most local galleries, many of our prominent arts institutions are directed by women, and many of our galleries are owned by women. Though women artists in Seattle affirm this apparent success, a closer look at statistics tells a different story. The Seattle Art Museum's "Documents Northwest" series gives nearly equal representation to women in their group shows, for instance, but only 7 women out of 32 were given solo shows between 1983 and 1992. At the University of Washington School of Art, 6 women out of 24 are full professors and 3 out of 8 are associate professors. The Seattle Art Commission's largest One-percent for Art project, entitled "In Public: Seattle 1991," was initially protested by the Seattle Art community because local artists, women and artists of color would not have a fair chance at funds.[1]

Though the work of women artists is visible in Washington, and Seattle in particular, there are few supportive spaces to present controversial work. As Cecilia Alvarez says in an interview with Alice Dubiel, "Since I am a Chicana (which means I am also female), people have permission to dismiss my art work. It doesn't have the concept of universality and transcendence. It's not 'good art' because it has content; it raises a subjective perspective."

Alternative exhibition spaces are usually multi-use facilities where art is not a priority. The public, and most gallery directors, are not prepared for work that addresses such issues as social injustice, child abuse, violence against women, ecological degradation, war, and racism. Seattle artist Sarah Teofanov says there is "no room for women who want to put forth a feminist political statement. We are the art — without the human connection, the context, you've lost it."

My first Seattle Women's Caucus for Art (SWCA) meeting took place in a member's basement apartment in 1985. Eight women convened to discuss a gallery of our own. The 25-member chapter had been meeting since 1983 in artists' homes and studios under the direction of first president, Patricia Zukas.[2] She was coming to the end of her term and vice-president, Barbara Bruch, was unable to take over. Armed with a computer (the only one in the chapter) and energized by my recent involvement in the WCA National Conference in Los Angeles, I accepted the office of president at the end of the year. The following year, SWCA inherited wall space in the Women's Cultural Center's meeting room in the University YWCA on Lake Union. The Center, directed by Sarah Teofanov from 1980 to 1982, was designed as a "learning" gallery where artists could develop exhibition and business skills rarely taught in academia. The SWCA continued this focus, coordinating 16 solo and group shows at A New Space gallery. Artists represented included Sara Adlerstein Gonzalez, Francie Allen, Denita Benechek, Carole Barrer, Katherine Carnell, Margaret Carson, Brooke Cottman, Marilyn H. Davis, Rachael Fefferman, Joe Hockenhull, Ruth Hooper, d'Elaine Johnson, Isabel Kahn, Pamela Mills, Rita Robillard, Helen Stout, Li Turner, Julie Vosoba, Louise Williams, Candace Zebell, Tammy Zlotnik. Encouraged by the exhibition opportunities at A New Space, membership grew over the next six years.[3]

In September 1986, the SWCA organized a Women Artists Visibility Event (WAVE), a national project in which many WCA chapters participated. The Seattle WAVE began with a salon-style exhibition, followed by a procession of creatively clad women artists with a banner proclaiming "Creativity is our Birthright." The parade culminated in Gasworks Park, where several noted Northwest artists and writers, including poet Sibyl James, writer and performance artist Annie Grosshans, and artists Jody Issacson, Marsha Burns, and Karen Guzak addressed women's issues in the arts. The SWCA also sponsored the Washington Women Artists Juried Exhibition at The Significant Form gallery in November 1987. In a notable show, 116 artworks by 80 Washington women artists were packed into this large gallery in Pioneer Square.[4]

With the relocation of the YWCA in 1988 and the closing of A New Space gallery, the SWCA continued its exhibition program in community college galleries. A second statewide juried exhibition was hosted by the SWCA in 1991, featuring the work of 16 artists at the Seattle Pacific University Art Center Gallery and juried by writer/curator Ruth Askey and artists Marita Dingus and Phyllis Yes. In October 1988, the Seattle and Oregon chapters

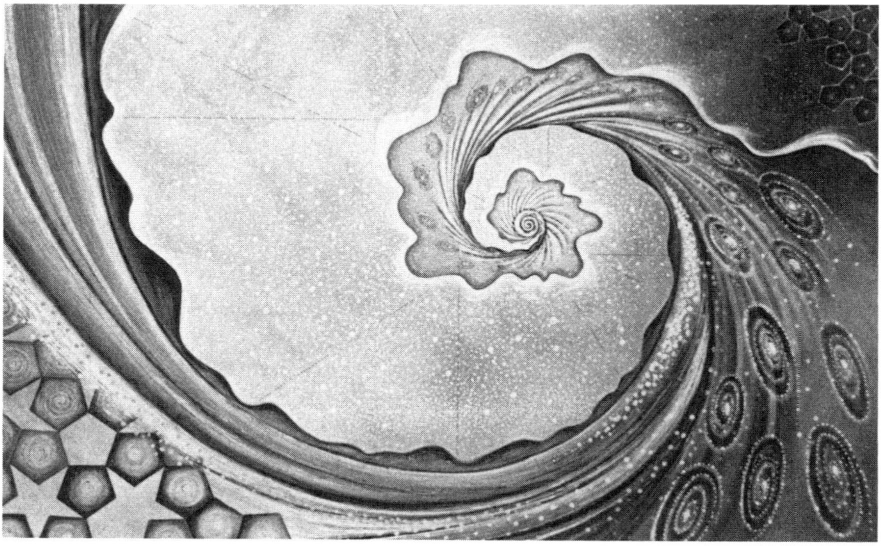

Barbara Bruch, *The Creation Process*, 1991, a/c, 56 x 88.

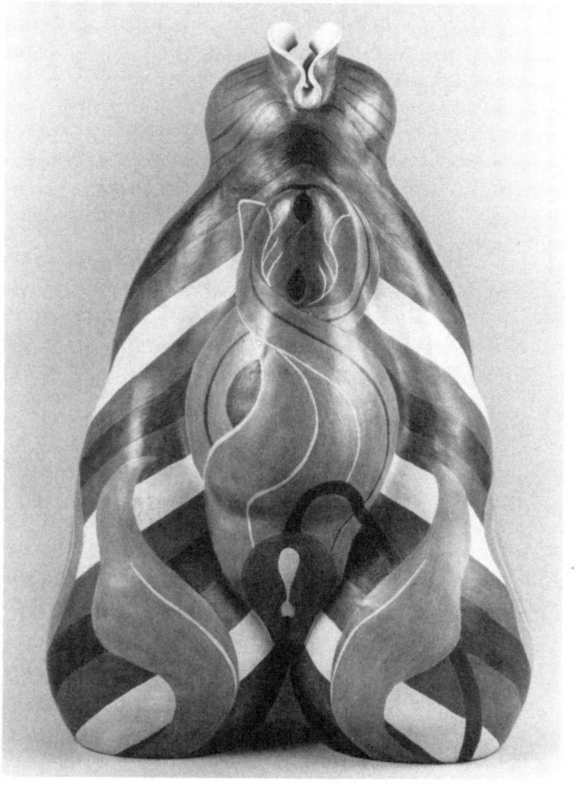

Joan Johnson, *Fertile Ground*, 1990, ceramic, 25 x 17 x 10.

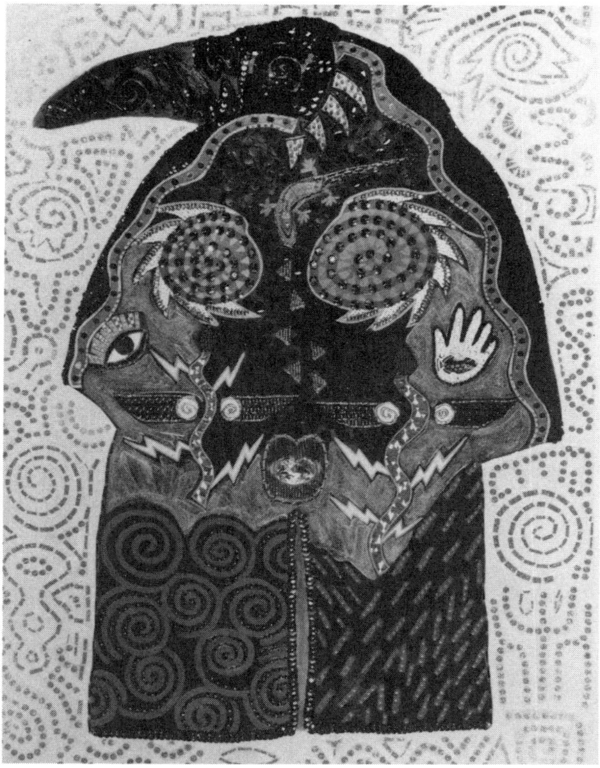

Sarah Teofanov, *Magic Coat Series: Crow Coat #3*, 1989, mixed media on paper, 27 x 34.

produced the first WCA Northwest Regional Conference in conjunction with the Northwest Women's Studies (NWWSA) bi-annual conference at Portland State University. The conference featured a wearable art fashion show, a day of panels including "Women Artists Many Colors," "Breaking the Exhibition Barrier," and "Feminist Art Criticism." Panelists included Barbara Coddington, Johanna Hays, Lydia Huante, Brooks Jacobsen, Claire C. Kelly-Zimmers, Betty LaDuke, Joyce Moty, Lillian Pitt, Susan Platt, Barbara Thomas and Gail Tremblay. An exhibition of women artists featured at PSU's Littman Gallery included many WCA members. In April 1991, the WCA again coordinated its Western Regional Conference with the NWWSA in Pullman, Washington. Panels addressed artist collaborations, censorship, and women artists with disabilities.

Barbara Bruch became the third president of the SWCA in 1991. Under her leadership, the SWCA continues to ensure that the work of regional women artists is visible and that our issues are represented in the art community.

Though far from equal, the opportunities for Washington women artists have improved. For 1993, the Seattle Art Museum has scheduled three major exhibitions by women artists, and the Seattle Art Commission's grants to visual artists is approaching equal gender representation.

Important work lies ahead in building a global community that embraces women's culture. Progress in networking in the Western United States was affirmed for me when the SWCA recently hosted a talk by Wyoming artist, Lynne Hull. She was introduced to the WCA through Southern California chapter members Lucy Blake Elahi and Katya Williamson, who were curating "Of Nature and Nation: Yellowstone: Summer of Fire." Elahi and Williamson had met through a WCA contact, and agreed to co-curate the exhibition, inviting Hull to participate. The exhibition at The Gallery in the Plaza, Security Pacific Bank in Los Angeles, in 1990, resulted in Elahi and Williamson becoming the first artists-in-residence in Yellowstone National Park in August 1991. Hull was granted a residency in June 1992.

We can create a feminist community by working together — a community that affirms our images, values, and concerns and supports our work in the world.

Research for this essay was contributed by Kari Morehouse.

NOTES:

[1] In a series of public discussions, this inequity was rectified.

[2] The SWCA is one of 39 chapters of the National WCA which was founded in 1972 at the annual meeting of the College Art Association. WCA founders recognized the importance of having a national network through which women in the visual arts professions could share their work with one another on an ongoing basis.

[3] The SWCA incorporated in February 1986 and received its non-profit status in September 1987. This was no small feat for a group of women who knew little of taxes, bylaws, bookkeeping and the IRS bureaucracy.

[4] *The Seattle Times* featured the exhibition on the front page of their Arts and Entertainment section of the Sunday edition. A discussion, moderated by Chris LaBeau of Channel 9 focused on jurors Layne Goldsmith, Karen Guzak, Wanda Westcoast, and artist d'Elaine Johnson. The exhibition was partially funded by a grant from the Washington State Art Commission.

A Conversation with Anne Focke

by Laura Brunsman

An important catalyst within the arts community, Anne Focke has been a low-key — but influential — conduit for early feminist ideas within the Puget Sound area. Her exposure to Lucy Lippard and various women's art networks of 1970-73 preceded and/or, the alternative arts organization she founded in 1974. And/or was remarkable as an alternative artists' organization that created a space for visual art, music, performance art, video art and post-production studio,and a library of periodicals, recordings, and artists books. Although and/or phased itself out in late 1984, it spawned other organizations that continue, including 911 Contemporary Arts Center (now 911 Media Arts Center), COCA (Center on Contemporary Art), Soundwork Northwest, and Artists Trust, as well as a for-profit business, Artech. Focke has continued her interests in artists' work and ideas, and is currently working on an interactive information network called ARTS WIRE, among other projects. We spoke on August 26, and September 14, 1992.

Laura Brunsman: How did your involvement with feminist ideas during the late '60s and early '70s develop?

Anne Focke: I give Lucy Lippard a lot of credit for helping me connect my life in the art world with my interest in feminism. Lucy came to Seattle in 1969 as an organizer with Seth Siegelaub of *557,087*, an exhibition sponsored by the Contemporary Arts Council of the Seattle Art Museum, and the first museum exhibition of conceptual art and earthworks. The title represented Seattle's population at the time. I was working at the museum, in the Education Department and got to know Lucy and helped her put the exhibition together.

About a year later, Lucy invited me to be part of the "West/East Bag," or "WEB," subtitled a "Liaison Network of Women Artists," a newsletter by and about women artists. Here were women artists whose work was about their lives as women, who were also activists in the art world, challenging discrimination against women in galleries and museums.

WEB was distributed in an unusual way. For each issue, one woman wrote about women's art activities in her own community, then sent her report to a list that included one woman from each of many cities throughout the U.S. Lucy asked me to be on this list. Each of us then took responsibility for copying, putting on postage, and getting the newsletter out to other women in the community. The first issue was from New York, then there were issues from San Francisco and Chicago, among others. I did one from Seattle that included information about women artists' activities here in 1971-72.

LB: What came out of WEB? Did it have anything to do with your forming and/or?

AF: In the late '60s, I was involved in the art world, both as an artist and as a staff person at the Seattle Art Museum. At the same time, I had begun to be very interested in feminism, following it through various publications from around the country, as well as talking and getting together with my own friends. WEB, and later other publications, drew these two parts of my life closer.

Whether I was conscious of it or not, this probably gave me a kind of encouragement to go ahead and do something. The publications about women artists showed women taking action. . . . The examples were powerful. Anybody who looks at the history of artists' organizations without looking at what was done specifically by and for women is missing a lot of history. Many of the earliest artists' spaces were women-run. There were a lot of very interesting projects, like the Womanhouse Project in L.A., The Feminist Studio Workshop, and the Women's Building. I don't think I said of myself, "Oh, if they can do it, I can." It was simply a matter of fact. I learned that people act. They start things when something is needed.

I had the chance to go to New York in 1974 after and/or opened and I looked up Lucy. We had corresponded, but hadn't seen each other since '69. She told me about an exhibition she had put together for Cal Arts, in the same series as *557,087*. It was called *c. 7,500*, because Cal Arts is in Valencia, which has a population of about 7,500. It showed pieces by women artists whose work had a conceptual base. We brought it to and/or in the spring of 1975, and it introduced me to the work of many artists I've followed since then. For example, there were photo-text pieces by Laurie Anderson and Mierle Laderman Ukeles; both came to and/or later.

LB: Was the show important for and/or at the time?

AF: Yes, both because it was work by women artists and because it was not conventional painting and sculpture. Also, it was a very easy show to ship around. The photos and texts and other wall pieces could be shipped in very small boxes. And/or had practically no budget at that point. We couldn't afford to do traveling shows.

LB: When did Lucy Lippard come back to Seattle?

AF: She came here to jury "Northwest Projects" for and/or in 1976. Northwest Projects let artists propose almost whatever was on their minds. Lucy chose three projects to be funded by and/or — "Museum of Neighborhood Phenomena" by Jack Baker, a performance titled "Public Document" by Gloria Bornstein with Annie Grosshans and Danae Wilson, and a photo documentary by Sherrie Markovitz titled "Women: Body, Space, and Personal Ritual." The expense of bringing Lucy here was shared with PCVA [Portland Center for Visual Arts]. PCVA brought Lucy out as juror for a large exhibition of Northwest artists that she titled "In Touch." PCVA and and/or were in good touch with each other in those days. We'd piggyback on each other's plans to bring artists to the region, sharing travel costs. We tended to put our money into bringing the artist, rather than shipping works. We'd focused on artists doing video, installation or performance. Ultimately, there was a lot of contact with the artists, not just with their "stuff." We did a lot for very little money.

LB: Then, later, Judy Chicago came to town?

AF: About 1975, several of us at and/or began to organize meetings for women artists to share slides of their work. People like Susan MacLeod, Judy Kleinberg, and Anita Fisk participated. Out of these evenings grew the Women Artists Group (WAG). There was no thought initially of starting anything ongoing, simply the desire to share work and ideas. WAG was the first activity that started at and/or and then became independent — which became almost a habit after a while.

This informal group began to talk about bringing Judy Chicago to town, and we found a way to get her here. Actually she came [in 1976] as part of a two-person show — she and her then-husband Lloyd Hamrol each had half of our gallery space. Judy involved a lot of women from the area in the construction and finishing of her installation, and many women got to know her in this working situation. She also gave slide talks in informal sessions.

LB: What other women came through and/or besides Lippard and Chicago?

AF: [There were enough that I couldn't trust my memory in the context of the interview. Laura Brunsman and I went to old and/or records and put together the following list, which I know, even so, is incomplete.] Among women who came here specifically to present their work, that is, not just to talk or be on a panel, were Jo Harvey Allen, Beth Anderson, Laurie Anderson, Jackie Apple, Lynda Benglis, Edit DeAk, Norma Jean Deak,

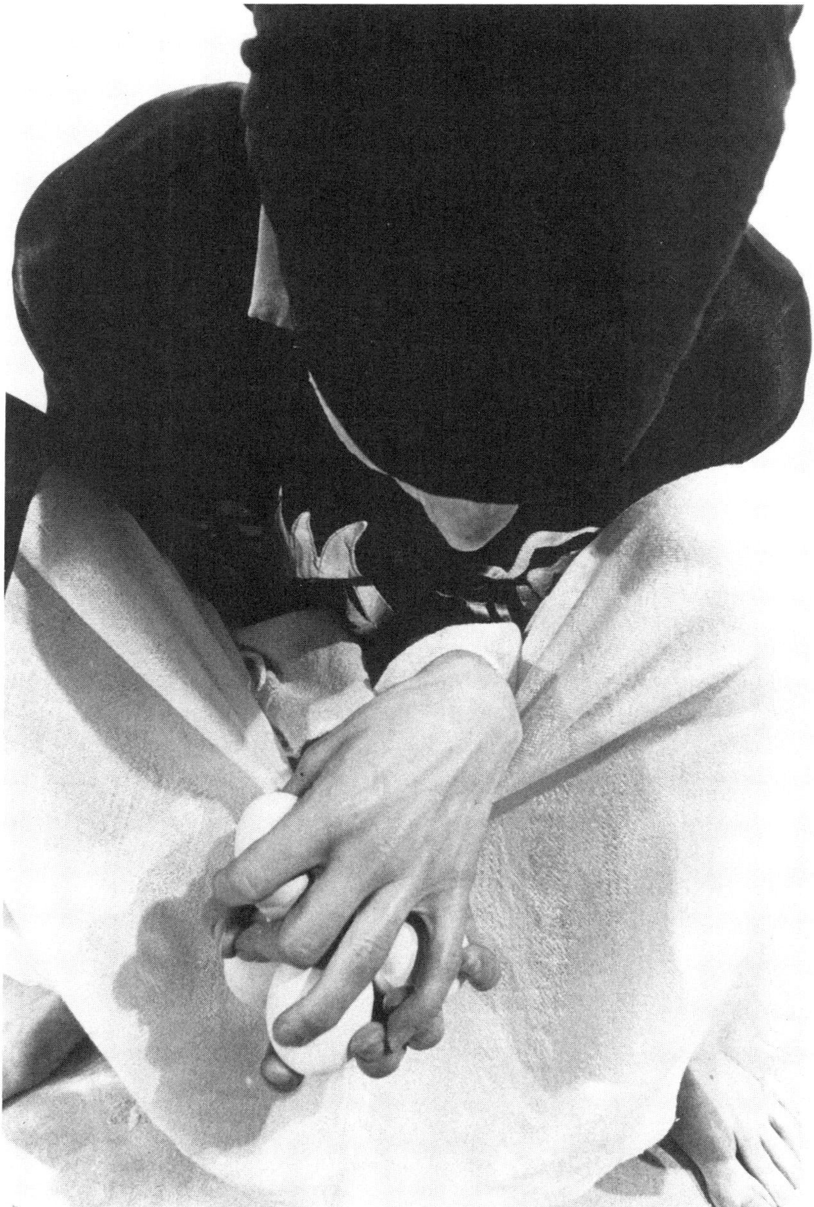

Gloria Bornstein, Annie Grosshans and Danae Willson, performing at and/or, Seattle, April 14 and 15, 1977; part of the *Northwest Projects* series.

Constance DeJong, Simone Forti, Sharon Grace, Nancy Holt, Jacquelyn Humbert, Joan Jonas, Nancy Karp, Katrina Krimsky, Shigeko Kubota, Suzanne Lacy, Joan Logue, Mary Lucier, Brenda Miller, Meredith Monk, Linda Montano, Pat Oleszko, Pauline Oliveros, Adrian Piper, Virginia Quesada, Ulrike Rosenbach, Martha Rosler, Elke Solomon, Mierle Laderman Ukeles, Steina Vasulka, and Joyce Wieland.

LB: But you didn't just work with artists from out of town. And/or was where women came together to collaborate in video, installation, and performance, which wasn't happening anywhere else in Seattle in the early days.

AF: A lot of Seattle artists put new work together for and/or and presented their work there. There were collaborations, as you say — performances by Gloria Bornstein, Miro FitzGerald, Annie Grosshans, Karen Helmerson, Chris Jonic, Laura Millin, Heather Ramsay, and Danae Willson, among others. Some of the artists were also involved in exhibitions and solo shows, as were many other women, such as Diana Aurigemma, Cheryl Cone, Rhoda Elend, Anita Fisk, Kathy Fridstein, Elise Lazzari, Helen Lessick, Susan McLeod, Marsha McMurray, Sherrie Markovitz, Maxine Nelson, Barbara Noah, Andy Ostheimer, Evelyn Roth, Shash Slettebak, Suzanne Tedesko, Barbara Tomash, Liza Zingarelli. Barbara Zusman and Susan Hereford of Portland were also included.

And we had many group shows, special events and projects, discussions, panels, and publications. Some involved women exclusively, like "You Guys Live Like Queens," an installation by a group of women who shared a home, and "Mamalookamumuday," a performance in celebration of Mother's Day. Friends of the Rag exhibited and performed at and/or; this was a loosely-knit group of artists and designers, both women and men, who made wearable art and clothing. I also remember a fairly wild early performance subtitled, "The Travelling Menstrual Show." In 1981, we sponsored an important conference titled, "The Art Politik" that brought Lippard and Martha Rosler back to town, as well as Judy Baca and Suzanne Lacy, among others.

I should also say that there were many women, as there were many men, whose names wouldn't necessarily show up on a list of artists presenting solo work or on a list of staff members, but who were very important to what happened at and/or. They organized shows, helped in the library or with events and mailings, and generally were there when the place needed them.

Though the core staff in the early days wasn't very large, it was fairly stable and included a high percentage of women — Annie Grosshans, Parker Lindner, Ann Obery, and Norie Sato, as well as myself. I wouldn't want to give the impression that and/or was just run by or for women, but there were a lot of women involved.

At the time, women seemed more prominent in some of the newer forms, like video and performance, than in older forms like painting and sculpture. There were also more women in central positions in artist spaces than in museums. I think women had greater access in new fields. It's probably economics on some level: new genres and new kinds of organizations didn't pay as well as established ones.

LB: In the late 1960s or early '70s, new forms were opening up, and feminist ideas were in the air. In terms of post-modernism, feminism is often credited with a portion of this opening up.

AF: Women were present and active when the forms were being defined, and therefore had much to do with how they got defined: video and performance come to mind.

LB: Do you feel there's a carryover of an experimental sense in women's exhibitions since and/or, or has the energy been somehow absorbed into a different way of thinking?

AF: Everything changes. I thought that when and/or stopped, other things would grow in its place. I'm sure this is true to some degree, though the parallels are not direct and we probably shouldn't expect them to be.

LB: There's an interesting passage in your book [*Writings* November 1973-May 1978, produced for an exhibition at PCVA, 1978] that deals with your thinking about art and artists' organizations. You mused then that, "traditionally, women's patterns have been less intense than men's, less absorbing, less directed. . . ." You wondered whether "values developed in/by women over time might be left behind." You suggested that these values might have a reverse relationship to intensity or aggressiveness and discussed ways women-based values might be incorporated into the patterns of organizations, values you related to your own "quiets" and "changes of focus."

AF: I guess I was feeling that one of the requirements for being "successful" in the world's eyes was to be totally consumed by one objective, pursued in an intensely directed way. This seemed to preclude a slower pace, or multi-faceted direction. I felt something valuable was probably left behind in such an all-consuming focus. I felt there was value in holding multiple focuses, in being interruptible and able to change course in midstream.

LB: Sort of a receptivity to chance, or other possibilities.

AF: I've come to appreciate that undirected, drift-like way of being, which is different than strategic. I think a lot happens when one lets oneself drift. I read about the pattern in a woman's life when she is a mom and at home taking care of the kids. She is constantly interrupted. That fragmentation and being responsive to interruption and to changes caused by people outside yourself is a very different sort of pattern than saying, "I'm just going to do this one thing." It's a different way of moving along; there's a strength in being able to handle things that way.

LB: This may be more a "working-through" process. Was there a synthesis with your ideas about feminism?

AF: I 'd say rather that feminism was a kind of ground within which I worked. I have a tendency to avoid rhetoric, or strong ideological stands, which always seem to close as many doors as they open.

LB: Also, feminist artists don't necessarily make big declamatory statements They might work quietly through autobiography or simply by noticing something or thinking.

AF: There's a real power in small, day-to-day actions,which begin to add up and have a larger power. I was very much affected by Mierle Ukeles's piece in *c. 7,500*, where I was asked, because I maintained the gallery space much of the time, to think of myself as making art at certain moments when cleaning the space. She just asked that I change my attitude about my work. Thinking about a small daily action, like maintenance, had a very strong effect on me — stronger, probably, than big, bold painting.

LB: A lot of the art of the '70s, and postmodernism in general, seems to be concerned with alternative ways of thinking, of taking control, getting away from the whole modernist machine.

AF: I'm not sure I'd put it quite like that, but I'm very interested in how we incorporate values into our lives in small, quiet ways.

Eastern Washington: Pullman and Spokane, 1970-1990

by Jo Hockenhull

The story of women's art in Eastern Washington during the 1970s and '80s is a tale of two cities: Spokane, the largest urban center east of the Cascades, and Pullman, small-town home of Washington State University (WSU).

I have always felt a difference between the arts of Pullman and Spokane, more than is warranted by size or distance. It wasn't until I began research for this essay that I started to understand it. The following observations are by myself and 35 women from Eastern Washington who have been generous with their time and thoughts.

PULLMAN:

I came to Pullman in August, 1972, the first woman hired for WSU's Fine Arts faculty in 20 years. The slide library held 25,000 slides, but included only four or five women artists. The first women's studies courses were offered through the extension program. I delivered my first lecture on women artists in 1976 as part of an introductory course taught *gratis* by women faculty from all over the university.

When Nancy Wriggle started teaching grade school art in Pullman in 1963, the only practicing women artists were Genevra Sloan, Mackey Roberts and Mary Kirkwood, all working in nearby Moscow, Idaho. By 1992, Washington State University's Fine Arts Department had six women professors: Ann Christenson, Sandra Deutchman, Deborah Haynes, Carol Ivory, Rita Robillard, and myself, plus two women adjuncts: Tamara Helm and Selene Santucci. Patricia Watkinson, director of WSU's Museum of Art, Nicole Taflinger, owner of the NICA Gallery, and Joanna Hays, director of the Pritchard Gallery in Moscow, have sponsored women artists' exhibitions and lectures. Karen Watts, an installation artist, has been appointed by the Washington State Arts Commission as liaison with WSU's Percent for Art projects. Heidi Uberheide, Canadian painter/

printmaker, recently moved to Palouse, Washington, 15 miles from Pullman. Things have changed.

Women graduate students at WSU in the '70s were serious, proficient, insightful artists, and in Spokane, many women exhibited and taught at a professional level. One afternoon in 1974, I stopped in Joy Broom's studio as she and another graduate student, Linda Okazaki, "transformed" a nudie men's calendar with magic markers, collage, and paint. With humor and irreverence, they laid the foundations for this change.

My interaction with women students (both graduate and undergraduate) during the 1970s led to a unique approach to watercolor in which the entire image is broken into hard-edge shapes, each carefully attended to according to the dictates of the work or personal interests of the artist — Linda Okazaki, Suzanne Lamon, Jennifer Stabler-Holland, and I enjoyed the swirls and contrasts created by adding and blotting up water in each shape; Joy Broom, Madge Gleeson, and Vickie Kallies tended towards a flatter application of paint. Joy used intricate patterns and "decorative" fabric references — getting cautious jabs from male faculty about the work being DECORATIVE (with negative overtones) but, we were having a wonderful time — full of ourselves!"

It has been exciting to watch content change in the work of these women. Joy Broom has always focused on relationships with family, friends, and objects. The strong patterning of the '70s has been concentrated into iconic, shrine-like images. Linda Okazaki and Suzanne Lamon explored a space reminiscent of Indian miniatures. Linda's narratives are sometimes frightening, dealing with the intersection of dreams and the world of daily events. She responds to the immense spaces of the surrounding landscape with paintings of birds, horses and rabbits.

In the '70s, influenced by Judy Chicago and the women's movement, Jennifer Holland painted large concentric, multi-petaled flowers, sensuous and meditative, while I discovered metaphors in the patterned arrangements of nature's elements. In the '80s, we both examined the impact of technologies, politics, and social traditions on the natural world. I combine computer printouts and photo-silkscreen in prints and paintings. Jennifer adds hand-painted images to huge photo-emulsions. For us the fractured pieces became symbolic of the fractured world.

This connection to natural forces is a theme in the work of Vickie Kallies and Sandra Deutchman, Art Education faculty members since 1971. Both are touched by their experiences with children's art. Kallies paints anthro-

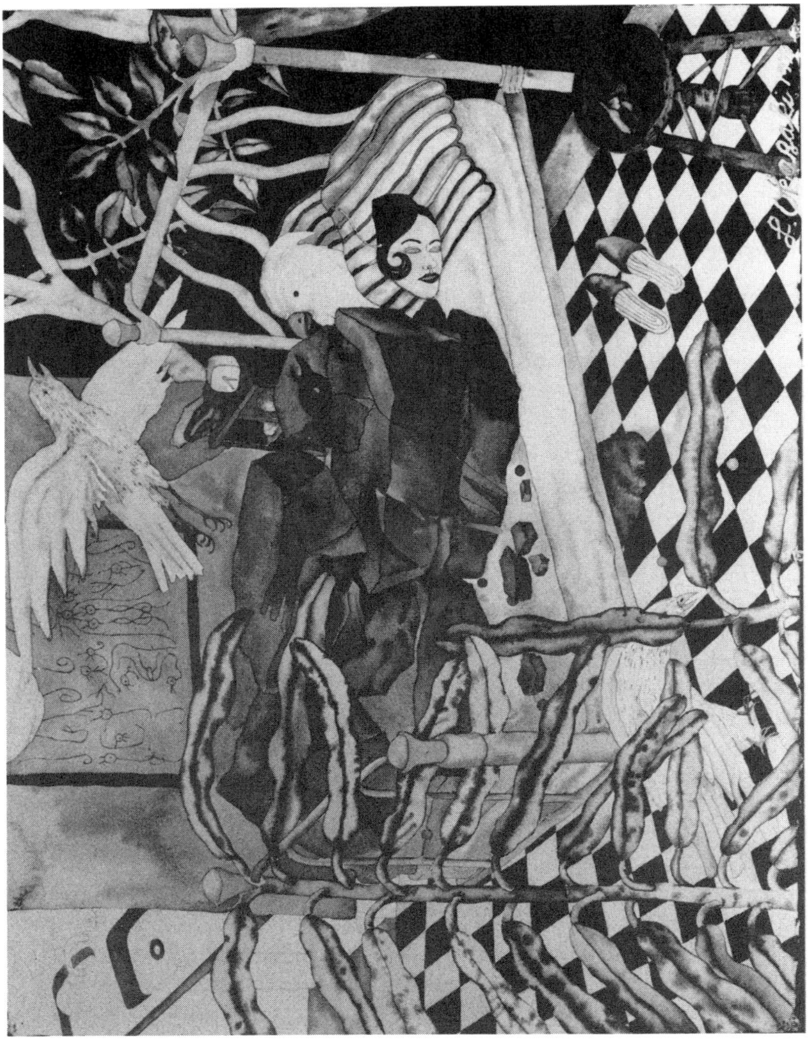

Linda Okazaki, *Night Journey*, 1979, watercolor, 20 x 30.

pomorphic self-portraits. In contrast to this whimsy, Deutchman's patterned, simplified figures are symbolic and mystical.

Three women have been prominent in sculpture. Nancy Wriggle, Alice Reedy, and Marilyn Lysohir. Wriggle constructed large multi-media sculptures; the luxurious fiber surfaces, encrusted with photos, tiny objects, and embroidered commentary directly addressed family and women's issues. During the late '70s and early '80s, both Reedy and Lysohir created monumental figurative clay pieces dealing with women's roles and responses to society.

Three painters of the '80s, Nancy Kiefer, Carson LeGree, and Nannette Pyron, took on these themes with a vengeance, twisting and manipulating forms into curious, sometimes creepy narratives. In Nancy Kiefer's words, "my work was about disabled midwestern housewives, nuns who wore spiked heels and *yearned*, and divorcées like myself who lit their cigarette butts much too early in the morning." Later in the '80s, influenced by storytelling, political activism, and the study of women, Kiefer added cheerleaders to her female protagonists. Carson LeGree studied and taught in Pullman from 1980-86, and influenced many students with her expressionistic color and style. In her tumultuous visualizations of everyday relationships and events, rooms slant precariously, beds fly though the air, bathtubs become ocean-going vessels. Nannette Pyron follows her inner questioning by constructing imaginative "portraits" and elaborate installations.

Painters Tamara Helm and Selene Santucci came to Pullman in the late '60s, attaining MFAs in the '80s. A moody stillness pervades Helm's work; frozen dolls act as metaphors for "humanness." Santucci's painterly canvases reveal struggles and resolutions of giving objects place and space.

Pullman women artists in the 1970s and '80s were trained largely by men. Their attitudes, in the main, are modernist — they work on their own and find their audiences in art centers outside Pullman, each going her own way. It's a small town, where it's impossible not to see each other at the market, drugstore, movie theater, and copy center. As Alice Reedy notes, "We have connections, but are not intimate. People's identities are important. There is no need to hold on to each other."

Of the dozen or so women artists active in Pullman during the '70s and '80s, all are connected to Washington State University — Sandra Deutchman and myself as faculty; the others as students who became artists. Many have been part-time instructors at WSU. (It's a company town.)

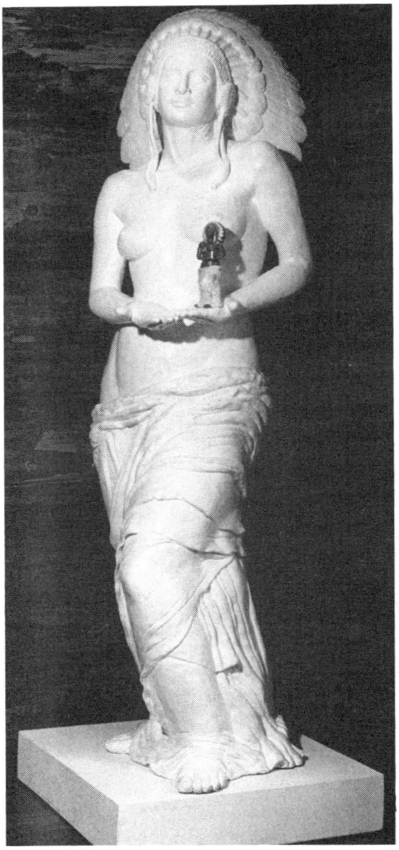

Marilyn Lysohir, *Maiden America*, 1978, clay, 17 x 68 x 18. Collection of Ed and Nancy Kienholz.

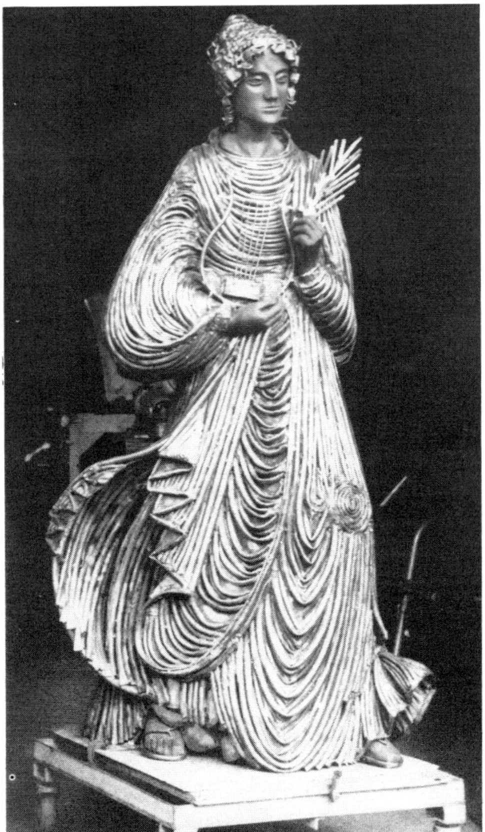

Paula Turnbull, *St. Cecilia*, 1987, 70 x 36 x 24 (approx.).

The work tends to be figurative, personal, and made with traditional art materials. Virtually every artist has been influenced by the landscape in some way and responds to nature and natural elements. Environmental concerns are also a priority. The illusionistic, spiritual, and metaphorical qualities of space are pervasive. Geographical isolation leads to meditative art, based on fantasy, dreams, and whimsical juxtapositions. These women draw heavily on their lives and relationships.

SPOKANE:

In contrast to Pullman, Spokane had a strong "first generation" of women artists in the 1950s and early '60s who displayed a professional commitment to both their art and community. Most taught, organized exhibitions, served on various community art boards, raised families and still continued to exhibit, win awards and start galleries. Pauline Haas remembers, "There is a group of us who have a special relationship of support — Lila Girvin, Kathleen Adkison, Joyce Atwood, Connie Huneke, Jody Sohlin, Sister Paula (Turnbull), Gayle Anderson and others of this vintage."

Women artists taught at every level in the Spokane of the '60s. Joyce Nichell Atwood, a jeweler, writes, "District 81 called on women artists to go out into the schools and teach — Jean Atwater, Connie Bagby and I went, plus many others. The Spokane Art School was brought along by strong women leaders with high energy and foresight — Maxey Megrue, Liz Plastino, Connie Huneke, Maxine DeBaney, and Pat Thompson, whose family were pioneers in the area, giving a building to the Art School for its present home." Atwood noted that "the teachers at the colleges have added to all our talents and growth." Area college art departments were chaired by women for long terms: Sister Paula Mary Turnbull at Fort Wright; Pauline Haas at Whitworth College; and Jo Fyfe at Spokane Falls Community College.

Painter Kathleen Adkison's story reveals the general environment for women artists in the '50s and '60s and their perseverance: "I came to Spokane, because of my husband's work, in 1950, after studying with Mark Tobey for three years. The only woman artist I knew then was Opel Fleckenstein who was teaching at Eastern State College (now Eastern Washington University). I was the only woman hired by Worth McCoy for the WSU extension course. I taught my women students to paint *first*, then tend to household chores. When I was invited to show at Woodside Gallery 25 years ago, I did not use my "Kathleen" name, because women artists were not thought to be *serious* painters." One of Pauline Haas's students, Jeanette Kirishian, now an instructor at Spokane Falls Community College, remembers that "the requirement for 'good art' was it had to look masculine."

The first major exhibition of women's work in Spokane was in 1969 at the Cheney Cowles Memorial Museum. "Eight Women Artists" included Lorraine Airey, Gayle Anderson, Jo Fyfe, Lila Girvin, Connie Huneke, Nancy McCutcheon, Ruth Whitehouse — all painters — and Sister Paula Mary Turnbull, sculptor.

In 1974-75, Pauline Haas organized two shows of area women artists at the Civic Theater Gallery in conjunction with the International Year for Women. In 1976, Cheney Cowles organized "Women in Art: Eastern Washington '76," which featured Spokane artists Lorraine Airey, Jo Fyfe, Pauline Haas, Cheryl Lepper, Kay O'Rourke, and Maxey Wolfe; Pullman artists Madge Gleeson, Jo Hockenhull, Suzanne Lamon, Linda Okazaki and Ellen Roberts; Ellensburg artists Margaret Sahlstrand and Constance Speth, also Ruth Allen, from Wenatchee; Kyle Berney from Chattaroy; and Brenda Jaeger from Pasco.

Through their own efforts, Spokane artists have built a strong support system. In 1969, Joanne Prigmore opened the Juniper Tree, the first contemporary art gallery in Spokane. Later it became part of Second City (1971-74), a complex of artists' studios and galleries organized by Joyce Atwood. In 1972, Allegra Askman began to write reviews and feature articles on art for the *Spokesman-Review*. Lila Girvin, who studied with Kenneth Callahan, Louis Bunce, Robert Sterling and Kathleen Adkison, shares their love of inner and outer landscapes in her paintings. She lobbied to get Maxine DeBaney (Martell) hired as art curator at Cheney Cowles from 1970-73. Kay O'Rourke, known for her complex, surreal, and painterly portraits, mentions the importance these three women had for her: "Maxine, Joanne and Allegra opened my eyes to a whole new world and to a world in myself I didn't know was there."

Since 1982, Beth Sellars, an artist herself, has been curator at the Cheney Cowles Memorial Museum. She works to promote regional art and to encourage a broader contemporary dialogue in Spokane. Sue Ann Heflin of the Spokane Arts Commission has also remained a stalwart advocate.

Carolyn Stephens, instructor at Spokane Falls Community College since 1974, rejoices: "We women found ourselves speaking to each other in a new art language — a visual language we hadn't learned in art school but

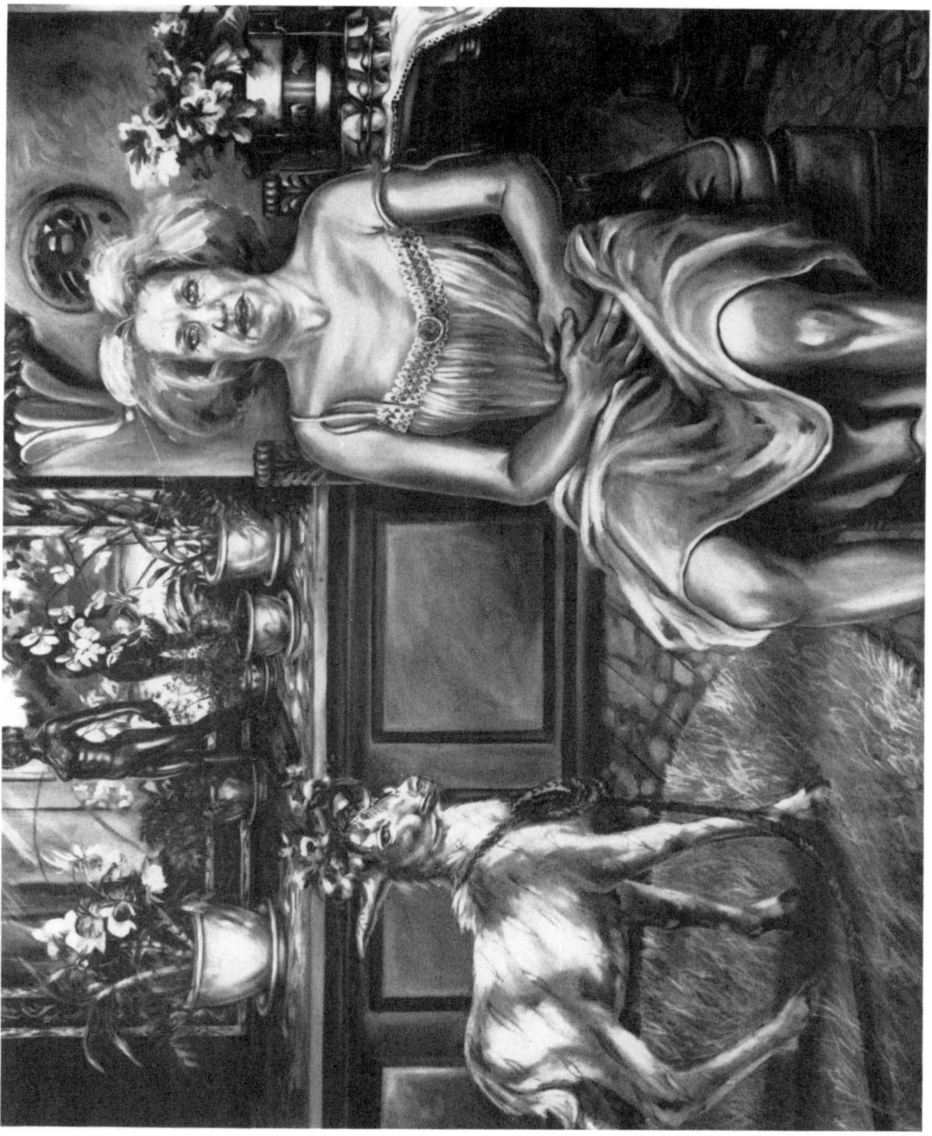

Kay O'Rourke, *Drawing of Visions of Her Needs*, 1989, oil, 48 x 60.

one we seemed to know intuitively. . . . Subject matter was equally anti-establishment; we talked about our love affairs, about children, about gardens, invented and real. It was a visual conversation among women — like talk over morning coffee — easy and unassuming." She notes that several of these artists were graduate students at Eastern Washington University during the '70s — Cheryl Lepper, Ann Reid Alfstad, Judy McMillan, Jean Atwater and herself. Both Barbara Hartman, director of the EWU art gallery, and Cecelia Alvarez, who worked as Academic Advisor to Native American and Chicano students, "made the scene change." Hartman organized a Washington Women Artists Symposium in 1981 accompanied by an exhibition, "Across the State: Different Points of View." Jean Atwater spent a year traveling the eastern half of the state, roughly 10,000 square miles, as part of the Washington State Arts Commission Visiting Artists Program. Judy McMillan and Ann Reid Alfstad were instrumental in forming TOUCHSTONE, an artists' cooperative performance and exhibition space.

The feminist art movement affected several artists working with fabrics and fibers. Ruth Beal, who exhibited at the Juniper Tree from 1969 on, found validity in her fiber-based sculptures through the "breakthrough internationally of women artists making fibers a fine art form." Later, her mixed media constructions incorporated family photographs and playful interactive elements such as music boxes, lights and tiny doors. Louise Kodis abandoned painting to present flowers, insects, birds and skies in translucent ripstop nylon banners, allowing breezes and sunlight to complete her pieces. Jeanette Kirishian used borders and patterns inspired by rugs of the Middle East to "explore various ethnic cultures beginning with my own Armenian background." Judy McMillan's watercolors grew out of her intricately embroidered fantasies.

Patty Haag, *Spokesman-Review* art writer, gallery director and instructor at Spokane Falls Community College, sees many similarities in the works of Spokane women artists throughout the '70s and '80s. "The use of lively, vibrant colors and metallic paints; tiny objects in the pieces; mainly figurative and narrative. There was much sharing of materials and no apologies for influencing each other. 'Originality' was not as important as personal expression."

Shani Marchant, Patty Haag, and Wendy Frankland Miller address the autobiographical, emotional, and social issues in their work. Marchant confronts deafness in her "Silent World" paintings. Large, colorful and richly textured, they depict an underwater world, separate from the "normal" world, layered with imaginative imagery and symbolism. Patty Haag's themes connect with her roles as mother and teacher. "Ideas of fear and protection play against each other" in her colorfully painted and fragile "shelters, or house shapes, usually empty, burning or floating in shark-infested waters." She claims that "we all long for safety, but there doesn't seem to be any." Likewise, Wendy Frankland Miller looks for a place of safety in her recent works, "Friendly Fire," dealing with issues of trust and vulnerability. For over ten years, she has done mixed-media painting using dyed paper pulp. In 1988 she did a series, "Witness," depicting the responses of both victim and family to Alzheimer's disease .

Jo Fyfe, Gina Freuen, Jean Atwater, Pauline Haas, and Judy McMillan are influenced by the history and geography of the region. Jo Fyfe's large,

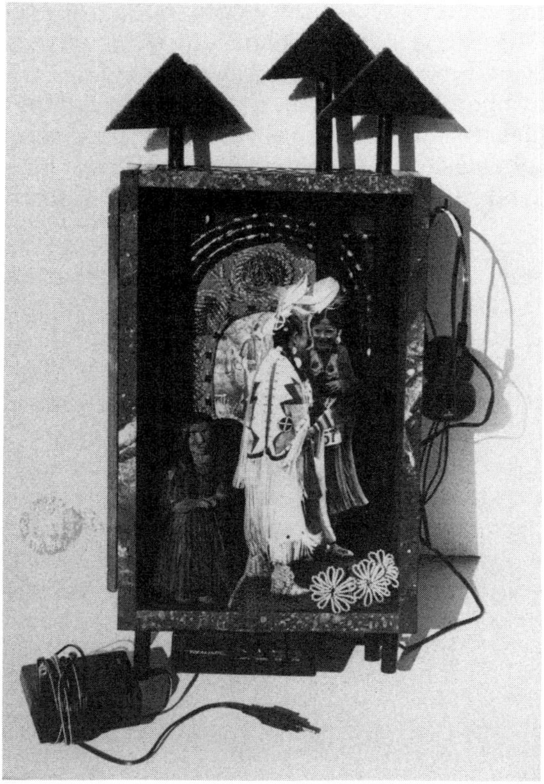

Ruth Beal, *Powwow*, 1991, mixed media with tape of Powwow music (recorded by the artists), 21 x 11 x 5.

shaped canvases explore variations of the "Cowboy and Indian" theme. Born on the Colville Indian Reservation, she has been "strongly influenced by the heritage of the Plateau and Plains Indians, especially that of Chief Joseph and his people." The white stoneware of Gina Freuen is based on the ceremonial paraphernalia of Northwest Coastal tribes. Jean Atwater paints "the landscape, the farms and irrigation ditches, what I see and love . . . a reminder of the beauty that we are so fortunate to live in, of its fragility and our duty to take care of it." Pauline Haas, too, sees her pastel landscapes as a "response to a threatened environment — a celebration of what is there for us to contemplate, enjoy and treasure." Judy McMillan, in her search for order and pattern, combines images of her family with the playground of her childhood — the woods. Sister Paula Turnbull has even made sculpture of the great Northwest myth of the Sasquatch.

Two artists combine their concern for the natural environmental with the human element. Kathleen Adkison, who paints from remembered experience, gave up figure painting in 1950 when she began hiking in the mountains around Spokane. She claims that "the interaction of life forces, such as water and lichen with inert matter influenced everything I did . . . but now, nature seems to have become a metaphor for human relationships." Cecelia Alvarez peoples her large paintings with strong women. Her work with indigenous students at EWU reinforced her own comfortable relationship with nature and made her look anew at its brutalization.

As one drives from Pullman to Spokane, the vast, uncluttered expanses of hill and valley change to clumps of Ponderosa pines springing from basalt rock. Similarly, women artists in Pullman seem to guard their individual space, while those in Spokane make a strong commitment to community as well as their own work. Both approaches consistently produce art that speaks of women's changing roles, perceptions, and definitions.

Feminism and Art in Vancouver: Time for Change

by Caffyn Kelley

I am keenly aware of problems in writing a survey article, making history out of my own point of view. I hope that by structuring this article through individual stories I indicate that it is a very partial view indeed.

"I'm not a feminist," says Haruko Okano, one of the most important figures on the women's art scene in Vancouver. "I'm *ganbari-ya* — a person who resists injustice."

Okano sees feminism as a movement of white women that has consistently failed to extend a hand to communities of color fighting racism. Her judgment is harsh. "Feminists leave out women of color, except when they want to claim our power or take credit for what we are doing," she says. But Okano affirms the possibility of cross-cultural collaboration, noting, "Not all feminists insist we be defined by their mandate. There *are* women who have learned to be strong allies, and who don't infringe on our right to represent ourselves."

Feminism is apparently gaining recognition in the established art world of Vancouver. The city's foremost public gallery, the Vancouver Art Gallery, responded to feminist criticisms of its policies and practice by instituting a Women's Committee of the Board of Directors in 1991. Public Programs Director Judith Mastai has run a series of programs and projects addressing feminist issues in the visual arts since 1988. Guest speakers have included such luminaries as Griselda Pollock, Mary Kelly and Laura Mulvey.[1]

While the vast majority of exhibitions at the Gallery honor great men in the Euro-American tradition, an exciting 1992 exhibition called "Memory and Desire: The Voices of Eleven Women of Culture" presented the work of ten local women artists, including Haruko Okano. The show was created through a Gallery workshop with visiting artist Sutapa Biswas, who wanted to do collaborative work with local women and sought a broad range of women to participate. The artists in "Memory and Desire" included professional and non-professional artists, women of many different ages from a wide variety of cultural backgrounds. Their work explored issues of voice, identity, and the interface of personal and cultural histories. The exhibition featured the first explicit lesbian image to appear at the Gallery, Shani Mootoo's *Memory and Desire/On Looking Back.*[2]

Vancouver has a lively art scene operating through government-funded, non-profit artist-run centers. The most consequential of these were established in the 1970s, when government funding was relatively accessible. Through the participation of feminists, along with consciousness-raising in the '70s and '80s, most of these non-profit, artist-run centers have incorporated feminist concerns within their mandate. Affirmative action, attention to gender parity, and artspeak fluent in feminist theories of gender and culture are commonplace. The six or eight centers comprise an alternative to the mainstream scene, where commercial and community galleries continue, uninformed by feminist concerns.

Vancouver's colleges and universities have long resisted the challenge of feminism. Emily Carr College of Art and Design, the local art college, finally met student demands for a program in feminist studies in 1991. At Simon Fraser University, the Women's Studies department has been a haven for feminists for many years, and the Fine Arts department has recently hired some distinguished feminists in response to ongoing criticisms.

Yet, even as feminism is institutionalized as a separate chapter within the master narrative, it is losing credibility at the grassroots and community levels, especially among women of color. Zainub Verjee, Director of the artist-run center, The Western Front, and long-time activist for women's rights in the cultural arena, as well as an art curator, programmer, distributor, and writer, explains, "In some contexts I describe myself as a feminist. But women of color certainly have a problem with that term. It has meant white, middle-class feminism."

In the past few years, through the activism of people of color, artists and feminists have been challenged by issues of race and difference. While many white feminists welcome these challenges, at the long-established feminist artist-run center, Women in Focus,[3] bitter divisions over issues of race have fractured all notions of a feminist "community."

Zainub Verjee was working as video distribution coordinator at Women in Focus in 1987 when she decided to address the low representation of women of color in that collection, as well as others in the city. Verjee initiated a group — all women of color — who worked as a distinct, separately-funded group within the Women in Focus society. The group, known as In Visible Colors, produced a five-day festival and symposium in November 1989, showcasing films and videos by women of color from around the world.

The festival was wildly successful. Attendance far exceeded expectations. Verjee says, "It was a real turning point in Vancouver. For the first time, local women artists and cultural producers could see their work in the context of a global effort to define themselves by historically silenced and oppressed people."

At Women in Focus, however, a rift developed between the white feminists who had owned the organization from the start, and the women of color working separately as In Visible Colors. In response to a financial crisis, the board of directors at Women in Focus put the profits from the festival in trust. In Visible Colors sued the Women in Focus society to have the money returned. The court eventually ordered that 75% of the money be paid to In Visible Colors while Women in Focus could retain 25%. But the director of the society refused to comply with the court order.

A coalition of white feminists and women of color came together with the purpose of returning In Visible Colors funds to that organization. Eventually, they had to vote out the society's director at a court-ordered meeting and take over management of the society early in 1992.

As Zainub Verjee comments, "It was a long, exhausting fight that depleted everyone of their energies." The process left Women in Focus accused of racism, while the myriad tasks of running the society and saving it from financial ruin took precedence over examining and transforming this legacy.

As I write this article in October 1992, Women in Focus is again embroiled in a controversy over race and representation. The first professional artist's show in the gallery after the In Visible Colors fiasco was by white feminist-artist Diana Kemble. Her semi-abstract paintings include representations of people of color which Kemble claims "have nothing to do with race. They are from my dreams." But other women found the pictures offensive and deeply painful. The gallery committee has unanimously resigned, calling on the society's board of directors to "immediately scrutinize and re-evaluate the society's goals, objectives, and structure," with the aim of addressing racism in the organization and, more broadly, in feminism and art critical practice.

Haruko Okano urges, "As women grow stronger, we have to make a choice to be responsible and powerful. Feminists have come into a position where they need to manifest their power with responsibility, using it with integrity and respect to break the negative ways power works in the world."

Reduced levels of funding for an ever-increasing number of cultural producers makes the struggle for recognition and authority especially critical. Shani Mootoo says, "For the existing system to include us means it will have to slowly deconstruct. People will have to give up power or step sideways; they will have to share. Who wants to do that?"

It is time to change; it is what cultural theorist Marlon Riggs calls "the best and the worst of times."[4] Women, feminists, people of color, gay men and lesbians are gaining unprecedented visibility and voice in the cultural arena, in Vancouver as elsewhere in North America. But in that arena as well as in the larger society, it is a time of increasing right-wing backlash against the small gains made by women and minorities. Cuts in government funding to women's publications, Native Communications, Multiculturalism, and the Court Challenges Program, among others, reflect this right-wing backlash and undermine cultural production by women and minorities at the community level. Our lives continue to be endangered by poverty and violence. Our actual social power does not change much, even when we gain space and voice in the closed world of art.

Haruko Okano is especially aware of the need to marry art and activism. In *Come Spring: Journey of a Sansei*, a multi-media project incorporating sculpture, essays and poetry that resulted in an exhibition and book published by Gallerie Publications in 1992, Okano describes her personal journey to power in a way she hopes will empower others. From earliest childhood, Okano's life was marked by trauma and displacement. She was born at the end of the war into a family torn apart by the forced relocation of Japanese-Canadians. Orphaned at the age of eight, she grew up in foster homes where she was tortured emotionally, physically and sexually. Finally she escaped into a marriage where the abuse continued and worsened until she had to flee, leaving two children.

From a place of bleak despair, she began a slow process of recovery. Through patient research, self-scrutiny, and the healing work of art, she has come to terms with her personal history and reclaimed her Japanese-Canadian culture and heritage.

In the meticulously crafted sculptures and writing that make up *Come*

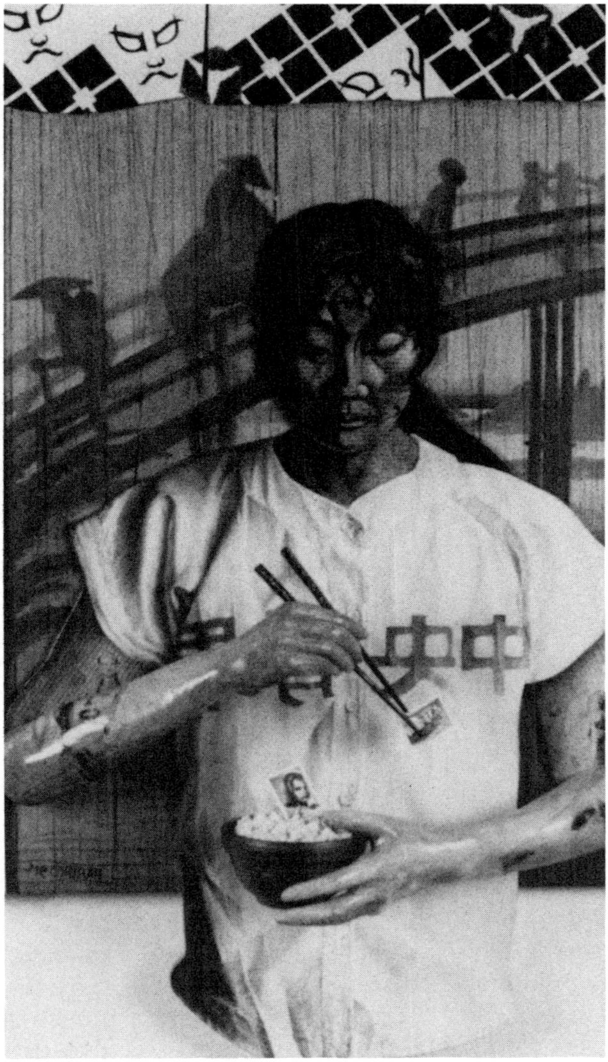

Haruko Okano, *Come Spring: Journey of a Sansei*, (detail), 1992, multimedia sculpture, 24 x 48 x 6.

Spring, Okano has made her personal journey accessible to all. As Shani Mootoo notes in the preface to the book, Okano makes art a "place of resistance — through memory and reclamation." Okano's project has been embraced by many in the Japanese-Canadian community, where she is a well-known human-rights activist.

Okano has compiled a major survey of non-western artists for The Western Front Society. She is curating a series of shows for the "grunt gallery," another artist-run center, where she intends to present important local artists whose work is ignored by existing institutions.

Okano's next book, *A Season of Hope*, will explore cross-cultural collaboration as a means of expressing and seeking hope. "Collaboration means working together with perfect integrity," She muses. "We are all so damaged it's hard to trust that things can be healed. But hope is what drives life."

Unlike many prominent women artists, Okano is not an academic and has never been offered a teaching position at any of Vancouver's colleges or universities. She recently refused several much-coveted offers of representation from Vancouver's best-known commercial galleries, because she was worried about the commodification of her creative process and her "Asian-ness." She has decided to travel a more difficult path, negotiating survival between non-profit artist centers, odd jobs, small grants and occasional sales of work from her studio.

"I'm driven," says Okano. "I'm a hope fanatic." Her passion is a critical element in the Vancouver scene.

Persimmon Blackbridge is an artist with deep roots in feminism. For over 20 years, her artwork has been intimately connected with what she describes as "seeing the ways I had accepted a really de-valued vision of myself through internalized sexism." She continues, "My art has always been rooted in feminism — it was a way of looking at ourselves as women, imagining other places, and telling the realities of our lives. It's also had to do with the anti-psychiatry movement or mental patients' liberation movement, as well as with being a lesbian. These things have everything to do with the kind of art that I make."

Blackbridge works collaboratively with the Kiss and Tell Collective. This group of three lesbian artists began meeting in 1985 to discuss the representation of sex. Blackbridge remembers, "My own early work on sexuality came out of a feminist analysis of pornography. I was honoring a concept of what sex should be like in opposition to sexism, instead of paying attention to the conflicted, often painful, yet empowering thing that sex can be for someone like me."

In 1987 Kiss and Tell changed from a discussion group to a group of three women who decided to actually make images of lesbian sex. They presented "Drawing the Line: Lesbian Sexual Politics on the Wall" at Women in Focus in 1988. The show consisted of a gallery full of photographs, taken by Susan Stewart, showing Persimmon Blackbridge having sex with collaborator Lizard Jones. The pictures represented a wide variety of sexual practices. Women seeing the show were encouraged to draw their lines, to say what pictures aroused them, and what pictures they considered pornographic or frightening.

"Drawing the Line" initiated a much-needed discussion of sexuality and censorship amongst lesbians and feminists. Viewers covered the gallery walls with comments. The interactive exhibit was a smash hit in Vancouver. It met with rave reviews throughout an ongoing tour of Eastern Canada, the United States and Australia. Of course, the tour was organized by feminist lesbians outside the institutional art world. A postcard book featuring 40 photographs from the exhibition along with selected viewers comments was published by Vancouver feminist publisher, Press Gang, in 1991.

In addition to this work on sexuality, Blackbridge makes powerful sculptures that describe mechanisms of social control — like mental hospitals and prisons — and the enduring ways people resist these mechanisms. Her work drew me, along with many other women, into feminism; I was astonished by her capacity to create images that dared to tell the grief and courage of women's lives.

Blackbridge has supported and been supported by the feminist community, along with people in other human liberation movements whose issues she shares. She was active in documenting and promoting work by women artists through the '70s and '80s, and is a founding member of a feminist artists' support group, East End Artists, that has been meeting regularly since 1978. Surprised by the level of art-world support accorded her work in recent years, she still cleans houses to supplement her income. Awarded the prestigious Vancouver Institute for Visual Arts award in 1991, she has many invitations to speak at conferences and universities. "Suddenly my art is very groovy and post-modern," she says. "But I'm not rooted in academia; I'm rooted in activism."

Shani Mootoo, *Backyard Jhundi*, 1991, mendi, plaster, acrylic, food coloring, sticks and stones, 60 x 20.

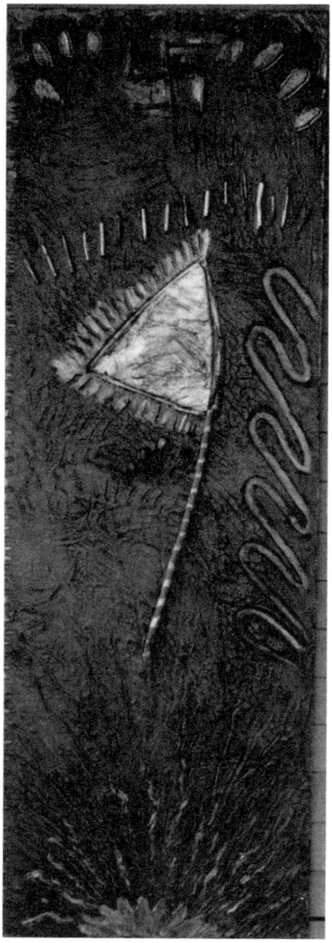

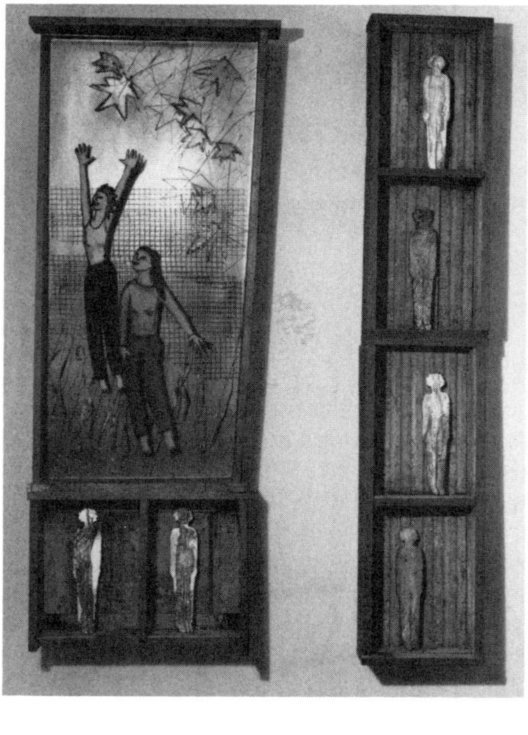

Persimmon Blackbridge, *A Canadian Landscape*, 1991, mixed media, 60 x 44.

Shani Mootoo refuses the feminist label. She uses the words of a Lillian Allen song to call herself "a woman-identified woman," adding, "I'm a woman-loving identified woman." Mootoo has been working as an artist in Vancouver since 1981. A painter, writer, and more recently a video producer, Mootoo tackles issues many would consider feminist, including sexual identity, gender oppression, and child sexual abuse. But she has never identified with the feminist movement, saying "Feminism is very much a white movement. It's been excluding."

In a remarkable 1989 exhibition and limited-edition book, *This is Our Little Secret*, Mootoo explored her childhood experience of sexual abuse. In probably the most mind-boggling effort I know of to connect art with social effect, Mootoo presented the powerful paintings to men who had been convicted of sexual abuse and were incarcerated at the Stave Lake Corrections Center. "As I began," Mootoo remembers, "I had a feeling that the men were quite scared, but after hearing about my feelings, some of them broke down, and disclosed how they had been abused as children. A lot of them were crying. They asked me to come back three times."

Mootoo received little support for her work until recently. Since her 1989 show at the Surrey Art Gallery and her participation in the Women in Focus self-curated group show by women of color, "Others Among Others," that year, there has been growing interest in her work. She is asked to sit on many arts panels and juries. She is co-curating a show of South Asian artists, *To Visit the Tiger*, which opens at the Community Arts Council this month. Women in Focus has scheduled a solo show of her work, and Press Gang will publish her first novel in 1993.

Kati Campbell's art is informed by feminist and psychoanalytic theory. Her installation, *Battle of the Titans*, in November 1992 at the Vancouver Art Gallery, incorporated a huge video projection of a 10-minute tape showing a mother dressing her toddler. Campbell explains, "I used the mother's struggle to dress the child as a metaphor for the child being socialized. And it really is a struggle — typical of children that age. They fight you tooth and nail, and there is a lot of jubilance in the struggle."

Campbell says she is immersed in psychoanalytic theory "because it's a theory of the subject. It's about how we devise our relationship with reality." In her focus on the mother-child relationship she says she is not proposing an overturning of Freudian or Lacanian discourse, where the father is the principal agent in establishing symbolic meaning. "But both mother and father have a role to play," Campbell says. "And of course the mother's role has been severely downgraded." She notes that though mothers are highly idealized, they are also blamed if anything screws up. Campbell laughs, "It's the way patriarchal discourse has its cake and eats it too about women!"

Campbell built her career through artist-run centers after graduating from Simon Fraser University in 1984. Her concerns with reaching past an art audience led her in 1986 to co-found an artists' collective which mounts public projects. She has exhibited widely in both Canada and Europe. In 1991, she moved her family to Leeds, England, for a year while she took a Masters of Art History with Fred Orton and Griselda Pollock.

Sara Diamond is an arts writer and teacher as well as a feminist artist who works with video as a primary medium and in an interdisciplinary way, incorporating text, computer technology, and furniture. In the 1980s she developed a course on feminist cultural theory for the local art college, Emily Carr College of Art and Design. When the college canceled the course in 1990, 1,000 students and faculty signed a petition of protest, calling for the establishment of a feminist and gender-studies program, which the college eventually instituted.

Diamond built her reputation in artist-run centers through the 1980s, particularly at Video In. She spoke eloquently against censorship in the feminist debate, organizing two important conferences on art and sexual representation in 1985 and 1986. She has recently accepted a job as Director of the Television and Video Program at the Banff School of Fine Arts. In 1992, the National Gallery of Canada held a retrospective of her work.

Before she got involved in art, Diamond was a prominent feminist and social activist. She says, "I realized that various social movements had failed to understand the role of both ideology and culture as very powerful mechanisms within contemporary society. The Left relied heavily on print as its primary form of communication, completely defying the notion that we live in a televisual culture." As a feminist, Diamond says, "the power of the images that articulate the gender construction of our culture is hard to miss." Diamond has used art strategies to address a wider audience, producing several tapes on labor history that have been broadcast on national television.

These are just five of the many important women artists working in Vancouver today. They all have in common a yearning for social justice and a critical art practice that incorporates their yearning.[5] Despite their very different work, and the huge differences in the level of support each is receiving from the institutional art world and feminist communities, they all agree on the need to weave art with the social fabric.

It's time for feminism to change, as women learn to speak across borders of race, cultural and sexual identity, and social class. At this exciting and exhausting time, when differences often seem to compete and collide, the work of women artists is more important than ever. They teach us to integrate our personal beliefs and experiences with creative work relevant to society. Their art is a powerful way of imagining and insisting on social change.

NOTES:

[1] Mary Kelly also taught two summer sessions at Simon Fraser University.

[2] According to popular belief, the exhibition was presented at the gallery only because of demonstrations by the Artists' Coalition for Local Color, which called the gallery to task for systemic racism and lack of support for local artists of color at a public meeting in December 1991. The Gallery denies this version of history, insisting that an exhibition was always planned.

[3] Women in Focus was established in 1974. It is currently located at 849 Beatty Street, Vancouver, B.C., Canada V6B 2M6.

[4] Marlon T. Riggs, "Ruminations of a Snap Queen: What Time is It?," *Outlook*, Spring 1991, pp 12-23. Riggs's analysis of the questions of difference informs this essay throughout.

[5] I use this word in recognition of the impact the cultural theory of bell hooks has had amongst cultural producers in Vancouver. See her book *Yearning: race, gender and cultural politics*, Toronto: Between the Lines, 1990.

Thanks to the many women who took the time to speak with me, and whose viewpoints inform this article, though I have not referred to them specifically, especially Doreen Jensen, Jill Pollock, Jill Baird, Lorna Boschman, and Judith Mastai.

For a comprehensive historical look at Vancouver's Feminist Art scene, see Carole Williams, "A Working Chronology of Feminist Cultural Activities and Events in Vancouver: 1970-1990," *Vancouver Anthology: The Institutional Politics of Art*, edited by Stan Douglas, Vancouver: Talon Books, 1991.

Afterword: Women in the Arts as Cultural Catalysts

by Julie Anderson

A surprisingly large number of women have influenced and guided successful arts organizations in the Pacific Northwest. Even limited research reveals dozens of outstanding women who deserve to be included when a complete history is written.

A whole chapter should be written about women as donors, acknowledging such crucial philanthropists as Margaret E. MacTavish Fuller, Virginia B. Wright, Anne Gould Hauberg, Anne Gerber, Katherine White and Elizabeth Bayley Willis. Another essay is waiting to be written on women in education, including Nellie B. Cornish, Annette Edens, Eugenie Worman, Lin Lipetz, Ruth Penington, Ramona Solberg, Hazel Koenig, Patti Warashina and Martha Kingsbury, among many others.

Maxine Cushing Gray, Betty Bowen, Rachael Griffin, Dorothy Malone and Zoe Dusanne deserve in-depth attention by younger generations of scholars.

Similarly distinguished lists can be drawn in other areas: curators, collectors, writers, designers and administrators have enriched the arts, often in difficult circumstances. They sometimes worked for low pay and without recognition. These women, perhaps without giving it a thought, opened doors of opportunity for those who followed.

Another piece should be written on voluntarism in the arts, saluting PONCHO, the Junior League, Northwest Designer-Craftsmen, Lambda Rho Alumnae, Allied Arts of Seattle, the Portland Art Association, the Henry Gallery Association, various museum guilds and arts and crafts clubs.

To exemplify high professional standards, intellectual acuity and individual style, I've chosen as examples a few women of distinction.

Alice Rooney headed to New York City with a degree in creative writing. She worked a few years at the Mutual Broadcasting System, before returning to her hometown of Seattle and a job with an advertising agency. There she wrote radio copy and served as executive secretary to the American Institute of Architects, an agency client.

From 1960 to 1980, she guided Allied Arts of Seattle to a leadership position in the city. Her primary gifts were an ability to gather and hold together coalitions of arts managers, architects, lawyers, preservationists and politically savvy idealists for the achievement of specific goals; and excellent communications skills with the press, elected officials and a wild assortment of "ordinary" citizens.

Allied Arts successfully lobbied the city to allocate a meaningful budget for its arts commission ($350,000) and endorse a 1%-for-the-arts ordinance. In the years since, these programs have benefited thousands of artists.

Rooney guided the Pilchuck School of Glass (1980 - 1990) through a major transition, preserving artistic vitality and growth, and adding 10 new buildings to an idyllic campus, while consolidating and increasing financial support. She brought Pilchuck from nearly total dependence on the generosity of a single donor to an internationally-acclaimed program with an $800,000 annual budget. She even established a $100,000 endowment,an enlightened move for such a young organization. Today, Pilchuck is recognized as a national treasure, in part because of her skilled commitment to making it so.

LaMar Harrington is perhaps best known for writing a definitive history of ceramics in the Pacific Northwest (1979) and as director emeritus of the Bellevue Art Museum. But her tenure at the University of Washington Henry Gallery (1957-1975) encompassed a stunningly diverse range of exhibitions, lectures and special events. She presented performances by Lee Breuer and Mabou Mines, sponsored happenings by Allan Kaprow, showed work by Cork Marchesci, Hans Haacke, Dan Flavin and Judy Chicago, introduced local and national video artists to Seattle, and collaborated with faculty, students, and ethnic and minority groups in mounting a string of first-rate exhibitions.

She created yearly series of lectures on photography, worked with Friends of the Rag and Bill Evans Dance company on media events, and developed and funded the first four books for the Index of Art in the Pacific Northwest, working closely with University of Washington Press. There were dozens of other exhibitions and programs under her guidance during those years. She opened up the University to the community and brought national attention to the Henry. In the process, the city grew accustomed to an exhilarating pace and breadth unmatched before or since.

Francine Seders arrived from France (with a law degree) in 1958 to receive a B.A. degree in English literature at the University of Puget Sound. By 1962 she had enrolled in the University of Washington, and, looking for part-time work, found Otto Seligman needed a secretary in his gallery. He wanted someone fluent in languages and struck gold with Francine, who speaks French, English and German.

It was the year of the World's Fair and Seligman had recently moved to a new space on University Way. He represented Mark Tobey, along with other important artists, and wanted someone to manage the gallery while he met with collectors here and in Europe. Seligman died in 1966, and Francine spent nearly four months helping sort out the estate, then acquired the gallery (calling it Francine Seders/Otto Seligman). In 1970 she moved the gallery to its current location and changed the name to reflect the reality of sole ownership. She also brought in a new generation of artists.

Seders has a special fidelity and integrity in dealing with artists. They, in turn, have shown unusual loyalty to her. Of the nearly three dozen artists she represents today, a core of 20 have been with her since the beginning. This mutual allegiance is testimony to her honesty and her faith in their work, sometimes in the face of harsh critical reviews or adverse economic realities.

Seders is a confident connoisseur and looks at deeper aspects of personality and character when she, with her staff, form partnerships with artists. This discipline and astute judgment have created a very high standard during a time of tumultuous growth in the arts. Because she is an intensely private person in a highly public profession, she has expected the art to speak for the gallery and, as a result, her own contribution is sometimes overlooked.

Ruth Nomura has managed the Northwest Craft Center since 1963, when Century 21 and the Northwest Designer-Craftsmen joined forces to dedicate the former Swedish pavilion at the Seattle World's Fair as a continuing public facility. Nomura manages a delicate balance of lively exhibitions and retail sales featuring ceramics, glass, jewelry, fiber, handmade papers, books and mixed media. By maintaining high standards, she encourages artists to explore a range of functional possibilities and stretches the imagination of shoppers. While the Center House has endured several costly remodeling projects to increase its appeal, Ruth Nomura continues to prove that an aging facility can attract local visitors and tourists without pandering or schlock.

She has an unerring eye and a curatorial understanding of the arts, combined with an intuitive business sense that make the Craft Center an institutional jewel. The considerable benefits accruing to both artists and the community have been achieved without acknowledgment or support from public funding agencies and philanthropic sources. This is a rare accomplishment in the non-profit sector, often overlooked by both business and arts leaders.

About the Authors

Lois Allan received her M.A. from Claremont Graduate School, California, and has been writing about the Northwest for the past 10 years. She is a contributing editor to *Reflex* and *Artweek.*

Julie Anderson, curator of the corporate collection of SAFECO Insurance Companies, was a member of the Seattle Arts Commission 1975-1978, and chair from 1977 to 1978.

Margery Aronson is an independent art advisor/curator for corporations and collectors. She is curator for the collections at Microsoft Corporation, the Sheraton Seattle Hotel, and The Prescott Collection of Pilchuk Glass at Pacific First Centre.

Ruth Askey, co-editor of *Modernism & Beyond: Women Artists of the Pacific Northwest,* has a special interest in women's art and issues through her work as a researcher on Judy Chicago's project, *The Dinner Party,* in California. Seattle-based since 1988, Askey writes for *Visions, Reflex,* and *Artweek,* works as an independent curator, is a board member of the Seattle Women's Caucus for Art, and serves on the Metro Arts Committee.

Laura Brunsman, project director and co-editor of *Modernism & Beyond: Women Artists of the Pacific Northwest,* is an art historian and instructor at Cornish College of the Arts. She writes art criticism for *Reflex, Glass,* and *Artweek,* and wrote the catalogue essay on "Viola Patterson: Northwest Modernist," for the SAFECO Insurance Companies collection.

Elizabeth Bryant is a painter and editorial director of the Northwest's *Reflex* magazine. She writes art criticism for *Artweek, Visions, New Art Examiner,* and the *Seattle Post-Intelligencer.*

Ann Focke, historian, was a founder of and/or, 911 Contemporary Arts Center, Center on Contemporary Art (COCA), and Artist Trust. She is currently working on an interactive information network, Arts Wire.

Ron Glowen teaches art history at Cornish College of the Arts. His criticism appears in *Artweek, Visions, Public Art Review,* and the *Everett Herald*. Glowen is editor of the *Glass Arts Society Journal,* former editor of the International Association of Art Critics newsletter, and has lectured widely — from the Straits of Juan de Fuca to the Gulf of Mexico.

Regina Hackett, art critic for the *Seattle Post-Intelligencer,* also wrote the catalogue essay for Alden Mason's 1989 exhibition at the Henry Art Gallery.

Nancy Weymouth Halbrooks, artist and educator, has taught painting at the University of Puget Sound in Tacoma and at Shoreline Community College. She was a member of WAG (Women Artists Group) in the 1970s.

Jo Hockenhull, painter and printmaker, is Professor of Fine Arts and Director of the Women's Studies Program at Washington State University, Pullman. She served as program chair for the Women's Caucus for Art National Conference in Seattle, 1993.

Matthew Kangas is an art critic and curator whose reviews have appeared in *Art in America, Artweek, Art Criticism, American Craft,* and *Glass.* Kangas served as Seattle Arts Commission Critic's Fellow, and as the James Renwick Fellow at the National Museum of American Art; he recently taught at the Aesthetic Design Research Laboratory of Shanghai Teacher's University.

Pam Keeley received her M.A. and M.F.A. from the University of New Mexico in Albuquerque and currently teaches at Cornish College of the Arts. She showed her performance/installation work, *A Wait, A Body* (1991), at the University of Colorado at Boulder/Fine Arts Center.

Caffyn Kelley is an arts writer, printer and publisher. She is the owner of Gallerie Publications, a feminist publisher of women artists and published an anthology, *Forbidden Subjects: Self-portraits by Lesbian Artists* (1992).

Martha Kingsbury is an art historian and professor at the University of Washington. As a scholar in the field of Northwest art, she has written essays including "Modern Art of the Pacific Northwest" (Henry Art Gallery) and "Northwest Traditions" (Seattle Art Museum).

Sandra Kroupa, curator of the Book Arts Collection of the University of Washington Libraries, is active in the Book Arts Guild and has organized book art exhibitions, including "Personal Form: Books and the Artist" at the Henry Art Gallery (1988).

Jennifer McLerran, a Ph.D candidate at the University of Washington, writes frequently for *Artspace* and *Reflex.* Her publications include *Old Age in Myth and Symbol: A Cultural Dictionary* (NY: Greenwood Press, 1991).

Lynn McAllister received her Ph.D. in art history from Cornell University. She wrote the catalogue essay for "Andy Warhol and Leroy Neiman, an exhibition of Sports Painting" for the Los Angeles Institute of Contemporary Art. Her gallery, opened in Seattle in 1983, focuses on Northwest art and glass art.

Kazuko Nakone, art historian and writer for *Reflex* and *Visions* magazines, has also worked on the Northwest Oral History Project archiving Asian-American artists.

Cherry Partee, a fiber artist, received her M.F.A. from the University of Washington in 1991. Her work has been shown at the Bernice Steinbaum Gallery, New York; Foster/White Gallery, Seattle; and in national quilt exhibitions.

Ann T. Rosenthal is an artist and curator, former president of the Seattle Women's Caucus for Art, member of the national board of directors and coordinator of the 1993 WCA National Conference in Seattle. Her work has been exhibited at the Tacoma Art Museum and the Art Center Gallery at Seattle Pacific University.

Index of Names

Page numbers in boldface type refer to illustrations.

CREDITS

Mike Seidl 21, 51, 82
Don Normark 24
Richard Nicol 26, 135
Jim Gorman / Vancouver Art Gallery 37
Roger Schreiber 44, 49, 60
Kim Zumwalt 53
Mark Van S. 61, 101
Mark Frey 62
Spike Mafford 74
Chris Eden 77,78
Christopher Dahl 96
Rob Vinnedge 96, 101
David L. Browne 108,110
Bill Bachhuber 113
David Potter 113
Eduardo Calderón 119
Moonphoto 145
M. J. Cody 150
Arthur Okazaki 156
Herman Joyner 161
Susan Stewart 172

Typographic design: Barbara Bergeron
cover: MOG